Sometimes They Even Shook Your Hand

Portraits of Champions Who Walked Among Us

John Schulian
Foreword by William Nack

University of Nebraska Press | Lincoln and London

Acknowledgments for the
use of copyrighted material
appear on pages 315–18,
which constitute an extension
of the copyright page.

Library of Congress
Cataloging-in-Publication Data

Schulian, John, 1945–
Sometimes they even shook
your hand: portraits of
champions who walked among
us / John Schulian; foreword by
William Nack.
p. cm.
Summary: "Profiles of one-of-
a-kind athletes from decades
past"—Provided by publisher.
ISBN 978-0-8032-3776-6 (pbk.:
alk. paper)
1. Athletes—United States—
Biography. 2. Sports—United
States—History. I. Title.
GV697.A1S418 2011
796.0922—dc22
[B] 2011015570

Set in Iowan Old Style
by Kim Essman.
Designed by R. W. Boeche.

For

Ernie Imhoff	Rob Fleder
Pat Ryan	John Walsh
George Solomon	Jay Lovinger
Ray Sons	Mike Rathet
Kerry Slagle	Brian Toolin
Marty Kaiser	Eliot Kaplan
Michael A. Davis	Paul Scanlon
Chris Hunt	Art Cooper (RIP)

— The editors who lit the way —

Contents

Part 3. Hoops and Horses and Everything in Between

Foreword
William Nack

For the better part of thirty-five years, for publications as far-reaching as the *Chicago Sun-Times* and the *Philadelphia Daily News*—for which he wrote as a columnist—and *GQ* and *Sports Illustrated*—for which he freelanced—John Schulian was among the keenest and most literate observers to work the arenas, ball fields, and fight gyms that defined the gaudy landscape of American sports.

To the noble enterprise of covering this rich slice of national life, Schulian brought the sensitivity of an artist seeking to craft something new out of the drama and mayhem going on inside the ropes, inside the chalk lines, and something original out of the private worlds from which the dramatists sprang. "My idea was to take the readers into places where cameras didn't go," he says, "or to places where other reporters did not choose to go."

The man succeeded deftly, even magically.

All anthologies such as this are really trips down the musty corridors of the past—nostalgic journeys to fights we once saw, to games we once witnessed, to the homes and playgrounds of athletes we thought we knew—and here Schulian acts the perfect tour guide all these years later, assembling sixty-four pieces that take us to places and events only dimly remembered and recall voices long silenced, long forgotten.

Most of the pieces in this volume were written for dailies under the hot poker of an a.m. deadline, and many of them—

particularly those describing the spiraling arcs of footballs and the smashing of fists on bone—still exude the force and fire that the writer felt as he glanced from clock to keyboard and chronicled what he had just seen and heard. After witnessing middleweight champion Marvin Hagler's savage dismemberment of Thomas Hearns, a barroom-like melee in which Hagler was bloodied early as the fighters hit each other with everything but their corner stools, Schulian wrote of Hagler: "Suddenly he was jerked out of 1985 and back into a time when warriors wore loin cloths instead of boxing trunks and did their hunting without benefit of eight-ounce gloves. He was a primitive and that splash down the middle of his face wasn't blood. It was war paint."

Schulian's cast of characters, the subjects of his long and short narratives, emerged full-blown across the whole range of American sports, but most of them come vibrantly alive on football fields, in basketball and boxing arenas, and in the country's baseball yards. As he wrote in a story on pitcher Nolan Ryan, "The pieces I liked doing best were about prizefighters bobbing and weaving with their dreams and the simple pleasures of baseball, from watching Mike Schmidt pickle a home run to listening to Bill Veeck's flights of fancy."

His long profile of the Philadelphia Eagles' Chuck Bednarik, the ferocious tackler and last of the two-way players, and his look at Chicago Bears safety Gary Fencik, a Yalie who read Kierkegaard on the side but hit like Bednarik on the chest, were written with intelligence and blessed with an abundance of the writer's manifest grace. And his shorter profiles—of the hell-raising Oakland behemoth, John Matuszak, and the Orioles' cussed manager, Earl Weaver—are filled with humor buoyed by genuine affection.

Of Matuszak, Schulian wrote: "He had a drink in each hand, although I doubt he knew what kind of drinks they were. Caring only that both contained alcohol, John Matuszak disappeared them in a gulp apiece. It was a classic maneuver by the Oakland

Raiders' wild man, who barged through his short, bacchanalian life with a lampshade on his head and a pair of panties dangling from the top of the shade."

And there was this gem on Weaver: "The profane potentate of the Orioles has spent the past thirteen seasons kicking dirt on home plate, tearing up rule books under umpires' noses, and generally behaving as if he were renting his soul to the devil with an option to buy."

Schulian was a throwback, to be sure, with an eye for detail, an ear for dialogue, and a feel for the lyric touch that put him in the company of the craft's old masters, of writers such as W. C. Heinz and Red Smith, both of whom he profiles in these pages. Of course, in laying bare the best of his life's work here, Schulian leaves something else behind quite as memorable—an enduring profile, revealed piece by piece, of the talent of the writer himself.

Acknowledgments

Some of these stories appeared in slightly different form when they were originally published. For the chance to write them and gather them here, the author would like to express his gratitude to the *Chicago Sun-Times, Sports Illustrated, GQ,* the *Chicago Daily News* (RIP), the *Philadelphia Daily News,* the *Baltimore Evening Sun* (RIP), the *Los Angeles Times, Sport* (RIP), *The National Sports Daily* (RIP), *Sport SCORE* (RIP), msnbc.com, and Danny Peary, editor of the book *Cult Baseball Players.*

Introduction

In an age when it seems that no royal perk is enough for the athletes who have been crowned our heroes, the helicopter that whisks Kobe Bryant to the Lakers' home games strikes me as more practical than self-indulgent. After all, the drive from his manse can take as long as two hours, even in a Lamborghini. What better reason to fly over the traffic jams that snarl the sprawling mess of Los Angeles, where his name and likeness are indelible in every subdivision and strip mall? L.A. is his kingdom, and a kingdom must be a hard thing to ignore when it is yours, but still I hope Kobe looks beyond it once in a while. I hope he looks until he sees the past.

He might get a glimpse of Steve Van Buren, the Philadelphia Eagles' fourteen-karat halfback, waking up one Sunday morning in 1948 and pulling back the curtain to discover that a blizzard had buried the city. The Eagles were supposed to play for the NFL championship that day, but Van Buren thought it would never happen, not with snow up to the rooftops, so he jumped back into bed. A phone call from his coach, Greasy Neale, coaxed him out again. There would indeed be a game. How Van Buren got to it from his suburban home was his problem. He couldn't extricate his car from his garage, so, like many another wage slave, he climbed aboard a trolley car, transferred to the subway, and walked the last seven blocks to Shibe Park.

The snow on the tarpaulin covering the field was so heavy that the Eagles and the Chicago Cardinals had to help the grounds crew roll it to the sideline. In action at last, Van Buren defied treacherous footing and nonexistent visibility to score the game's only touchdown. Then he celebrated the Eagles' championship by walking back to the subway and riding it to where he could catch the trolley home.

And there you have the difference between yesterday's heroes and today's: Van Buren's trolley and Kobe's 'copter.

There, too, is the inspiration for this book.

It is a cross-section of newspaper columns and magazine stories I wrote about the last heroes who at least gave the impression that they walked among us. I want to offer proof that they actually existed for both the fans who cheered them and the writers who chronicled their exploits. The heroes the press anointed could be irascible—one of my contemporaries got stuffed in a trashcan, another thrown in a swimming pool—but enough questions were answered for human beings to emerge from behind the headlines.

Once, it was a sports page staple to paint a picture of a hero and attempt to show the good and the bad of him, the happy and the sad. But these days, with the newspaper business reduced to rubble, character sketches are in increasingly short supply. For one thing, the heroes have too much at stake to risk revealing their true selves—too much money, too much fame, too much everything. They are further afflicted by social media eager to catch them shooting off their mouths, canoodling with coeds gone wild (if Madonna isn't available), or drunk and drugged-up enough to win a ticket to rehab. It might be TMZ, *Deadspin*, *US Weekly*, or some rat-faced kid who gets lucky with the camera in his iPhone, but our heroes live in fear that someone will nail them for something. The result is a stifling paranoia and a furtive, cliché-hugging air that wouldn't become a DMV clerk let alone a world-class athlete who stares down blitzing linebackers or hundred-mile-an-hour fastballs for a living.

My friend Alex Belth, mastermind of the wide-ranging and ceaselessly entertaining Bronx Banter Blog, traces the change in athletes to the early nineties. That, he says, was when salaries became otherworldly and the big names in sports packed their bags and headed for whatever their idea of Mount Olympus was, be it a mansion on a Florida golf course or a horse ranch in that part of Montana favored by moguls and movie stars. It was also the time when more and more newspaper sports columnists began giving up on writing about people and started spouting opinions loudly, endlessly, and, too often, artlessly. The noise they made was the print and Internet equivalent of the soulless jumble that assaults us on sports talk radio and the worst of cable TV's yak fests. What none of the shouters and screamers seemed to realize was that when something truly deserving of comment occurred, they had no way to differentiate it from their blathering about the inconsequential. And they still don't.

The tenor of the times makes me glad I'm no longer a sports columnist, and yet my affection for sportswriting remains undiminished. I was lucky enough to count old masters such as W. C. Heinz and Red Smith as my friends as well as my heroes, and I am proud to have been part of a generation in which press boxes overflowed with talent that regularly awed me and left me reeling with envy. There are those of us who like to think the standard we set will never be equaled, but it is, time and again. Just read the books by Mark Kriegel and John Ed Bradley, the magazine pieces by S. L. Price and Wright Thompson, and anything and everything from the pens of Charlie Pierce, Joe Posnanski, Sally Jenkins, and Mark Kram Jr. These contemporary big hitters embrace the language, challenge the ruling mindset, and operate with a time-honored blend of heart and humanity. To say thank you scarcely seems sufficient when I consider the obstacles that face them at every turn. Better I could give them the kind of subjects I have included in this book.

The first one I crossed paths with was Willie Mays, a year after the World Series in which he closed out his magnificent career by proving he could no longer walk on water in center field. I was still a cityside reporter at the *Baltimore Evening Sun* and the sports department should have handled his visit, but there I was watching Willie grump through breakfast. I wrote the story that way, too, right up to the pleasant surprise it had for an ending.

Not for nothing had I read the advice Red Smith got from his favorite sports editor, Stanley Woodward: "Stop godding up those ballplayers." I tried to apply that edict to everything I wrote about sports for the next thirty-five years. The heroes on my watch were first and foremost human beings, whether it was Walter Payton, who had little to say, or Muhammad Ali, who said enough to fill the entire sports page. Both of them gave me something special to write about, as did Pete Rose and Pete Maravich, who sank under the weight of forces they couldn't control, and Reggie Jackson, whose mood swings were as mesmerizing as his home run swing. And then there were those who were heroes strictly by my definition, the fight guys who gave their cruel sport a heart and the high school basketball star cut down by a bullet before his name could be writ large.

Of all the heroes I encountered, though, the one who best fit the description was Stan Musial, who managed to be a regular guy even with a statue of him standing outside old Busch Stadium, just as it does now in front of new Busch. In 1982, with the Cardinals on their way to the World Series, it seemed fitting that I should write about him. We met at the restaurant that bore his name, and as soon as I mentioned an obscure teammate of his—Eddie Kazak, a third baseman in the forties—it was like we were old friends.

When I finally ran out of questions, Musial offered to drive me back to my hotel. We made our way through the restaurant's kitchen, pausing every few steps so he could say hello to a cook or slap a dishwasher on the shoulder. At last we reached the small parking lot in back. The only other people in sight were two teenaged boys with long faces. Musial was unlocking his Cadillac when one of them said, "Hey, mister, you got any jumper cables? Our car won't start."

"Lemme see, lemme see," Musial said. He repeated himself a lot that way. It only added to his charm.

He opened his trunk and started rooting around, pulling out golf clubs, moving aside bags and boxes until, at last, he found his cables. By then, however, I was more interested in watching the boys. One of them was whispering something to his buddy and I could read his lips: "Do you know who that is? That's Stan Musial."

The statue in front of the ballpark had come to life.

1

Hundred-Yard Warriors

Chuck Bednarik
Concrete Charlie

Sports Illustrated
September 6, 1993

He went down hard, left in a heap by a crackback block as naked as it was vicious. Pro football was like that in 1960, a gang fight in shoulder pads, devoid of the high-tech veneer its violence has taken on today. The crackback was legal, and all the Philadelphia Eagles could do about it that Sunday in Cleveland was carry a linebacker named Bob Pellegrini off on his shield.

Buck Shaw, a gentleman coach in this ruffian's pastime, watched for as long as he could, then he started searching the Eagle sideline for someone to throw into the breach. His first choice was already banged up, and after that the standard thirty-eight-man NFL roster felt as tight as a hangman's noose. Looking back, you realize that Shaw had only one choice all along.

"Chuck," he said, "get in there."

And Charles Philip Bednarik, who already had a full-time job as Philadelphia's offensive center and a part-time job selling concrete after practice, headed onto the field without a word. Just the way his father had marched off to the open-hearth furnaces at Bethlehem Steel on so many heartless mornings. Just the way Bednarik himself had climbed behind the machine gun in a B-24 for thirty missions as a teenager fighting in World War II. It was a family tradition: Duty called, you answered.

Chuck Bednarik was thirty-five years old, still imposing at

six-foot-three and 235 pounds, but also the father of one daughter too many to be what he really had in mind—retired. Jackie's birth the previous February gave him five children, all girls, and more bills than he thought he could handle without football. So here he was in his twelfth NFL season, telling himself he was taking it easy on his creaky legs by playing center after all those years as an All-Pro linebacker. The only time he intended to move back to defense was in practice, when he wanted to work up a little extra sweat.

And now, five games into the season, this: Jim Brown over there in the Cleveland huddle, waiting to trample some fresh meat, and Bednarik trying to decipher the defensive terminology the Eagles had installed in the two years since he was their middle linebacker. Chuck Weber had his old job now, and Bednarik found himself asking what the left outside linebacker was supposed to do on passing plays. "Take the second man out of the backfield," Weber said. That was as fancy as it would get. Everything else would be about putting the wood to Jim Brown.

Bednarik nodded and turned to face a destiny that went far beyond emergency duty at linebacker. He was taking his first step toward a place in NFL history as the kind of player they don't make anymore.

✫ ✫ ✫

The kids start at about 7:00 a.m. and don't stop until fatigue slips them a Mickey after dark. For twenty months it has been this way, three grandchildren roaring around like gnats with turbochargers, and Bednarik feeling every one of his years. And hating the feeling. And letting the kids know about it.

Get to be sixty-eight and you deserve to turn the volume on your life as low as you want it. That's what Bednarik thinks, not without justification. But life has been even more unfair to the kids than it has been to him. The girl is eight, the boys are six and five, and they live with Bednarik and his wife in Coopersburg, Pennsylvania, because of a marriage gone bad. The kids' mother, Donna, is there too, trying to put her life back together, flinching every time her father's anger erupts. "I can't help it," Bednarik says plaintively. "It's the way I am."

The explanation means nothing to the kids warily eyeing this big man with the flattened nose and the gnarled fingers and the faded tattoos on his right arm. He is only one more question in a world that seemingly exists to deny them answers. Only with the passage of time will they realize they were yelled at by Concrete Charlie, the toughest Philadelphia Eagle there ever was.

But for the moment, football makes no more sense to the kids than anything else does about their grandfather. "I'm not *one* of the last sixty-minute players," they hear him say, "I am *the* last." Then he barks at them to stop making so much noise and to clean up the mess they made in the family room, where trophies, photographs, and game balls form a mosaic of the best days of his life. The kids scamper out of sight, years from comprehending the significance of what Bednarik is saying.

He really is the last of a breed. For fifty-eight and a half minutes in the NFL's 1960 championship game, he held his ground in the middle of Philly's Franklin Field, a force of nature determined to postpone the christening of the Green Bay Packers' dynasty. "I didn't run down on kickoffs, that's all," Bednarik says. The rest of that frosty December 28, on both offense and defense, he played with the passion that crested when he wrestled Packer fullback Jim Taylor to the ground one last time and held him there until the final gun punctuated the Eagles' 17–13 victory.

Philadelphia hasn't ruled pro football in the thirty-three years since then, and pro football hasn't produced a player with the combination of talent, hunger, and opportunity to duplicate what Bednarik did. It is a far different game now, of course, its complexities seeming to increase exponentially every year, but the athletes playing it are so much bigger and faster than Bednarik and his contemporaries that surely someone with the ability to go both ways must dwell among them.

Two-sport athletes are something else again, physical marvels driven by boundless egos. Yet neither Bo Jackson nor Deion Sanders, for all their storied shuttling between football and baseball, ever played what Bednarik calls "the whole schmear." And don't try to make a case for Sanders by bringing up the turn he took at wide receiver last season. Bednarik has heard that kind of noise before.

"This writer in St. Louis calls me a few years back and starts talking about some guy out there, some wide receiver," he says, making no attempt to hide his disdain for both the position and the player. "Yeah, Roy Green, that was his name. The writer's talking about how the guy would catch passes and then go in on the Cardinals' umbrella defense, and I tell him, 'Don't give me that b.s. You've got to play *every* down.'"

Had Green come along thirty years earlier, he might have been turned loose to meet Bednarik's high standards. It is just as easy to imagine Walter Payton shifting from running back to safety, or Lawrence Taylor moving from linebacker to tight end and Keith Jackson from tight end to linebacker. But that day is long past, for the NFL is a monument to specialization.

There are running backs who block but don't run, others who run only from inside the five-yard line, and still others who exist for no other reason than to catch passes. Some linebackers can't play the run and some can't play the pass, and there are monsters on the defensive line who dream of decapitating quarterbacks but resemble the Maiden Surprised when they come face mask to face mask with a pulling guard.

"No way in hell any of them can go both ways," Bednarik insists. "They don't want to. They're afraid they'll get hurt. And the money's too big, that's another thing. They'd just say, 'Forget it, I'm already making enough.'"

The sentiment is what you might expect from someone who signed with the Eagles for ten thousand dollars when he left the University of Pennsylvania for the 1949 season and who was pulling down only seventeen grand when he made sure they were champions eleven years later. Seventeen grand, and Reggie White fled Philadelphia for Green Bay over the winter for, what, $4 million a year? "If he gets that much," Bednarik says, "I should be in the same class." But at least White has already proved that someday he will be taking his place alongside Concrete Charlie in the Hall of Fame. At least he isn't a runny-nosed quarterback like Drew Bledsoe, signing a long-term deal for $14.5 million before he has ever taken a snap for the New England Patriots. "When I read about that," Bednarik says, "I wanted to regurgitate."

He nurtures the resentment he is sure every star of his era shares, feeding it with the dollar figures he sees in the sports pages, priming it with the memory that his fattest contract with the Eagles paid him twenty-five thousand dollars, in 1962, his farewell season. "People laugh when they hear what I made," he says. "I tell them, 'Hey, don't laugh at me. I could do everything but eat a football.'" Even when he was in his fifties, brought back by then coach Dick Vermeil to show the struggling Eagles what a champion looked like, Bednarik was something to behold. He walked into training camp, bent over the first ball he saw, and whistled a strike back through his legs to a punter unused to such service from the team's long snappers. "And you know the amazing thing?" Vermeil says. "Chuck didn't look."

He was born for the game, a physical giant among his generation's linebackers and so versatile that he occasionally got the call to punt and kick off. "This guy was a football athlete," says Nick Skorich, an Eagle assistant and head coach for six years. "He was a very strong blocker at center and quick as a cat off the ball." He had to be because week in, week out he was tangling with Sam Huff or Joe Schmidt, Bill George or Les Richter, the best middle linebackers of the day. Bednarik more than held his own against them, or so we are told, which is the problem with judging the performance of any center. Who the hell knows what's happening in that pile of humanity?

It is different with linebackers. Linebackers are out there in the open for all to see, and that was where Bednarik was always at his best. He could intercept a pass with a single meat hook and tackle with the cold-blooded efficiency of a sniper. "Dick Butkus was the one who manhandled people," says Tom Brookshier, the loquacious former Eagle cornerback. "Chuck just snapped them down like rag dolls."

It was a style that left Frank Gifford for dead, and New York seething, in 1960, and it made people everywhere forget that Concrete Charlie, for all his love of collisions, played the game in a way that went beyond the purely physical. "He was probably the most instinctive football player I've ever seen," says Maxie Baughan, a rookie linebacker with the Eagles in Bednarik's whole-schmear season. Bednarik could see a guard inching a foot backward in preparation for a sweep or a tight end setting up just a little farther from the tackle than normal for a pass play. Most important, he could think along with the best coaches in the business.

And the coaches didn't appreciate it, which may explain the rude goodbye that the Dallas Cowboys' Tom Landry tried to give Bednarik in '62. First the Cowboys ran a trap, pulling a guard and running a back through the hole. "Chuck was standing right there," Brookshier says. "Almost killed the guy." Next the Cowboys ran a sweep behind the same pulling guard, only to have Bednarik catch the ball carrier from behind. "Almost beheaded the guy," Brookshier says. Finally the Cowboys pulled the guard, faked the sweep, and threw a screen pass. Bednarik turned it into a two-yard loss. "He had such a sense for the game," Brookshier says. "You could do all that shifting and put all those men in motion, and Chuck still went right where the ball was."

Three decades later Bednarik is in his family room watching a tape from NFL Films that validates what all the fuss was about. The grandchildren have been shooed off to another part of the house, and he has found the strange peace that comes from seeing himself saying on the TV screen, "All you can think of is, 'Kill, kill, kill.'" He laughs about what a ham he was back then, but the footage that follows his admission proves that it was no joke. Bednarik sinks deep in his easy chair. "This movie," he says, "turns me on even now."

Suddenly the spell is broken by a chorus of voices and a stampede through the kitchen. The grandchildren again, thundering out to the backyard.

"Hey, how many times I have to tell you?" Bednarik shouts. "Close the door!"

The pass was behind Gifford. It was a bad delivery under the best of circumstances, life-threatening where he was now, crossing over the middle. But Gifford was too much the pro not to reach back and grab the ball. He tucked it under his arm and turned back in the right direction, all in the same motion—and then Bednarik hit him like a lifetime supply of bad news.

Thirty-three years later there are still people reeling from the Tackle, none of them named Gifford or Bednarik. In New York somebody always seems to be coming up to old number 16 of the Giants and telling him they were there the day he got starched in the Polo Grounds (it was Yankee Stadium). Other times they say that everything could have been avoided if Charlie Conerly had thrown the ball where he was supposed to (George Shaw was the guilty Giant quarterback).

And then there was Howard Cosell, who sat beside Gifford on *Monday Night Football* for fourteen years and seemed to bring up Bednarik whenever he was stuck for something to say. One week Cosell would accuse Bednarik of blindsiding Gifford, the next he would blame Bednarik for knocking Gifford out of football. Both were classic examples of telling it like it wasn't.

But it is too late to undo any of the above, for the Tackle has taken on a life of its own. So Gifford plays along by telling what sounds like an apocryphal story about one of his early dates with the woman would become his third wife. "Kathie Lee," he told her, "one word you're going to hear a lot of around me is Bednarik." And Kathie Lee supposedly said, "What's that, a pasta?"

For all the laughing Gifford does when he spins that yarn, there was nothing funny about November 20, 1960, the day Bednarik handed him his lunch. The Eagles, who complemented Concrete Charlie and Hall of Fame quarterback Norm Van Brocklin with a bunch of tough, resourceful John Does, blew into New York intent on knocking the Giants on their media-fed reputation. Philadelphia was leading 17–10 with under two minutes to play, but the Giants kept slashing and pounding, smelling one of those comeback victories that were supposed to be their specialty. Then Gifford caught that pass.

"I ran through him right up here," Bednarik says, slapping himself on the chest hard enough to break something. *"Right here."* And this time he pops the passenger in his van on the chest. "It was like when you hit a home run, you say, 'Jeez, I didn't even feel it hit the bat.'"

Sam Huff would later call it "the greatest tackle I've ever seen," but at the time it happened his emotion was utter despair. Gifford fell backward, the ball flew forward. When Chuck Weber pounced on it, Bednarik started dancing as if St. Vitus had taken possession of him. And as he danced he yelled at Gifford, "This game is over!" But Gifford couldn't hear him.

"He didn't hurt me," Gifford insists. "When he hit me, I landed on my ass and then my head snapped back. That was what put me out—the whiplash, not Bednarik."

Whatever the cause, Gifford looked like he was past tense as he lay there motionless. A funereal silence fell over the crowd, and Bednarik rejoiced no more. He has never been given to regret, but in that moment he almost changed his ways. Maybe he actually would have repented if he had been next to the first Mrs. Gifford after her husband had been carried off on a stretcher. She was standing outside the Giants' dressing room when the team physician stuck his head out the door and said, "I'm afraid he's dead." Only after she stopped wobbling did Mrs. Gifford learn that the doctor was talking about a security guard who had suffered a heart attack during the game.

Even so, Gifford didn't get off lightly. He had a concussion that kept him out of the rest of the season and all of 1961. But in '62 he returned as a flanker and played with honor for three more seasons. He would also have the good grace to invite Bednarik to play golf with him, and he would never, ever whine about the Tackle. "It was perfectly legal," Gifford says. "If I'd had the chance, I would have done the same thing to Chuck."

But all that came later. In the week after the Tackle, with a Giant-Eagle rematch looming, Gifford got back at Bednarik the only way he could, by refusing to take his calls or to acknowledge the flowers and fruit he sent to the hospital. Naturally there was talk that Gifford's teammates would try to break Concrete Charlie into little pieces, especially since Conerly kept calling him a cheap-shot artist in the papers. But talk was all it turned out to be. The Eagles, on the other hand, didn't run their mouths until they had whipped the Giants a second time. Bednarik hasn't stopped talking since then.

"This is a true story," he says. "They're having a charity roast for Gifford in Parsippany, New Jersey, a couple of years ago, and I'm one of the roasters. I ask the manager of this place if he'll do me a favor. Then, when it's my turn to talk, the lights go down and it's dark for five or six seconds. Nobody knows what the hell's going on until I tell them, 'Now you know how Frank Gifford felt when I hit him.'"

★ ★ ★

He grew up poor, and poor boys fight the wars for this country. He never thought anything of it back then. All he knew was that every other guy from the south side of Bethlehem, Pennsylvania, was in a uniform, and he figured he should be in uniform too. So he enlisted without finishing his senior year at Liberty High School. It was a special program they had: Your mother picked up your diploma while you went off to kill or be killed.

Bednarik didn't take anything with him but his memories of the place he called *Betlam* until the speech teachers at Penn classed up his pronunciation. Betlam was where his father emigrated from Czechoslovakia and worked all those years in the steel mill without making foreman because he couldn't read or write English. It was where his mother gave birth to him and his three brothers and two sisters, then shepherded them through the Depression with potato soup and second-hand clothes. It was where he made ninety cents a round caddying at Saucon Valley Country Club and two dollars a day toiling on a farm at the foot of South Mountain and gave every penny to his mother. It was where he fought in the streets and scaled the wall at the old Lehigh University stadium to play until the guards chased him off. "It was," he says, "the greatest place in the world to be a kid."

The worst place was in the sky over Europe, just him and a bunch of other kids in an Army Air Corps bomber with the Nazis down below trying to incinerate them. "The antiaircraft fire would be all around us," Bednarik says. "It was so thick you could walk on it. And you could hear it penetrating. *Ping! Ping! Ping!* Here you are, this wild, dumb kid, you didn't think you were afraid of anything, and now, every time you take off, you're convinced this is it, you're gonna be ashes."

Thirty times he climbed behind his .50-caliber machine gun on bombing runs. He still has the pieces of paper on which he neatly wrote each target, each date. It started with Berlin on August 27, 1944, and ended with Zwiesel on April 20, 1945. He looks at those names now and remembers the base in England that he flew out of, the wake-ups at four o'clock in the morning, the big breakfasts he ate in case one of them turned out to be his last meal, the rain and fog that made just getting off the ground a dance with death. "We'd have to scratch missions because our planes kept banging together," he says. "These guys were knocking each other off."

Bednarik almost bought it himself when his plane, crippled by flak, skidded off the runway on landing and crashed. To escape he kicked out a window and jumped twenty feet to the ground. Then he did what he did after every mission, good or bad. He lit a cigarette and headed for the briefing room, where there was always a bottle on the table. "I was eighteen, nineteen years old," he says, "and I was drinking that damn whiskey straight."

The passing of time does nothing to help him forget, because the war comes back to him whenever he looks at the tattoo on his right forearm. It isn't like the CPB monogram that adorns his right biceps, a souvenir from a night in some Army town. The tattoo on his forearm shows a flower blossoming to reveal the word MOTHER. He got it in case his plane was shot down and his arm was all that remained of him to identify.

There were only two things the Eagles didn't get from Bednarik in 1960: the color TV and the thousand dollars that had been their gifts to him when he said he was retiring at the end of the previous season. The Eagles didn't ask for them back, and Bednarik didn't offer to return them. If he ever felt sheepish about it, that ended when he started going both ways.

For no player could do more for his team than Bednarik did as pro football began evolving into a game of specialists. He risked old bones that could just as easily have been out of harm's way, and even though he never missed a game that season—and only three in his career—every step hurt like the dickens.

Bednarik doesn't talk about it, which is surprising because, as Dick Vermeil says, "It usually takes about twenty seconds to find out what's on Chuck's mind." But this is different. This is about the code he lived by as a player, one that treated the mere thought of calling in sick as a betrayal of his manhood. "There's a difference between pain and injury," Maxie Baughan says, "and Chuck showed everybody on our team what it was."

His brave front collapsed in front of only one person, the former Emma Margetich, who married Bednarik in 1948 and went on to reward him with five daughters. It was Emma who pulled him out of bed when he couldn't make it on his own, who kneaded his aching muscles, who held his hand until he could settle into the hot bath she had drawn for him.

"Why are you doing this?" she kept asking. "They're not paying you for it." And every time, his voice little more than a whisper, he would reply, "Because we have to win."

Nobody in Philadelphia felt the need more than Bednarik did, maybe because in the increasingly distant past, he had been the town's biggest winner. It started when he took his high school coach's advice and became the least likely Ivy Leaguer that Penn has ever seen, a hard case who had every opponent he put a dent in screaming for the Quakers to live up to their nickname and de-emphasize football.

Next came the 1949 NFL champion Eagles, with halfback Steve Van Buren and end Pete Pihos lighting the way with their Hall of Fame greatness, and the rookie Bednarik ready to go elsewhere after warming the bench for all of his first two regular-season games.

On the train home from a victory in Detroit, he took a deep breath and went to see the head coach, who refused to fly and had one of those nicknames you don't find anymore, Earle (Greasy) Neale. "I told him, 'Coach Neale, I want to be traded, I want to go somewhere I can play,'" Bednarik says. "And after that I started every week—he had me flip-flopping between center and line-backer—and I never sat down for the next fourteen years. That's a true story."

He got a tie clasp and a $1,100 winner's share for being part of that championship season, and then it seemed that he would never be treated so royally again. Some years before their return to glory, the Eagles were plug-ugly, others they managed to maintain their dignity, but the team's best always fell short of Bednarik's. From 1950 to 1956 and in '60 he was an All-Pro linebacker. In the '54 Pro Bowl he punted in place of the injured Charlie Trippi and spent the rest of the game winning the MVP award by recovering three fumbles and running an interception back for a touchdown. But Bednarik did not return to the winner's circle until Norm Van Brocklin hit town.

As far as everybody else in the league was concerned, when the Los Angeles Rams traded the Dutchman to Philadelphia months before the opening of the '58 season, it just meant one more Eagle with a tainted reputation. Tommy McDonald was accused of making up his pass patterns as he went along, Tom Brookshier was deemed too slow to play cornerback, and end Pete Retzlaff bore the stigma of having been cut twice by Detroit. And now the Eagles had Van Brocklin, a long-in-tooth quarterback with the disposition of an unfed Doberman.

In Philly, however, he was able to do what he hadn't done in L.A. He won. And winning rendered his personality deficiencies secondary. So McDonald had to take it when Van Brocklin told him that a separated shoulder wasn't reason enough to leave a game, and Brookshier, fearing he had been paralyzed after making a tackle, had to grit his teeth when the Dutchman ordered his carcass dragged off the field. "Actually Van Brocklin was a lot like me," Bednarik says. "We both had that heavy temperament."

But once you got past Dutch's mouth, he didn't weigh much. The Eagles knew for a fact that Van Brocklin wasn't one to stand and fight, having seen him hightail it away from a post-game beef with Bob Pellegrini in Los Angeles. Concrete Charlie, on the other hand, was as two-fisted as they came. He decked a teammate who was clowning around during calisthenics just as readily as he tried to punch the face off a Pittsburgh Steeler guard named Chuck Noll.

Somehow, though, Bednarik was even tougher on himself. In '61, for example, he tore his right biceps so terribly that it wound up in a lump by his elbow. "He just pushed the muscle back where it was supposed to be and wrapped an Ace bandage around it," says Nick Skorich, who had ascended to head coach by then. "He hardly missed a down, and I know for a fact he's never let a doctor touch his arm." That was the kind of man it took to go both ways in an era when the species was all but extinct.

The San Francisco 49ers were reluctant to ask Leo Nomellini to play offensive tackle, preferring that he pour all his energy into defense, and the Giants no longer let Gifford wear himself out at defensive back. In the early days of the American Football League, the Kansas City Chiefs had linebacker E. J. Holub double-dipping at center until his ravaged knees put him on offense permanently. But none of them ever carried the load that Bednarik did. When Buck Shaw kept asking him to go both ways, there was a championship riding on it.

"Give it up, old man," Paul Brown said when Bednarik got knocked out of bounds and landed at his feet. Bednarik responded by calling the patriarch of the Browns a ten-letter obscenity. Damned if he would give anything up.

All five times the Eagles needed him to be an iron man that season, they won. Even when they tried to take it easy by playing him on only one side of the ball, he still wound up doing double duty the way he did the day he nailed Gifford. A rookie took his place at center just long enough to be overmatched by the Giants' blitzes. In came Bednarik, and on the first play he knocked the red-dogging Sam Huff on his dime. "That's all for you, Sam," Bednarik said. "The big guys are in now."

And that was how the season went, right up to the day after Christmas and what Bednarik calls "the greatest game I ever played." It was the Eagles and Green Bay for the NFL championship at Franklin Field, where Bednarik had played his college ball, and there would be no coming out, save for the kickoffs. It didn't look like there would be any losing either, after Bednarik nearly yanked Packer sweep artist Paul Hornung's arm out of its socket.

But there was no quit in Lombardi's Pack. By the game's final moments, they had the Eagles clinging to a 17–13 lead, and Bart Starr was throwing a screen pass to that raging bull Jim Taylor at the Philadelphia twenty-three-yard line. Baughan had the first shot at him, but Taylor cut back and broke Baughan's tackle. Then he ran through safety Don Burroughs. And then it was just Taylor and Bednarik at the ten.

In another season, with another set of circumstances, Taylor would have been unstoppable. But this was the coronation of Concrete Charlie. Taylor didn't have a chance as Bednarik dragged him to the ground and the other Eagles piled on. He kicked and cussed and struggled to break free, but Bednarik kept him pinned where he was while precious seconds ticked off the clock, a maneuver that NFL rule makers would later outlaw. Only when the final gun sounded did Bednarik roll off Taylor and tell him, "Okay, you can get up now."

It was a play they will always remember in Philadelphia, on a day they will always remember in Philadelphia. When Bednarik floated off the field, he hardly paid attention to the news that Van Brocklin had been named the game's most valuable player. For nine-of-twenty passing that produced one touchdown—an ordinary performance, but also his last as a player—the Dutchman drove off in the sports car that the award earned him. Sometime later Bednarik caught a ride to Atlantic City with Retzlaff and halfway there blurted out that he felt like Paul Revere's horse.

"What do you mean by that?" the startled Retzlaff asked.

"The horse did all the work," Bednarik said, "but Paul Revere got all the credit."

☆ ☆ ☆

In the mornings he will pick up his accordion and play the sweet, sad "etnik" music he loves so much. As his football-warped fingers thump up and down the keyboard, he often wishes he and Emma and the girls had a family band, the kind Emma's father had that summer night he met her at the Croatian Hall in Bethlehem. Not what you might expect, but then Bednarik is a man of contradictions. Like his not moving any farther than his easy chair to watch the Eagles anymore. Like his going to 8:00 a.m. Mass every Sunday and saying the Rosary daily with the industrial-strength beads that Cardinal Krol of Philadelphia gave him. "I'm a very religious person, I believe in prayer," Bednarik says, "but I've got this violent temper."

Sixty-eight years old and there is still no telling when he will chase some joker who cut him off in traffic or gave him the finger for winning the race to a parking place. If anybody ever thought he would mellow, Bednarik put that idea to rest a few years back when he tangled with a bulldozer operator almost forty years his junior. As evening fell the guy was still leveling some nearby farmland for housing sites, so Bednarik broke away from his cocktail hour to put in a profane request for a little peace and quiet. One verb led to another, and the next thing Bednarik knew, he thought the guy was going to push a tree over on him. He reacted in classic Concrete Charlie fashion and got a fine that sounded like it came from the World Wrestling Federation instead of the local justice of the peace: $250 for choking.

That didn't change him, though. It slowed him down, made him hope that when he dies, people will find it in their hearts to say he was a good egg despite all his hard edges. But it couldn't stop him from becoming as gnarly as ever the instant a stranger asked whether he, Chuck Bednarik, the last of the sixty-minute men, could have played in today's NFL. "I wasn't rude or anything," he says, "but inside I was thinking I'd like to punch this guy in the mouth."

Of course he did. He is Concrete Charlie. "You know, people still call me that," he says, "and I love it." So he does everything he can to live up to the nickname, helping to oversee boxing in Pennsylvania for the state athletic commission, getting enough exercise to stay six pounds over his final playing weight of 242, golfing in every celebrity tournament that will invite Emma along with him, refusing to give ground to the knee replacement he got last December. "It's supposed to take older people a year to get through the rehab," he says. "I was done in four months." Of course he was. He is the toughest Eagle there ever was.

But every time he looks in the mirror, he wonders how much longer that will last. Not so many years ago he would flex his muscles and roar, "I'm never gonna die!" Now he studies the age in his eyes and whispers, "Whoa, go back, go back." But he can't do it. He thinks instead of the six teammates from the 1960 Eagles who have died. And when he sees a picture of himself with six other Hall of Fame inductees from 1967, he realizes he is the only one still living.

It is at such a moment that he digs out the letter he got from Greasy Neale, his first coach with the Eagles, shortly after he made it to the Hall. "Here, read this out loud," Bednarik says, thrusting the letter at a visitor. "I want to hear it."

There is no point in asking how many times he has done this before. He is already looking at the far wall in the family room, waiting to hear words so heartfelt that the unsteady hand with which they were written just makes them seem that much more sincere.

Neale thought he hadn't given Bednarik the kind of introduction he deserved at the Hall, and the letter was the old coach's apology. In it, he talked about Bednarik's ability, his range, his desire—all the things Neale would have praised if his role as the day's first speaker hadn't prevented him from knowing how long everybody else was going to carry on.

"If I had it to do over again," he wrote in closing, "I would give you as great a sendoff as the others received. You deserve anything I could have said about you, Chuck. You were the greatest."

Then the room is filled with a silence that is louder than Bednarik's grandchildren have ever been. It will stay that way until Concrete Charlie can blink back the tears welling in his eyes.

Walter Payton
The Poetry of Silence

Chicago Daily News
November 21, 1977

There will only be a number by his name. It will tell everybody who looks in the NFL record book that he ran for 275 yards in a single game, and nobody ever ran for more. Such a pity, for what Walter Payton accomplished Sunday was poetry, even if he never used a word.

Where Jim Brown's every slam-bang carry was a study in onomatopoeia, where Gale Sayers floated across the turf with strides as graceful as Elizabethan couplets, Payton performed in free verse. One time the little big man of the Bears would barge into the biggest defensive tackle he could find, the next time he would skitter around end like a rabbit with his tail on fire. And all the befuddled Minnesota Vikings could do was react in the manner of the first critics to see E. E. Cummings' unstructured poesy. They let Payton sail right by them.

It was the last thing he thought he would be able to do. He had missed practice Wednesday and he could barely get through half of Thursday's session. The team doctor blamed it on the flu. Payton's diagnosis was "hot and cold flashes." Whatever, he felt like the dog's breakfast Sunday as he waited to step into Soldier Field under a weeping dishrag sky. "I didn't know if I was going to make it through the introductions," he said.

He didn't complain about it, though, because complaining would have involved talking, and talking is something he would rather not to do with anybody—friend, foe, or poetry lover.

"Walter Payton is really a weird individual," said left guard Noah Jackson, who is in his third season of blocking for him. "Not weird in a derogatory way, but weird in a respectable way. He just won't let you get to know anything about him. When he's not on the football field, he's an off- to-hisself type person."

Actually, Payton has those tendencies on the field, too. "I don't like people talking to me during a game," he said. "Never." The last time anybody broke that unwritten rule was a year ago. Payton went into the season finale against Denver leading O. J. Simpson by nine yards in their duel for the league's rushing championship. "We concentrated on proving to Walter that we were trying for him so much that we forgot about the game," right guard Revie Sorey said. First, Payton got distracted, then he got injured, and then he got his balloon punctured. He had failed to topple Simpson.

The Bears dared not tempt fate with their last best hope for the playoffs at stake Sunday. As they poleaxed Minnesota 10–7, nobody said a word to Payton about his assault on the one-game rushing record established just last Thanksgiving when Simpson—him again—juiced Detroit for 273 yards.

"Did you set up that last run so Walter could break the record?" someone asked head coach Jack Pardee afterward.

"Did he break a record?" Pardee said, his eyes widening in surprise. "You're the first person who's told me."

All he cared about after Payton high-stepped fifty-eight yards through right tackle was getting him—or anyone else, for that matter—into the end zone from the Vikings' nine-yard line. And if the Bears couldn't do that, then Pardee, who probably plays field position in the shower, wanted them to drive as deep as possible, field goal be damned. "We didn't think the Vikings could go ninety-five yards into the wind for a touchdown," he said.

The Bears began painting them into an inescapable corner when Robin Earl, the rookie mastodon, plowed straight ahead for three yards. Payton jacked his total for the afternoon up to 271 yards by sweeping left end for three, and after quarterback Bob Avellini botched a handoff to him, Payton made amends on the next play. He didn't get the six points he was looking for, but with the Vikings' Matt Blair clinging to his knees, he made one of those long, strong lunges that have become his trademark. His reward this time was a four-yard gain. And the record.

"Somebody told me that was the fortieth time I carried the ball," said Payton, who needed one more carry to set an NFL record in that department. "It only felt like twenty."

Payton rarely comes closer to bragging than that, although he was tempted Sunday after realizing that the 1,404 yards he has gained in the first ten games put him within 599 of Simpson's single-season record of 2,003.

"How would you defense Walter Payton?" someone asked.

"I'd probably kidnap him the night before the game," he said, giggling.

He looked at his questioners with those large, startled eyes that give away his innocence and uncertainty. Nobody is supposed to think he has the slightest bit of ego, and now he had to prove it again. He talked about the way Earl, Jackson, and Sorey had mowed down the Vikings for him. "Revie got two of them with one block," he said. It was surprising he noticed. "Usually I don't watch numbers, just bodies."

Running is like that for Payton. It is instinctive, intuitive, for he is a natural. What does not come naturally to him is this business of meeting the press. For one thing, he despises the microphones with which radio people are forever threatening to unwittingly knock out his teeth. For another thing, he wonders what can possibly come from attempts to read his mind.

"It's an impossible task," he said. "I don't think anybody could analyze me."

Those who insisted on trying, however, were given some tips by the great man himself. "I used to do sports interviews down in Mississippi, at Channel 3," he said. "If you give a man some room, you get good stuff. But if you crowd him, he forgets what he's thinking about."

He waited to see if his message had sunk in.

"Could I ask you all a question?" he said at last.

"Sure," someone said.

"Naah," Payton said. "I'm just kidding."

He was hurrying to vacate the spotlight now. He bandaged a gouge on his left arm that he said hurt more than any of the Vikings' tackles. He tied his tie hastily and buttoned his blue sweater high enough to cover it. And then it was as if he heard a snap count that sent him weaving through the crowded dressing room and out the door and into the night. He left no poetry behind, just the spaces between the words where silence dwells.

It doesn't matter to me that four running backs have since broken Payton's record. I still think of him as the greatest all-around football player it has been my privilege to watch. Once upon a time, I might have also described Payton as indestructible simply because of the way he punished the poor devils who had to tackle him. But I learned that wasn't true when cancer killed him in 1999.

Terry Bradshaw
A Country Boy Can Survive

Chicago Sun-Times
January 22, 1979

MIAMI—They were surging around the platform where Terry Bradshaw stood, waving microphones and shouting questions and forcing him backward until he was pressed against a white pillar. At the rear of the truth-seeking mob, one of Bradshaw's friends cranked up and threw him the good ol' boy equivalent of a life preserver—a bag of Red Man chewing tobacco.

It wobbled through the air like a wounded mallard. Any other time, under any other circumstances, the bag would have come open and the journalists would have worn tobacco back to their hotel rooms. But Bradshaw, risking impalement on a sea of pens and pencils, steadied himself with his left hand and leaned out to grab the bag with his right. It was an impossible catch, a catch worthy of Lynn Swann, yet Terry Bradshaw made it. And why not? On Sunday he could do anything.

He even took the Super Bowl, that bore of bores, and turned it into a masterpiece in his own image. Never in nine years as the Pittsburgh Steelers' quarterback had he thrown four touchdown passes in a game, but he did in this one. Never had he passed for more than three hundred yards in a game, but he did in this one. And when he was done, he had hornswoggled the Dallas Cowboys 35–31 and made the Steelers the first team to win three Super Bowls. If there is any justice, they will engrave his Ozark Ike likeness on their championship rings.

And if there is anybody with any sense at NFL headquarters, they will take the words Bradshaw uttered in his victory speech and chisel them in stone, to be handed down from generation to generation.

"Shoot, I wasn't gonna change my style just because we were playing in the Super Bowl," he said. "Passing was what got us here—play-action passes and like that—and I was gonna keep on passing. Everybody always tightens up when they get here, but I didn't give a hoot whether we won or lost. I was gonna play the game my way. I was gonna have a good time."

Hear that, George Allen? How about you, Red Miller? And you, Don Shula? And what about all the rest of you troglodyte coaches who are afraid to throw on anything less than third-and-eighteen? It really is possible to play in football's biggest game and induce thrills instead of a deep sleep.

There was Bradshaw running around the tatty old Orange Bowl Sunday, living out his fantasy as a happy bombardier. Seventy-five yards to John Stallworth. Touchdown. Twenty-eight more to Stallworth. TD again. A shorty of seven to Rocky Bleier, but it was good for six points just the same. And then one last fling to Lynn Swann as the overworked scoreboard wheezed and sputtered.

You had to love it unless you were betting on Dallas or wearing a Cowboy uniform. And if that was the case, you wondered why your team, with all its computers and IQ tests and well-advertised wizardry, hadn't thought of letting one of the inmates run the asylum.

"We confused Bradshaw with our defenses, but damned if it mattered," safety Cliff Harris said. "He didn't know who to throw to, and because he didn't, he'd just throw to whoever and complete it. What do you do?"

The Cowboys could start by telling Bradshaw they're sorry they wondered publicly if he was smart enough to play Pick-Up

Sticks. After all, he did outfox them completely by sending Franco Harris up the middle for an eighteen-yard scoring run when the Cowboys were guessing pass. And perhaps the menacingly mischievous Harris in particular could apologize for threatening Bradshaw's well-being before the game.

"I still think Cliff's a heckuva guy," Bradshaw said. "We talked a little after the game and I told him I'd see him at that Christians' conference in Dallas."

Give Bradshaw an amen for needling Harris so deftly. And keep in mind that he was just as uncharacteristically unexcitable during the game. Maybe he would have been different if Swann had been called for offensive pass interference on the play that set up Pittsburgh's last touchdown. But Bradshaw wasn't going to talk about that, probably for fear he would upset the football gods who had been smiling on the Steelers. "I'm just leaning back and having fun," he said, leaning back and having fun.

He had earned his leisure by doing more than completing seventeen of thirty passes. For one thing, this was Super Bowl XIII and the superstitious had sworn that the game was cursed. Bradshaw had more to fear than a number, though. Two Dallas muggers stripped him of the ball in the second quarter, and while one of them skedaddled for a touchdown, Bradshaw lay writhing on the greensward. "When they told me on the sidelines that my left shoulder was separated, I about flipped out," he said. The team physician pacified him, however, by hastily revising the diagnosis to a strained shoulder. "I still felt kinda sick to my stomach," Bradshaw said. But he could play—that was the important thing.

Bradshaw had to grit his teeth and prove something to the detractors who had nipped at his heels even in his finest season. He had to prove it and then have the supreme pleasure of not bragging about it. "I'm right where I should be," he said. "Roger Staubach is at one level and I'm right below it."

But think about this: Staubach quarterbacks the Cowboys, and after what happened Sunday, the Cowboys are right below the Steelers. Staubach did not make the Super Bowl a game worth watching. Terry Bradshaw did. He made you wish the NFL put on a show like this every year. And maybe it would if he was always the quarterback.

Bear Bryant
A Win, and a Coach, for All Time

Chicago Sun-Times
November 29, 1981

BIRMINGHAM, Alabama—Legends grow scarce in this era of prying electronic eyes and unblushingly indiscrete memoirs. The man who can maintain his dignity while he buffs his image is a rare creature, one worth treasuring and maybe even coddling. So it came as a surprise Saturday to watch the University of Alabama's usually well-mannered football team spend three quarters treating an aging two-legged keepsake like something the cat dragged in.

Life is tough enough for Bear Bryant, who in the best of times describes himself as "tired and dotty-headed" when he isn't gulping down the eleven pills he needs each day to keep his engine running. But now he was going for the 315th victory of his thirty-seven-year career, the bauble that would make him the winningest college football coach ever, and his beloved Crimson Tide was acting as if it didn't believe the Bear is the truth and the light. It was letting Auburn, forgettable Auburn, pull ahead by three points and waiting as long as it could to salvage the 28–17 triumph that pushed Bryant ahead of Amos Alonzo Stagg in the record book.

Surely this would be grounds for the hide-tanning that underscored the Bear's nickname not only at Bama but at Maryland, Kentucky, and Texas A&M. Surely there would be a post-game uproar to summon the kind of fear he once instilled with sand crabs, mosquitoes, and his own willingness to hunker down in practice without pads and take on all comers. Oh, he used to be fierce, Paul William Bryant did, but when he came off Legion Field Saturday to hosannahs and hallelujahs, he couldn't help showing that his rock-hard heart has a big tender spot.

"Hell, it wouldn't have been any fun if we'd gotten a big lead right away and just breezed," he said in that sour-mash-and-cigarettes voice of his. "I think it was one of the greatest victories I've ever been associated with. If I had to chart a way to get the record, I'd want it just like this, comin' back in the fourth quarter. It showed the players what they can do. It proved they've got a lot of class."

And class is something Bear Bryant demands.

It is why he suspended All-Southeastern Conference tackle Bob Cayavec and guard Gary Bramblett two days before the victory that left 78,170 people chanting, "Three-fifteen, three-fifteen, three-fifteen!" It is why the Bear has spent the past twenty-four seasons hovering in his fabled crimson tower on the Tuscaloosa campus and stopping practices cold by bellowing through a bullhorn: "Goddammit, do it again! You're better than that."

Bryant teaches hitting and hard work because he knows there are rewards to be gleaned from them. How else would he have risen from his hillbilly roots in Moro Bottom, Arkansas, and become a legend to be mentioned in the same breath with the Halases and Lombardis? How else would he have been standing in the Alabama dressing room Saturday, sixty-eight and bone-tired, with President Reagan's voice caressing his ear. "He recalled he'd been to practice in a tuxedo a few years ago, which he did," the Bear said with a raspy laugh. Lord, all the big shots were calling him as night fell on a sun-dappled autumn day—Jimmy Carter, congressmen, wheeler-dealers—and you knew the old rascal was loving every second of it. But there was still nothing to compare to the glow that wreathed his craggy face when he spotted the people who had been with him along the way, the people he still calls "family."

All he had to do to see them during the game was glance around the sideline. Joe Namath was there, at least until the third quarter, when the suspense drove him to the shelter of the press box. John David Crow managed to go the distance. Danny Ford, the coach of the Clemson team that will now be jousting with 'Bama for number one in the wire-service polls, hung on till the end, too. And when the Bear opened the door to the interview trailer, there was another one—Pat Dye, the ex-assistant who kept his Auburn team in the game until the Crimson Tide's talent and tenacity took over.

"What the hell you doin' in here?" Bryant asked.

"I told you we were gonna get after your ass," Dye said, laughing.

Then they embraced.

There is nothing manufactured about the affection that Bear Bryant elicits. He sends birthday cards, goes to funerals in the snow, keeps track of his extended family through every twist and turn. Even as he sat relishing his 315th victory, he couldn't help remembering old friends sick with cancer and bad hearts, and others he has simply outlived. "I'm just thankful that the good Lord made it possible for me to be associated with so many good people," he said. And after the way his Crimson Tide performed in the fourth quarter, running their record to 9-1-1 and driving Auburn to extinction, it's safe to say that Bryant remains a sterling judge of character.

There was Walter Lewis, the third of the three quarterbacks he used, spearing the Tigers with a thirty-eight-yard touchdown pass that put Alabama ahead 21–14 with barely seven minutes left. There was halfback Linnie Patrick, suspended for insubordination earlier this season, inactive for all but one play in the first three quarters, banging fifteen yards around right end and through a half dozen would-be tacklers to reach the end zone and put the game on ice. And there was the Bear himself saying afterward, "I'd have carried every one of my players off the field one at a time if I'd had the strength."

Instead, he settled for shaking their hands and letting them see what might have been a tear in his eye. "It's been a hard year for me," he said. "I wasn't strong enough or bright enough for it to be otherwise." He was going home now, home to his wife and grandchildren, home to have "some milk, bread, and an onion" while he watched game film. He was going home with a piece of history that makes you wonder if a story they tell in Alabama is truth or fiction.

There was a coach who died, you see, and when he got to heaven, St. Peter welcomed him with a tour of the grounds. The last stop was the football field, where a lanky old gent in a houndstooth hat paced the sideline.

Peering in disbelief, the coach asked St. Peter, "Isn't that Bear Bryant?"

"Oh, no," St. Peter said. "That's only God. He just thinks he's Bear Bryant."

The Bear died a little more than a year later. It was the same week as the Super Bowl between the Redskins and the Dolphins, a game that featured five of his players. They all had good things to say about their old coach, but the one I remember best is the Dolphins' Don McNeal. "We were farmers, both of us," he said. "I grew up working behind a mule, farming and growing crops for my father, and so did he. He never forgot that. He never forgot that, down deep, he was the same as me. You want a reason why he was so great, there it is. He was one of us." It was a remarkable thing to hear from a black man about a white coach who, it was said, began caring about racial equality only when it was necessary to help him win football games.

Dan Hampton
A World of Hurt

Chicago Sun-Times
December 2, 1983

Pain is relative, which may be as good an explanation as any for why Dan Hampton could go from knee surgery back to defensive end without fretting about what haste might to do his chances of playing mumblety-peg at forty. Although the Bears' mountainous All-Pro aches and limps and generally behaves like a candidate for premature arthritis, he will swear on his playbook that the ring finger on his right hand has caused him more grief than his knee. On a good day, the misshapen finger only swells to the size of a golf ball. As for his knee, Hampton keeps it where neither friend nor foe can see it, beneath his pants.

So you take his word about the pain ratio and listen to team trainer Fred Caito recall the preseason scrimmage in which Hampton's finger got twisted into the shape of a hickory walking stick. "I could see Dan out there jerking it around for four or five plays," Caito says. "Finally he came out and said he needed some attention." Dislocations usually do. Indeed, a lesser man might have called in sick the rest of the season. Hampton just cussed about losing the strength in the hand he uses to throw blockers around like sacks of potatoes.

His injured finger plagued him most on a soggy Sunday in Philadelphia just as he thought he was regaining his grip on things. He tried to grab an offensive lineman's jersey and spin into the Eagles' backfield, only to discover that he was a beat slow—a perfect target for a leg whip. "I've taken the spin out of my repertoire," Hampton says. To convince him to do so, it took torn cartilage in the knee that got kicked, arthroscopic surgery, three weeks in sick bay, and, most important by his lights, the sight of his name in the NFL's weekly injury report.

"I don't want anybody reflecting on me because they think I'm not gutting it up," Hampton says. "All that questionable-probable stuff is a bunch of crap. They'd be a lot closer to the truth if they made the categories 'Sissy,' 'Punking Out,' and 'Squirreling Out.' There's no other way you can think in football. Everybody's got to be doing his day's work."

This play-now, heal-later ethic has been part of the Bears' tradition for as long as the feud they will renew with the Packers Sunday at Green Bay's Lambeau Field. Hampton became a believer the instant he read Dick Butkus' *Stop-Action*, in which the iconic monster of the Midway left no doubts that, his future as a cripple notwithstanding, he wished a pox on every man in the whirlpool. "I know just how he felt," Hampton says. So it is that the hard guy revered as Danimal refuses to cave in to his knee, won't even dignify the damned thing by putting it in his personal top ten of pain.

If he did, how could he ever look fellow pass rusher Mike Hartenstine in the eye? Two years ago, Hartenstine insisted on terrorizing quarterbacks even though his broken thumb was held together by pins. "God, he had one pin that stuck out of his cast," Hampton says. "Looked like a horseshoe nail—really nasty."

And then there is former safety Doug Plank, who would have risked paralysis if the Bears' doctors had let him. What would he say if he paused from retirement and listened to Hampton whine about something as inconsequential as a ravaged knee? "Calcification of the spine," Big Dan says, musing over Plank's career-ending injury. "Maybe that's the only way to go out, with a real showstopper."

So the beating goes on. And no matter how fierce the blows he catches, Hampton will tell anyone who asks that he has been on the receiving end of worse. The worst, in fact, was the first. He was a fifth-grader when he fell from an oak tree near his Arkansas home, breaking his left leg and crushing his right heel so badly that half of it had to be removed and the rest held together with the medical version of catgut and baling wire.

"I couldn't get my brother to believe I was hurt," Hampton says. "I had to wait until a neighbor boy went and got my mom. Then the doctors at the clinic I went to were out to lunch, and then they decided they had to send me to downtown Little Rock. I guess it was three and a half, maybe four hours before I got taken care of. And pain? I've never felt anything that bad."

Not any of the various lacerations that have moved his stitch count to two hundred. Not the hole he bored in his leg with a motorcycle as a high school senior and played on despite an infection that bordered on gangrene. Not the cartilage he broke in his sternum at the University of Arkansas, an injury that made him click like a six-foot-five, 255-pound castanet every time he breathed. Not the back injury in his second season with the Bears that made it impossible for him to touch his toes even though he never missed a game. And certainly not the knee injury that has underscored his proclivity for pain.

"I think I'm a masochist at heart," Hampton says, laughing as though he really does play to see how many purple hearts he can collect. But when he returned to combat two weeks ago against Tampa Bay, his sense of humor disappeared as soon as the Buccaneers' offensive linemen started diving at his bum knee. "He came off the field screaming, 'Can you believe it, those mother lovers are cutting me!'" says Gary Fencik, a Bear casualty himself. Of course everyone could believe it. In the NFL, they call it the taste test.

Those who administer it, however, had best be aware that there is no hiding from Hampton. "I'll pay them back someday," he says. And his targets can only hope it will not be with the same finality he wrought upon the tree whose branches long ago refused to hold him. After it was struck by lightning, he fetched a power saw and, with a murderous gleam in his eyes, cut it into firewood. "Actually, the whole thing was kind of cute," he says. In a world of hurt, it is better to give than receive.

John Matuszak
Me and the Tooz

Sports Illustrated
February 2, 2004

He had a drink in each hand, although I doubt he knew what kind of drinks they were. Caring only that both contained alcohol, John Matuszak disappeared them in a gulp apiece. It was a classic maneuver by the Oakland Raiders' wild man, who barged through his short, bacchanalian life with a lampshade on his head and a pair of panties dangling from the top of the shade. Nothing in that pre-thong era could change him, least of all Super Bowl XV, in New Orleans. The Tooz always reserved Wednesday for getting loose, and when the Raiders imposed an uncharacteristic curfew before the game, he boogied all over it.

"Too early for my game face, Johnny," the Tooz shouted to me over the Bourbon Street din as available babes pressed close and strangers fought for the privilege of buying the next round. I have a feeling he used the diminutive when addressing anybody—it seemed to come naturally to a six-foot-eight, 285-pound defensive end built like a municipal statue. Once you got past the stories about the drugs and the .44 Magnum and the machete (love that machete), he was the world's largest puppy dog. He started calling me Johnny when I wrote about his two-week incarceration with the Washington Redskins under George Allen, a match as odd as Kid Rock and John Ashcroft. In Oakland he celebrated his salvation with the Raiders by taking me to an after-practice haunt where one of the team's closet crazies was quietly getting pie-eyed as we walked in. Five seasons later the Tooz was in the Big Easy, hailing me with a *Johnny* at Tuesday's press conference and practically asking the Raiders if they wanted him to pay his thousand-dollar fine in advance for breaking curfew.

When I chanced upon him committing that sin, he was grinning like Mephistopheles and letting his adoring public sweep him toward ever more raucous surroundings. By the time the sun came up on Thursday, it was said that he had danced with other men's wives, landed in bed with a presumably unmarried woman, and put himself in prime position for a hangover bigger than he was. Though he had gone his way and I had gone mine—to sleep—he told me all I needed to know about just how good a time he'd had when I caught up with him after the devil's spawn from Oakland had throttled Dick Vermeil's Philadelphia choirboys. Somewhere between calling Al Davis a genius and mocking the straitlaced Vermeil, the Tooz saw me out of the corner of his eye and did a double take. "Hey, Johnny," he said, genuinely puzzled, "when did you get to town?"

The Other Side of the Story

Chicago Sun-Times
December 13, 1981

The questions started when the baby died. Johnny couldn't have been more than twelve or thirteen then, and he wanted to know what kind of god would take away his brother after only two years. Not long afterward, Johnny stopped going to mass.

Life wasn't fair and neither was death. Those were terrible thoughts for a shy, spindly kid who was already stumbling over his own gawkiness, but Johnny couldn't escape them. He had seen how the baby's feet puffed up as cystic fibrosis claimed another victim, and he had heard his mother sob that her angel would have to go to his grave without shoes.

Maybe it is at such moments that boys become men. If nothing else, it was when Johnny's mother decided that the only survivor of the three sons born to her was steeped in kindness.

"He got some money from me and walked all the way to the store to buy some shoes," she says. "Oh, he loved that baby."

And John Matuszak, who grew up to be portrayed as the Marquis de Sade of the NFL, would see to it that the baby was buried with dignity.

How strange the story seems when it is placed beside the boozing, wenching, brawling caricature that passes for the real Tooz. In Oakland, where he regularly leads the Raiders to the other side of midnight, and in all the other cities where he has spit in propriety's face—Washington, Kansas City, Houston, Tampa,

Columbia, Missouri—he is supposed to be the twentieth-century equivalent of the caveman he played in the movies. Forget that he bulwarked the defensive line for the Super Bowl champions. Matuszak watchers giggle about the pantyhose draped over his lampshade, nod knowingly at recollections of the Air Force cadet whose face he rearranged, and try to remember what he had in his car when he got tossed in jail last summer.

Let's see, there was a .44 Magnum, a bayonet, and some dope, hardly the staples of a candidate for sainthood.

"Well," Audrey Matuszak says, "Johnny is a little rowdy."

But she can overlook that because he doesn't have to beat the drum for macho in front of his mother, and couldn't if he wanted to. After all, Mama Tooz patted him on the back when his junior high classmates were teasing him mercilessly about his height. She watched him romping on the living room floor with his nephews and listened to him on the phone trying to explain how terrible he felt about John Lennon's murder. "Johnny was such a Beatles fan," Mrs. Matuszak says. "I even had to buy him a Beatles suit when he was in school." Of course he was a kid then. Nobody expected him to be different.

He was from a distinctly middle-class family—his father still works as a supervisor for Wisconsin Electric, and his mother has taken up clerking at a drugstore—and the greatest dilemma in his life could well have been moving from Milwaukee to suburban Oak Creek as a bewildered teenager. But he grew up to stand six foot eight and weigh 285 pounds, grew up with the kind of muscles that make sexpots and football scouts drool, grew up to star in the ribald tales that make the old neighborhood rush to his defense.

"Why, the last time my neighbor lady read something about Johnny in a magazine, she wanted to sue," Mrs. Matuszak says. "She remembers seeing me carrying Dawn—Dawn's the youngest of our three girls—and how Johnny used to come running up to the corner so he could take her the rest of the way. He really was a good boy, tender and loving and deep feeling. I guess you don't forget that."

Granted, there have been occasions when Mama Tooz was tempted. She detests the thought of her outsized offspring switching from beer to hard stuff. "Every time Johnny takes a drink of Yukon Jack, he hurts me," she says. The pain, however, is only momentary, a mere flash compared to the deep ache she felt when she learned that he was embarking on a marriage that soon went *pffft*.

"My husband and I weren't home when he called to tell us they'd taken out a license," she says, "so he let my sister-in-law give us the news. I could have killed him for that. I really could have."

Audrey Matuszak has dreams for her Johnny and they extend far beyond his pummeling quarterbacks for the greater good of the Raiders or following up on his success as an actor in *North Dallas Forty* and *Caveman*. She dreams of seeing him with an adoring wife and a flock of children, but she always seems to collide with the same problem: Big Tooz is still a kid.

Even at thirty-one, he is imbued with the same sense of mischief that got his high school rival locked out of the football dressing room in a jockstrap just as the cheerleaders walked by. There is no predicting when Matuszak's funny bone will start itching, it just does. How else can you explain his going on a toot the Wednesday before the Super Bowl, thousand-dollar team fine be damned?

"He was going to be so good, he was going to have such a good image," Mama Tooz says. "Well . . ."

At least she has the memories to reassure her that he doesn't always have to be kept under armed guard. Just listen to her talk about how he learned sign language so he could shoot the breeze with a deaf Oakland fan. And then there was the night he kept the Sears store in Oak Creek open until he could sign autographs for everybody who had showed up to see him. The stories go on and on, a mother's kisses for her misunderstood son.

"He isn't a bad boy," Mrs. Matuszak says.

But it is so much easier to believe that if you can picture her crying over her dead baby's swollen feet while Johnny trudges off to buy the shoes that will cover them.

The last time I saw the Tooz, he was laying down some additional dialogue for an episode of Miami Vice *called "Viking Bikers from Hell." He played one of the bikers, naturally. I was one of the show's writers. "Cool," he said when I told him I'd made the jump from the sports page. I thought I'd see him again somewhere in Hollywood, but I was wrong. He died in 1989, at thirty-eight, most likely from too much living.*

John Riggins
Runaway

Chicago Sun-Times
January 31, 1983

PASADENA, California—He was all alone now, thundering down the sideline with nothing in front of him but the end zone. The last Miami Dolphin had lost his grip on him, and he was free at last, with the wind whipping through his helmet's ear holes and the roar of the crowd growing louder and louder. They weren't going to catch John Riggins this time. Nobody was going to catch him.

He wasn't supposed to be shooting for anything more than a first down, but this was his little joke. On fourth-and-inches at Miami's 43, the Washington Redskins had ordered up a blue plate special called "Chip 70," and suddenly Riggins was turning those inches into yards. When he wheeled around left end, every yard he covered seemed to put another mile between him and the Dolphins, between him and the NFL's bureaucrats, between him and everybody who has ever tried to make him dance to their fiddling.

After his bold fourth-quarter gallop had given the Redskins their first lead Sunday, after he had pointed the Redskins toward their 27–17 Super Bowl victory, the air was filled with talk that President Reagan wanted to change his last name to Riggins. And Big John, this runaway dump truck disguised as a fullback, swatted down the joshing request as if it were just another underfed cornerback.

"Ron's the president," he said, "but I'm the king."

Could there be any question about it? Nobody else pounded 166 yards out of Miami's grim reaper defense. Nobody else carried the ball thirty-eight times for a Super Bowl record. Nobody else set an NFL playoff record with four straight 100-yard-plus games. Nobody else gained 610 yards for the tournament, 57 more than he gained during the strike-broken season. And nobody else could think back two years, the way Riggins did, and say, "I remember sitting out on my farm, listening to the coyotes howl."

He was pro football's unrepentant dropout then, angling for a contract extension he never got and playing hard-to-get whenever the Redskins had a peacemaker knocking on his door. A lot has been written about his self-imposed exile—a lot he didn't like, a lot that made him take an 18-month vow of silence—but the point that may have been touched on least was that the coyotes made music he could understand. They bayed at the moon, just the way he has been known to in his own distinctive way.

You may remember how Riggins was once moved to shave his head like a Mohican Indian, leaving nothing but a strip of his thick hair down the middle of his scalp. Even in New York, when he was a Jet and anarchy ruled, the locals didn't know what to make of that. They thought he was a rabble-rouser, a troublemaker, maybe even a Commie, for God's sake. But all he was, was a free spirit gasping for air in the stuffy world of corporate sports.

That's not a sin, by the way, and he tried to explain as much when he checked into Redskin Park seven seasons ago. When he talked his way into a fat paycheck as a free agent in 1976 and promptly laid an egg, he smiled and said, "Maybe I'm a better businessman than I am a football player." Alas, nobody got the joke.

Riggins had to wait until now for people to cling to his every word. He had to wait until he was thirty-three years old, with eleven seasons' worth of campaign ribbons on his broad chest, for anyone to leap to his aid the way Redskin owner Jack Kent

Cooke did Sunday when a TV sportscaster suggested that Riggins is, ahem, "crazy." "He is not," Cooke huffed. You have to think that nobody laughed harder about that than Riggins. Of course, he really is crazy.

He'll tell you so himself, in so many words. Just think of what he said when someone forgot that he had studiously ignored questions about retirement and asked once more, with feeling. "You know me," he said. "I'm kinda like the wind. I can change directions in five minutes."

For the Dolphins, however, Riggins was more than the wind. He was a hell-bent storm, one of those three-day blows off the Pacific that has been washing Malibu's million-dollar homes into the surf. He tore into the heart of the Miami defense again and again, following the blocks of the beasts the Redskins call "The Hogs" and seemingly feeding on the weight of the load he was carrying.

"Actually, I only told Joe Gibbs I wanted to run this much against Detroit," he said of the Redskins' coach. "I think he got carried away."

The audience laughed. Riggins just smiled.

"Do this in regular season?" he asked, surprised that anyone would ask. "Listen, there's an old fella in Centralia, Kansas—name's Glenn Jacobs—and if I tell him the coyotes might be getting on my nerves, he says, 'I've killed about two hundred of 'em. They don't exactly raise the hair on the back of my neck anymore.' It's the same with me and the regular season. I've played about 130 regular-season games, and they don't exactly raise the hair on the back of my neck anymore."

Ah, but the playoffs and the Redskins' improbable march to their first Super Bowl championship—that was different, that was special. In an era when the NFL has gone airborne, John Riggins reveled in the joys of being a mastodon. He hammered away at a defense that was supposed to be made of granite, and he turned it to dust when he wasn't supposed to be doing anything more than loosening another little piece of it.

The demolition began with "Chip 70." Clint Didier, the Redskins' man in motion, did an about-face, and Don McNeal, the Dolphin cornerback who was supposed to be trailing him, slipped when he tried to do likewise. By the time McNeal was back on his feet, Riggins had the ball and was veering around left end. "I remember one guy had a hand on me," he said, "but he couldn't hold on." That was McNeal, and as he lay where he had fallen, he watched something that has been a long time coming.

John Riggins was finally out there by himself, out where he has always wanted to be.

Dan Marino
A Kid Among Legends

Philadelphia Daily News
November 27, 1984

MIAMI—The rogues' gallery doesn't exist that could make room
for Dan Marino without an uncomfortable pause. His is a coun-
tenance rich in dimples and curls, a visage unencumbered by
wrinkles, seams, and scars. He represents youth in bloom, and
when people see his picture hung beside shots of George Blanda
and Y. A. Tittle, they are going to wonder what he could possibly have in common with those old buzzards.

They were finished as quarterbacks almost before Marino was
as big as the ball they threw. "The only thing I remember Blanda
doing is kicking," he says. Tittle, on the other hand, isn't even a
memory, just a name in the record book. The thirty-six touchdown passes he threw as the hairless, fearless leader of the 1963
New York Giants matched the single-season standard established
two years earlier by the grimly purposeful Blanda. Embittered
by his wars with George Halas in Chicago, Blada was hell-bent
on creating a new frontier in Houston. And his crusade and Tittle's crust make it that much harder to imagine Marino in their
company.

Marino is twenty-three, and the only thing that has raised his
ire so far is the *Miami Herald*'s revelation that he is engaged to
marry his sweetheart from New Lebanon, Pennsylvania. The rest
of the time he is PG-rated sweetness and light, uttering scarcely
a sentence that isn't brimming with praise for his elders. But he

changed the equation last night by unfurling four touchdown passes in the Dolphins' 28–17 escape act against the New York Jets. Now he has thirty-six for the season, too. Now he is one with Blanda and Tittle.

Of course the era he's playing in gives him an advantage they didn't have. They played twelve games in a season while last night's game was Marino's thirteenth, and he has three more in which to turn Blanda and Tittle into statistical afterthoughts. So give him an asterisk if you must. But be advised that none but a blockhead would underestimate him.

"He's very aware of what he's doing, he's not awed or intimidated," said Dolphins coach Don Shula. "You could see it when we played Pittsburgh. Pittsburgh's his hometown and I thought he might be a little shaky, but he just went in there and went after it. He's in every game that way." Shula raised his right hand as high above his head as he could and said, "He's in it way up to here."

Without that level of commitment from Marino, the Dolphins certainly wouldn't own a 12-1 record and they might even be hard-pressed to equal the Jets' 6-7. "I don't spend any time with speculation like that," Shula said. "I don't see any point in it. We've got Marino and that's all that matters to our team.

In Shula's jut-jawed world, strangers might never hear anything closer to a sigh of relief than that. But relief was certainly what the Dolphins needed when they tiptoed into the Orange Bowl last night. Their only defeat of the season was eight days behind them, and there was no forgetting that they had warmed up for it with stinkers against the Eagles and the very same Jets who lay in ambush again. Suddenly you could hear unhappy rumblings about the Dolphin's collapsible defense and Uwe von Schamann's misguided kicking.

The rumblings turned to anguished screams last night when Jets quarterback Ken O'Brien faked to Freeman McNeil up the middle, then hit him with an over-the-shoulder pass for the game's first score. "That young quarterback of theirs kept coming up with answers on third down," Shula said. "I was waiting for him to throw one up to us, but it never happened."

The Jets picked O'Brien over Marino in the 1983 draft, and their reasons were as plain as the statistics that O'Brien left behind last night: twenty-one pass completions in thirty-nine attempts for 267 yards and a touchdown. But there were subtleties woven into the 192 yards that Marino wrung out of his nineteen-of-thirty-one performance, and they proved once again why he is old beyond his years.

It did no good to listen to him wax rhapsodic about the brilliant catch that wide receiver Mark Clayton made in the fourth quarter, somehow keeping his feet in bounds while he leaned out to catch the ball as if there were a safety belt around his waist. Clayton got a lot closer to the truth when he said, "The reason that play was so tough was because I screwed it up. I was supposed to keep sliding to the outside, but I let the defensive back get in my way."

Marino still delivered the goods. It was what he always demands of himself. It was what he always demands of his teammates. "Sometimes when they have me throw a reverse pass or something," the talkative Clayton said, "he'll tell me to just shut up and throw the bitch."

There is no arguing with Marino, not after the performance he has put on for the Dolphins. Any time he settles behind center, he is capable of doing what he did last night with Bruce Hardy twice and Clayton and Dan Johnson once apiece. "How can a quarterback lead by example any better than by throwing a touchdown pass?" Hardy asked. "We're lucky Dan's on our team. Or maybe we're on his team."

You assume that George Blanda's teammates felt the same way. Y. A. Tittle's, too. But they had age on their side. They wore campaign ribbons from wars that captured the imagination and stirred the competitive juices. They represented things that Dan Marino will need another decade to grow into.

For the present, the kid in him simply won't go away. A magazine photographer approached him the other day, for example, and complained that he was impossible to capture in action because he releases his passes so quickly. "Yeah? Yeah?" Marino asked delightedly. He wants to get rid of the ball in haste, wants to get it to the open man as fast as he can, wants to keep piling up the yards and the scores as rapidly as history can make room for him.

"Have you ever seen a more precocious quarterback?" someone asked Shula last night.

"What does precocious mean?" the man who coached Johnny Unitas and Bob Griese asked back.

He knew perfectly well, of course. Dan Marino defines the word every time he plays.

Joe Montana
Easy to Underestimate, Hard to Beat

Philadelphia Daily News
January 21, 1985

STANFORD, California—He was the other quarterback. It was a role without the legal complications that come with being the other woman, but it still left him feeling trapped and embarrassed. Every day last week, he had to answer reporters' questions about Dan Marino, the Miami Dolphins' golden child. And though he always found the right thing to say, the other quarterback couldn't help wondering if anyone remembered what he had done. But the past was not what people were here for.

So he could take the twenty-eight touchdown passes he threw during the regular season and his unsurpassed computer rating and even his three-year-old Super Bowl championship ring—he could take them all and dump them in the Pacific. All the media wanted to hear about was the bazooka Marino has for an arm, and how he stands taller than almost every other quarterback as he looks regally over pass rushers in his search for receivers.

"I'm sorry," the other quarterback kept saying. "I'm not fortunate enough to have the size and arm he does."

In rare moments of charity, someone would ask the other quarterback if the Dolphins' long-ball offense might make him look bigger, more powerful, more majestic. But it did no good.

"Maybe I don't have a strong arm," the other quarterback said. "Maybe I like to throw short."

From here on, though, no apologies are necessary. What we have before us is the man who engineered the San Francisco

49ers' 38–16 Super Bowl humiliation of Miami, a dervish who not only passed for three touchdowns and a record 331 yards but ran for an equally historic 39 yards and one more score. You can call him a winner, and you can call him the game's Most Valuable Player, too. He has captured the award twice now, a feat that only Bart Starr and Terry Bradshaw have accomplished, and if their names will never be forgotten, maybe the other quarterback's name shouldn't be, either.

It is Joe Montana.

He isn't much to look at even if he does have a movie starlet for a fiancée—just a thin, slouchy figure who doesn't blossom in bright lights. And he isn't big on small talk in public places, particularly when it involves how great he may or may not be. But his performance in Stanford Stadium was not that of someone filled with self-doubt. "I don't see how he could have played any better," said wide receiver Dwight Clark. Maybe Joe Montana never has.

The other quarterback, indeed.

He shed that label with the subtlety that is part and parcel of San Francisco's offense. He threw no passes that were particularly long, and he made no moves that were particularly startling, and in the game's early minutes, Marino made him look as if he might be finished before he started.

Miami opened with a hurry-up attack designed to negate the depth of the 49ers' defense, and there was Marino heaving the ball every which way. "He's a great quarterback," Montana said, and the kid seemed determined to prove it as he began the festivities by launching a twenty-five-yard completion to Tony Nathan. Marino hopscotched the Dolphins down the field for a field goal, and then he erased a 7–3 San Francisco lead by completing five straight passes, the last a sweet lob to tight end Dan Johnson. If anyone ever looked unbeatable, it was Marino.

But Montana had been hearing that ever since the Dolphins arrived at Pete Rozelle's version of the Sweethearts' Ball. All the

49ers had. "It was Miami, Miami, Miami every time we turned around," Montana said. "You people were overlooking us."

And we did it again when Marino completed nine of his first ten passes. We hardly noticed that Montana was going seven-for-nine in the same stretch and using the unheralded Carl Monroe to set the tone for the day. On first and ten from the Miami thirty-three, Monroe curled out of the backfield on a pattern called "Roll Right, Halfback Sail." When he got to the five, Montana deposited the ball in his hands and all Monroe had to do was avoid tripping over Renaldo Nehemiah on his way to the end zone. The 86,059 paying customers called it a touchdown. The 49ers called it a harbinger of things to come.

They could play their short game almost at will not because the Dolphins' inside linebackers, Jay Brophy and Mark Brown, were babes in the woods, but because the Miami defense made them sacrificial lambs. "We thought it was a perfect fit for our offense," Montana said. Even when he was hurling long-range missiles to the wing-footed Nehemiah, there were reports that Clark and Freddie Solomon were open underneath. So underneath Montana went.

"Your confidence builds so much, you almost feel you can execute anything," he said. "Our offensive line was picking up their blitzes, Roger Craig was making great catches, Russ Francis was sliding and catching the ball."

And Joe Montana was running. "They never told me not to," he said. Discretion seemed advisable, though. Those 195 pounds at which the 49ers' press guide lists him must include a pocket full of rocks. There is no such generosity involved, however, when defenders beat him about the head and shoulders. "It can be kind of scary," he said, "especially when you're running up the middle and sliding."

But the Dolphins were vulnerable there, too. They kept leaving the middle open as they scattered on pass defense, so Montana kept scrambling for first downs. "Sometimes I wouldn't even look down the field," he said. On those rare occasions when he did, he saw Miami defenders chasing their quarries with their backs to him, never suspecting what he was up to. And one time, all he saw was the goal line.

He was supposed to be looking for Clark, but the sight of five yards of open road rearranged his priorities. He could apologize when he was back on the sideline. He could even admit he was doing something Marino couldn't. "But he's had a couple knees, hasn't he?" Montana asked. "Knees" is NFL shorthand for surgery on that most vulnerable body part, and the answer to his question was yes. "That makes it tough to move," Montana said. There would be no gloating, no rubbing it in.

"Joe is a gentleman, his teammates are very close to him," said Francis, the tight end with the well-developed sense of the ridiculous. "I know he always opens the door for me. Of course, I'm bigger than he is."

Maybe Montana likes it that way. Maybe the shadows are right for his understated personality, just as the spotlight seemed perfect for Marino as he rewrote Super Bowl history by passing fifty times yesterday. But Marino was the loser despite his twenty-nine completions, the poor devil who will have to live with the memory of four sacks and two interceptions. Montana, meanwhile, was sacked but once and his jersey bore nary a grass stain.

So he came away the winner and still flinched when people pointed it out to him. "It wasn't me against Marino," he kept saying. He tried to build a case for teamwork by talking about the three touchdowns Craig scored, and the wall the 49ers' offensive line built around him, and a hundred other things that would do nothing to make him a star. But there was no denying what he had done. He had pitched a perfect game, and the questions about it stuck to him like flypaper.

"Were you always confident you could do it?" someone asked.

Joe Montana's sly smile tipped his hand at last.

"Why not?" he said.

Gary Fencik
Boola! Boola!

GQ
September 1986

Class of '76, wasn't he? They worry about such things at Yale, you know. Maybe the Chicago Bears worry about them, too, even with their Super Bowl championship. Maybe they look at Gary Fencik, the Yalie who upholds their honor at free safety, and figure he has the wherewithal to sample delicacies that will always be beyond their grasp. Surely an Ivy Leaguer ought to be able to order the right wine at dinner, and it's a matter of record that Fencik has tasted the kisses of at least one *Playboy* centerfold. But even so, that messy business involving his mouth and a runaway fullback's shoe last season must have made the Bears wonder how much a fancy education can really do for you.

When the Washington Redskins' 230-pound George Rogers slammed through the line, it didn't matter that Fencik could discuss America's nuclear policy or that he would wind up playing golf in February with the chairman of Mobil. He had to ignore his thirty-five-pound disadvantage and pray that colliding with Rogers would leave him with nothing worse than a headache. "Maybe that's why I didn't graduate *summa*," Fencik says. "I was just dumb enough." Dumb enough to what? Or do dumb and smart and variations thereof bear any relation to the way he picked up the pieces after Rogers's heel caught him flush in his cover-boy smile?

"I was afraid to open my mouth when I got back to the huddle,"

Fencik says, gingerly touching his fractured left front tooth. "Real root-canal work. Well, at least it hasn't started to discolor yet."

Then he laughs.

"I'll tell you what was really bad. Rogers gained about thirty yards after he got away from me."

Which is exactly what you would expect a football player to say. And, for the time being, a football player is exactly what Gary Fencik is.

Sometimes the free agents who drift into the Bears' camp for tryouts can't understand that. They are either too young or too desperate to see how a brain can make a body perform better than it ought to. "They must look at me," says Fencik, "and tell each other, 'He ain't that big and he ain't that fast. What the fuck is he doing here?'"

How easy it is to forget that Fencik has prospered with the Bears for a decade, winning All-Pro honors once, going to the Pro Bowl twice, and breaking Dick Butkus's team record for tackles in a career. Yes, the same Dick Butkus who became a legend at middle linebacker by bending every bone he couldn't break and dreaming of knocking off a quarterback's head and watching it roll down the field.

Yale is hardly a standard launching pad for inclusion in such red-blooded company. "Just a little school that plays shitty football," sniffs Bears defensive tackle Steve McMichael, who developed his perspective at the University of Texas. And McMichael is a *friend* of Fencik's, a broad-backed brawler whom Fencik considers a bridge to the saltier side of life. So you can imagine what opponents and strangers must think, particularly after the Yalie spent last season piling every radio and TV gig he could find atop his Consort styling-mousse ad and his magazine fashion spreads. "Fence is extremely hot right now," says his Chicago-based agent, Charles Besser. "I think he could easily be the next Frank Gifford." Then again, he might decide he would rather be "a player" in real estate. "Player" is Besser's word, a tribute to the success Fencik has already had at real-life Monopoly and a sample of the code the agent speaks with friends. They are lawyers, investment bankers, and wheeler-dealers—yuppies, if you will—and they are proud to include Gary Fencik in their starting lineup.

But Fencik, though he treasures both their friendship and his shiny-bright image, balks at being pigeonholed so blithely. The days when he took piano lessons and a wine-tasting class are no more. "The piano is gone," he says, "and I drink a lot more beer than wine." He drives American cars, not imports; he knows that "leverage" is a noun, not a verb; and he's so busy he's lucky to read a book a month, not the well-advertised book a week. He didn't appreciate it one bit last year when *Sports Illustrated* called him the "Pride of the Yuppies," nor does he like the idea that the Hunt Club, the Chicago bar of which he's part-owner, has become a roost for people who think he should be proud of the label. "Too many Top-Siders," he explains.

It doesn't seem a politic thing to say unless you realize that Fencik has never cut the pattern of his life to fit anyone else's fashion. Maybe that was the greatest lesson he learned at Yale. "When you looked at all those amazingly bright people around you, you saw that they had an ability to be comfortable with their own style," he says. So it is with him, as he proved while performing at one of the media inquisitions the week before the Super Bowl.

The Bears had literally put Fencik on a pedestal, the same status accorded the venerable Walter Payton and the outrageous Jim McMahon, and there were those in the audience who wondered if he wasn't enjoying it a little too much. It might have been the sunglasses he was wearing indoors at ten-thirty in the morning, or the way his shirt collar was turned up, or the fact that he had arrived late. Whatever, some reporters were muttering about arrogance while Fencik was trading bon mots with a writer who kept making him laugh.

"Where are you from?" he asked at last.

"Los Angeles," the writer replied.

"Yeah?" Fencik said, his brow wrinkling. "What's your name?"

"Jim Murray, *L.A. Times*," said the nation's reigning sports-page wit.

"I've read your articles," Fencik said. "Enjoyed them a lot."

And as he reached down to shake Murray's hand, he blushed. It was, by the standards of professional sports, an unnatural act. But Fencik didn't apologize for it any more than he backed away from George Rogers the day he got his smile rearranged. For there are two sides to the man, and every once in a while they converge. Thus did John Madden, the amiable Vesuvius of TV's color commentators, describe him as "clean dirt." Fencik loved it, and his mother did, too. There has been no official reaction from Yale, but at least the great thinkers there needn't worry that he has soiled his diploma by sweating for a living.

☆ ☆ ☆

Friends and strangers call Gary Fencik special. His parents cannot, for they have five other children whose feelings they cherish and protect. "I would never want anything written," Adeline Fencik says, "that would suggest that Gary is more special to us than any of the others." And yet, after watching him play in the Super Bowl, after letting him treat them to vacations in Europe and Hawaii, they can't deny that he is more something. "I guess the best way to describe Mr. and Mrs. Fencik," says a family friend, "is goggle-eyed."

Yale was the start of it. Here were these two humble, hard-working people from the South Side of Chicago—a coach who had become an assistant principal at Barrington High and his devoted wife—and their first son was leaving his father's school to go to college with budding moguls and aristocrats. They thought back to how he had made money painting houses and working for a veterinarian, how he had saved it by seldom going on dates, how he had even survived a crushing C in chemistry. Then he was gone, and they could only wonder how he was doing. "He could have at least said he was homesick," his mother says, smiling.

They got the message anyway when his father slipped off to Yale for a weekend and found Gary warming up for a freshman football game. "I yelled, 'Hey, hot dog!'" his father, John, recalls, "and you could just see him go, 'Where have I heard that voice before?' Then he turned around and ran over to the fence where I was standing and gave me a big hug. He was so glad to see me I still don't think he realizes he hit me with his helmet."

In truth, Fencik was in one kind of a daze or another throughout his freshman year. "It was kind of like the army—they wanted to break you down and build you back up," he says. "It was a very intense environment; I'd never been around so many bright people. I spent the whole year worrying that I was going to flunk out." Obviously, he didn't; in fact, he would graduate with a B average as a history major. But his memories of freshman life are a compendium of nonstop studying and a familiar stunt, sleepwalking.

"I did it a lot," Fencik says, "and I did it with my eyes open. That took some getting used to for my roommates."

Though his sleepwalking continued, Fencik woke up in a lot of other areas. He realized he was good enough to become Yale's all-time leading pass catcher—a record since surpassed—and he came to understand that it didn't hurt to study between breakfast and the time he went to the Yale Bowl for a game, just as long as no one knew about it. "I like people to think I don't work hard," he says, "but I really plan very thoroughly." Sometimes his strategy paid off, as when he was able to vacation in Kenya after spending the spring of his junior year in England. Sometimes it didn't, as when his senior thesis, on England's World War I war cabinet, got the best of him. "I didn't do real well," he says. "I don't even know where it is anymore." But that was part of his education, too. By the time he graduated, Fencik understood what he was, and wasn't.

"There are geniuses at Yale and there are drones," he says. "I was one of the drones. I partied hard, but I had to work hard, too. When I think about it, it seems that to be a top student there, you have to be original. You take something that has been studied for years and years and you try to see it in a different way than anybody else. You're creating. And in that sense, I guess the only place I ever really succeeded was football."

★ ★ ★

Jake Scott had the eyes of a hawk and a head so free of hair that you could have mistaken it for the top of his helmet. He played free safety for Miami's championship teams in the early seventies, providing the barbed wire that lashed together the defensive secondary and warding off intruders with his mordant wit. If he had hated Gary Fencik on sight, it wouldn't have been a surprise.

But none of the veterans were cut that way when Fencik tried out for the 1976 Dolphins as a tenth-round selection in the National Football League draft who didn't care that he would have needed spelunking gear to go any lower. The kid liked the pro game more than he thought a gentleman and a scholar from Yale could, or should. There wasn't any homework, and he got switched from wide receiver to safety, the position he had always wanted to play. The vets even took him and some of the other rookies drinking, a slice of life that introduced him to the pepperoncini peppers he still can't live without. Eventually, though, Jake Scott had to break the news to him.

"Funny thing," he said, surveying the 43 on Fencik's chest. "I've never seen anybody with that number make this team."

Fencik didn't break the tradition.

He punctured a lung in his first scrimmage, and by the time he got out of the hospital, he was so far behind his competition he could never catch up. After the Dolphins' final cut, it looked as if his next stop would be the management-training program at Citibank in New York. But before he could get his tie knotted and his collar buttoned down, the Bears beckoned.

"I remember calling to tell him how tickled I was that he was coming back to town," says Glenn Reed, Fencik's lawyer as well as a friend since high school. "He was really excited. He kept saying, 'Glenn, I can play for this team,' and all the while I was thinking, Good Lord, what does it matter? Just enjoy it. But he's had a tremendous amount of confidence in his ability every step of the way—making the team as a free agent, becoming a starter, making All-Pro. Well, I better stop before I get to the Super Bowl. I don't think he believed it himself last season."

Now it is done. Fencik stands with the NFL's conquerors after too many 7-9 seasons when the offense consisted of fumbles and offside penalties and the defense called itself either "Limburger" or "Swiss"—one stank, the other had holes in it. In retrospect, maybe it should have been easy to spot him as a survivor. When the Bears issued him the dread No. 43, he quickly traded it to the teammate he later replaced in the starting lineup. As No. 45, he has prospered one way or another ever since, though never quite as lavishly as in the wake of the Super Bowl. "It's like looking in the looking glass," he says. "You'll never be the same."

No longer do his shades hide him from autograph seekers as he walks down Chicago's streets. And when he and William "the Refrigerator" Perry, the Bears' rookie behemoth, made a personal appearance at a department store, the crush of humanity was so great they couldn't even put their pens to paper. They could only wave helplessly—presumably for help.

Fencik's refuge from such madness is the condominium on the North Side that has always separated him from the herd as well as from most of his married, suburban teammates. The music on the stereo may be Talking Heads or Chicago bluesman Buddy Guy or Chopin; the books and magazines on the shelf include back issues of *Foreign Affairs*, *Masters of French Impressionism*, and *Charlotte's Web*, the children's classic by E. B. White; and the conversation of an evening may jump from venture capital to the audacity of making a movie like *Brazil* in the Reagan era. It is a vibrant jumble that seems perfect for someone who has spent his off-seasons running with the bulls in Pamplona and traveling the Far East by himself. Nobody beyond Chicago really cared, though, until the Bears' howling success. Before that, Fencik was the only thing he could be on a team that defined failure—a cult figure.

It wasn't just that he was an Ivy Leaguer and the Chicago press's idea of a Renaissance man. There was also an irreverence about him that he never tried to muzzle. His teammates nicknamed him "Doom," his general manager settled on "Bitch." He raised hell about the constipated offense, the insanity of having to stay in a hotel the night before home games, and the size of the salary (now $400,000 a year) his historically penurious employers paid him. "I wasn't critical," Fencik says. "I was honest." If he seems quieter now—the younger Bears have taken the lead in the bitching-and-moaning department—it's because vindication breeds silence. It isn't because he's paying more attention to his job. His opinions never got in the way of that.

For his first seven seasons, Fencik played strong safety, a most un-Yalie position that required him to sacrifice his body and level blockers so others could make tackles. Though he excelled at it—All-Pro in '79, all everything else in '81—only the Bears understood how far his skills went beyond the physical to the cerebral.

Other safeties came and went, taking with them bodies that looked like palaces compared to his six-foot-one cracker box. These were studs who could fly, too, thoroughbreds he would race only if someone stuck a gun in his ear. And yet Fencik was always the one who watched them pack their bags. "He's an overachiever, plain as that," says Dan Hampton, the Bears' mountainous defensive end. "When the game changed, he changed with it. He's always made it so we couldn't do without him."

Perhaps the greatest tribute to Fencik's status was delivered backhandedly by Buddy Ryan, the hard case who masterminded the Bears' defense until he parlayed their Super Bowl success into a head-coaching job with Philadelphia. The occasion was a particularly graceless defeat in San Francisco, and Ryan was steaming.

"He was so mad he actually had tears in his eyes," recalls Doug Plank, who used to provide the *Sturm* to Fencik's *Drang* in the secondary. "He still used all the adjectives, though: 'Most of you assholes are just dumb football players. I understand that. You're going to screw up, you're going to go the wrong way, you're going to play like fucking idiots. But, goddammit, there are two or three of you I depend on to tell the rest of you dumb assholes what to do. And you didn't fucking do it. And . . .'"

Everybody knew Fencik was one of the guilty parties. Maybe guiltier than the rest, because he was smarter than the rest. "You try writing a story with somebody hitting you over the head with a baseball bat," Ryan says. "That's what it's like for Gary, and he can handle it. Brain-wise, he's got to be in the top 5 percent of all the players I've ever coached." To earn such praise—hell, to keep his job—Fencik can't allow more than a few mistakes a season. Any more than that and the Buddy Ryans of the world would make more of his deficiencies on one-on-one pass coverage. They might even remember that he hasn't run a forty-yard dash for time since Lake Michigan was a puddle. But as the Sundance Kid told Butch Cassidy, "You keep thinking, that's what you're good at." One way or another, the Bears deliver the same message to Fencik.

His brainpower mattered more than ever when he moved to free safety three years ago as Ryan threw his ballyhooed 46 defense into high gear. The 46 takes its name from the number Doug Plank wore and its strength from the confusion it creates with a variety of exotic maneuvers. "You have to do two whirly-whirls and a loop before you get to hit somebody," Plank says.

"I believe the 46 was made for me," Fencik says. "You have to do more than prepare yourself mentally for a game; you have to be able to flow with what's actually happening on the field. You need cognitive skills. You have to be able to feel pass patterns, feel the flow of where running plays are going, feel where your people are, whether they're inside or outside. And every year you play, your knowledge of these thing increases exponentially."

It all seems so clean, the same as Fencik's observation about the silence that wraps itself around each game no matter how loud the roar of the crowd. "It's like living in the city," he says. "Pretty soon you don't hear the traffic anymore." But the root of football is contact; you have to be willing to get hit, and you have to have the blood lust to hit back even harder. As Ryan puts it, "You've got to drop your nuts."

Indeed, a Bear cornerback of recent vintage actually did lose a testicle after a low blow. Fencik has been luckier, although you would have had a difficult time convincing him three years ago, when a groin injury cost him half the season. "I felt like I'd been shot by a sniper in the upper deck," he says. By then, however, he knew he could survive. He had endured 1979. That was the season he knew he would have his left ankle restructured when it was over. In the Bears' first game, he broke his left arm, an annoyance that never kept him out of action even though he couldn't straighten it. For a grand finale, when the Bears went to Philadelphia for a playoff game, he ravaged his left knee almost irreparably and punched his ticket to surgery two days before Christmas.

"It's gone," he told his mother when he called home at halftime.

"Oh, Gary," she said, fighting back tears for fear he would start crying, too. "It's not."

"Yes, it is," he whispered.

Fencik never came close to quitting. He was devastated by the sight of his scarred, withered leg when the cast was finally removed, and his rehabilitation exercises left him in puddles of sweat and anguish. But he made it back for reasons as varied as his fiercely competitive nature and the idea that he *plays* football, he doesn't work at it. Mixed in was a wry understanding of the role pain plays in his life. "Where," he wonders, "would this world be without Darvon?"

He needs it, as do the men he hits. A few seasons back, the Redskins accused him of being one of the NFL's dirtiest players, a charge he shrugged off as guilt by association with the take-no-prisoners Plank. There are those among the Bears, however, who will tell you that Fencik really does have a mean streak, that simply making a tackle doesn't satisfy him as much as knocking the prunes out of someone. It is not the kind of thing a Yale grad readily fesses up to. But in the aftermath of the game that sent the Bears to the Super Bowl, he came as close as he ever has to stripping the veneer from his violent work ethic.

He was talking about the first play of the Bears' 24–0 victory over the Los Angeles Rams. He had slipped up to linebacker and crashed into the Rams' backfield. He got there as Eric Dickerson was taking a handoff, the same Eric Dickerson who had run for 248 yards and stomped the Dallas Cowboys flat the week before. Fencik drove his head into Dickerson's churning legs, stopping him with a measly two-yard gain and setting the tone for the day.

To look at Fencik in the locker room afterward was to think there must have been someone else in his uniform. His hair was combed, he had a fresh shirt on, and a towel covered what no TV camera was allowed to show. His legs were crossed as if he were at a board meeting, and his calm, reasoned tone belied the chilling message he delivered.

"Everyone's knees," he said, "are the same."

Valentine's Day, 1986. The phone in the kitchen rings for the third time in the last fifteen minutes. When Gary Fencik answers it, he does so with the smile that moved the *Chicago Tribune* to describe him as "a heartthrob" and a female editor at *Playboy* to call him her "cream dream."

"Hello," he says in a tone that has a smile of its own. "Yes, who's this?"

The answer he gets is a quick disconnection.

"Sounds like somebody who shouldn't have my number."

The mysterious admirers are everywhere, regardless of how often Fencik changes his number. Even if he did hide successfully, they would still pester his parents the way they did last night. And always there is the mail that gets delivered to the Bears' offices. "The letters usually begin, 'I've never done anything like this before. . . ,'" Fencik says. But now there has been a change of approach in this assault on his heart. "You've got to see this picture," he says. At first glance it appears to show nothing more than a pretty girl with two boldly colored swatches of cloth hiding her charms. The cloth is attached to a transparency covering the picture, though. When you lift the transparency, you can examine the girl modeling the skimpiest of underthings. That may not be much compared to the pubic hair that gets mailed to Don Johnson and Philip Michael Thomas, the sexual lightning rods on *Miami Vice*, but it's pretty impressive for someone who wouldn't go to his senior prom in high school.

"I wasn't into that sort of thing then," Fencik says. "Even now I won't date just for the sake of dating. I don't have the energy for it. I mean, it's flattering that someone would want to meet you. But I like to see a woman and make my own decision rather than be—I'm searching for the right word here—solicited."

Fencik's instincts in this department are unpredictable at best. While it seems entirely fitting that his current girlfriend attends Harvard Business School, he went against form—intellectual form, that is—when he dated Charlotte Kemp, *Playboy*'s Miss December of 1982.

"I forgot to ask your mother about her," a visitor tells Fencik.

"It was just as well," he replies, laughing. "My mother thought Charlotte was charming until she was the centerfold. Then she wouldn't allow her in the house. Strict Catholic, you know."

Though the romance is long since over, Fencik keeps in touch with Charlotte, tracking the highs and lows of her life. It is a gentlemanly touch, one he quickly dilutes by describing the rigors of being a dashing bachelor with a stake in a fashionable bar. "There are a lot of women," he says. "A lot of skeletons too." Fortunately, his horizons go beyond the Hunt Club to places where the dreamer in him can roam unfettered. So it was that at a party in San Francisco three years ago he met a Stanford graduate named Julia Kennedy, who captured his imagination before waltzing off to Europe for eight months. "There were plenty of much prettier girls vying for his attention," Kennedy says, "but I guess he was fascinated by someone who wasn't that easily accessible."

She reached that conclusion after she returned home from Europe and was awakened by a 3:00 a.m. phone call. On the line were her old boyfriend Ken Margerum, a Stanford grad who plays wide receiver for the Bears, and this guy Fencik. "They were both drunk," she says. They were also convincing, for they persuaded her to fly to Chicago for their next game. Ostensibly, she was to visit Margerum. She didn't believe it for a minute.

Fencik was waiting, and he hasn't been far from Kennedy's life since, despite the distance between Chicago and Harvard or the few letters he writes her in his perfect hand. They are bright, strong-willed, talkative people, and it's easy to imagine them having a relationship a la David Addison and Maddie Hayes of TV's *Moonlighting*. He gave her the flu when she joined his family and friends at the Super Bowl—"Very touching," she says—and she responded by laughing at the girls who whined to interviewers about the ailing Fencik's absence from the Bears' victory parade. "I can't kid him too much, though," she says. "I think he really enjoys it."

Likewise, Fencik must be careful with his words around her. "Julia just doesn't accept careless statements easily," he says. "I end up having to justify myself with rational arguments a lot of times. Boy, do I hate that." His smile calls him a liar.

☆ ☆ ☆

It is almost over, and Gary Fencik, at thirty-two, knows it. He is the third-oldest player on the Bears no matter how youthful he looks, no matter how boyish his enthusiasm for life remains. When he looks around the locker room now, there is hardly anyone else who remembers the old farts he broke in with, nervously smoking their cigarettes before a game, then racing into the can to puke their guts out.

All that the new Bears have experienced is the funk thumping out of Walter Payton's ghetto blaster. And winning. "They have no concept of what it used to be like," Fencik says. "Of blocked punts or field goals that hit the uprights, of losing 6–3 a week after losing 10–9, of playing hard but playing stupid, of trying to be satisfied with saying, 'Well, we really beat them up.'" Listen to him long enough and you can almost hear the words he won't say: fucking kids.

They will never know him when he was at least sneaky fast, when he had enough pop to put your lights out with a tackle. They will only see him hoping he can walk away without another injury, yet fighting not to let it rob him of his boldness on the field. They will see him battling to remain a starter even though the Super Bowl season may have been his best ever, for what has he done for the Bears' new defensive coordinator? Buddy Ryan is gone, so is his 46 defense, and when Fencik thinks of the standard (i.e., boring) 34 defense with three linemen and four linebackers that is likely to be thrust upon the team, he can't help balking. Even in his sleep.

"I had a dream last night," he says. "We were playing a game—I can't remember who it was against—and we were using the 34 with a zone. All of a sudden we started playing the 46 and the crowd went crazy. They loved this act of defiance, and when we came off the field, we were heroes. Of course, we were all gone the next day."

At best he has only a year or two left. "His future," says agent Charles Besser, "is beyond the NFL." Down deep, Fencik has realized that since the day he left Yale, but he didn't really start working at it until his knee came apart in '79. He has had some nice off-season jobs with Morgan Guaranty Trust of New York and the First National Bank of Chicago, but lying there in the hospital, uncertain he would ever take another quick step, he wondered if he had gotten sidetracked.

"You come out of Yale thinking you have an obligation to contribute something to society," he says. "So with me, football was just supposed to be a sidelight. Then I got a little panicky; I started thinking, jeez, maybe I don't like anything *except* football, maybe I can't do anything else with my life. Maybe I was programmed a certain way and lost it."

Fencik regained his bearings at Northwestern, where he earned a master of management degree by going to school even during the season. On plane rides home from road games, with the other Bears either drowning their sorrows or shouting out victory toasts, he kept his nose in *Quantitative Concepts for Management*. "He couldn't even have a drink," Julia Kennedy says. "He used to complain about it all the time." He was rewarded for his abstinence and his remarkable concentration, though, when he received his degree in 1985. The problem now is, he can't figure out what to do with it.

Fencik likes the idea of having one friend who just took command of a lottery consulting firm in Chicago and another who runs a $160 million venture capital fund in Boston. Nor are they the only well-connected people he knows. When his phone rings, it may very well be someone trying to convince him he can make another killing in real estate. "But I'm not sure I want to get up to go to work at eight in the morning or whenever it is they have to leave," Fencik says. He proved it this past off-season when he shied away from most jobs that might lead to employment after football. Oh, there was the matter of an operation to remove some cartilage in his left knee, but he could have gone to work on crutches. Instead, he flirted with a part in a TV movie that never came to be, talked to several publishers about a book, and worked the banquet circuit shamelessly. "Easy money," he says.

His hardest work, if you don't count digesting rubber chicken, was smiling into a camera. Building on his regular post-game spot of last season, he put together two sports features a week for WMAQ-TV, the NBC affiliate in Chicago. He was spurred by both his curiosity about the business and his agent's "next Frank Gifford" refrain. Rest assured he wasn't spinning his wheels. "If Gary decides on television full-time," says Dick Reingold, WMAQ's news director, "I can definitely see him as a local sports anchor or a network commentator." *If* is the big question, of course. Because Fencik doesn't know what to do next.

"All I'm sure of is that I'm not going to be the president of a Fortune 500 company," he says. "You've got to start toward that when you're in your twenties."

So should he settle for TV or business, or should he try to balance the two? If he chooses the balancing act, will he be able to have the wife and family he readily admits wanting? Or should he chuck everything and opt for a do-nothing existence in a do-nothing place he identifies only as "la-la land"?

That wouldn't be what his public expects, but, really, how much longer will he be the man everybody wants anyway? Won't there come a time when someone displaces him, someone who sounds even better than a Yalie who played for a Super Bowl champion and courted a *Playboy* centerfold and ran with the bulls in Pamplona? And doesn't he know it?

"Sooner or later, I've got to jump," Gary Fencik says.

The smart ones don't wait to be pushed.

2

Legends of the Box Score

Willie Mays
Out of the Past

Baltimore Evening Sun
October 9, 1974

The public relations man wasn't Willie Mays' kind of guy. He was in a hurry, and Willie never hurries, not any more.

He used up all his hurrying playing a kid's game until last year when he was forty-two and too creaky to move across a baseball diamond the way he had for twenty-three seasons. Yesterday morning he just wanted to eat his sausage and eggs in peace and maybe doctor the cold he thought he was catching from the arctic air conditioning in his hotel suite. He would worry about the rigors of being a legend later.

But the public relations man kept after him: "Half an hour until we leave for the Babe Ruth House, Willie . . . Twenty minutes until we leave, Willie . . . Fifteen minutes, Willie . . . Five minutes."

"Shoot, man," Willie said at last, stretching in the chair he hadn't budged from. "I'll get there when I get there. Those people aren't doing anything for me. I'm doing something for them."

The day's itinerary called for him to sign autographs and talk into the microphones thrust in his face at the Ruth House, eat lunch with a sportswriter, and tape two TV shows, all in his role as goodwill ambassador for a soap company. The company's latest promotional gimmick is to spread more than three hundred thousand dollars among six national youth groups, and Willie is supposed to explain how the money will be divvied up. But when a reporter tried to pin him down yesterday, he said, "You'll have to ask somebody else about that."

There has always been somebody else where Willie Mays is concerned. He came to baseball with the gift of his talent—the rest he left to the fates, and the fates were kind. Leo Durocher, as flinty a manager as ever cursed an umpire, put an arm around his shoulder when he was a trembling rookie with the New York Giants. Once he emerged as arguably the greatest player ever, he found himself in the company of rich men who cultivate friendship with their heroes. One of them, a Boston bank president, made sure Willie got to know the president of the soap company as well as the head of an outfit that operates concession stands at race tracks. Naturally, the concessionaire wanted to take care of him, too.

"I go around and they put on Willie Mays races," Willie said. "I got to be up in Boston next week at—what do you call it?—yeah, Suffolk Downs. Man, I don't know nothing about race tracks except you lose all your money there."

The tracks he visits want nothing more than his name, which still surprises him because he never thought the living outside baseball would be so easy. He was scared as his playing days drew to an end, and he admits it. He engraved his image on the national consciousness with 660 home runs, miraculous catches, and a cap he was forever running out from under. But the last the public saw of him, he was staggering around centerfield for the Mets in the 1973 World Series, his talent eroded by time and his future filled with he knew not what.

Only then did he discover that to the power brokers he would always be the Say Hey Kid, a symbol of their youth and the possessor of a hand they not only wanted to shake but to fill with money. They came with so many offers that he could pick and choose, and once again it was good to be Willie Mays.

The surprising thing is he doesn't spend much time thinking about baseball. When he arrived here Monday night, he didn't know the Orioles were in the American League playoffs. Not that he would have watched them if he could have.

"I went to the ballpark in New York every day I could this summer, you know, to take batting practice and work out in the outfield and infield," he said. "But I never stayed and watched a game. I'd go home and watch them all on TV. If I stay at the ballpark, I get depressed."

It's difficult to picture Willie with the blues, just as it was difficult to see how weary he looked yesterday as he made his way through the hotel lobby and out to a waiting limo. If the wrinkles come in right on his face, he will end up looking like one of those beautiful old jazzmen you see in New Orleans, but now he was just someone who had played too many gigs, and it quickly got worse. He wanted to know what was going to happen at the Babe Ruth House, and the representative from the Baltimore Promotion Council didn't have an answer for him.

A storm warning crossed Willie's face. "When they don't tell you the program," he muttered to the man beside him, "you got to watch out."

There was no ambush waiting for him at the Ruth House, though, just the usual horde of kids wanting autographs, which they got, and the usual group of reporters seeking answers to routine questions, which they got. Only a burly Southwestern District cop named Dan Markowski was out of the ordinary. Ten years ago, he was Willie's caddy in spring training, an eager minor leaguer who took the legend's place in centerfield midway through each game.

Willie couldn't pronounce Markowski's name, so he called him McCookie. When McCookie hit a home run, Willie bought him a steak dinner. It made a nice memory for a ballplayer whose professional career moved no farther than Fresno. Markowski was on his way home from a court appearance yesterday when he decided to thank Willie for it one more time.

"Remember me?" he said. "You used to call me McCookie."

Willie looked at the cop uncertainly. He has met a lot of ballplayers in his time, and it isn't always easy to put a name with a face from the past. Then a light went on in his eyes and he smiled and said, "Yeah, I remember you." Now Markowski was smiling, too.

He had made Willie Mays young again, if only for a moment.

Stan Musial
The Man, Forever

Chicago Sun-Times
September 21, 1982

ST. LOUIS—He looks the way you've always thought an old baseball star should: turned out in a handsome gray suit and a sub-
tly striped tie, ready with an eye-crinkling grin and a glad hand
for everybody who approaches him in the restaurant that bears
his name. His kingdom encompasses every inch of the city and
all the hamlets and burgs where the Cardinals' games floated in
by radio in a simpler time. But the mayor can keep City Hall and
the folks at home their front-porch swings. Stan Musial needs
nothing more than his corner table to gaze back down the road
he traveled from a place once distant and now nonexistent.

The minor leagues ceased to dip as low as Class C years ago,
but Class C was indeed where Musial could be found at the start
of the 1941 season, a dead-armed pitcher trying to find a second
life as an outfielder. He was one bus ride from oblivion with the
Cardinals' Springfield, Missouri, farm team when the home office
in St. Louis started getting reports that there looked to be magic
in his bat. The Cards hustled him to Rochester, New York, for a
trial by fire against Triple A pitching. Soon enough, a well-trav-
eled third baseman pulled Musial aside and told him he wasn't
long for the bushes. Musial eyed the old bird suspiciously and
asked, "What do you mean?" That's how new he was to success
back then: He didn't trust it.

But he finally got the message in the form of a telegram from the Cardinals summoning him to St. Louis. They were still battling Brooklyn for first place even though their lineup seemed to be made of broken bones, and they wanted to find out if Musial could apply first aid at the plate. After one game as a spectator, there he was digging in against the Boston Braves to face the unknown in the truest sense of the word.

"Their pitcher was Jim Tobin, who threw a knuckleball, and I'd never seen a knuckleball before," he says. "My first time up, I saw the ball floating around and dancing, and I said, 'My God, what's that?'"

He popped out, but that was the end of the pitcher's fun. Musial came to bat twice more that day, stroked two line drives for hits, drove in two runs, and won the game for the Cardinals. They would live another day in a pennant race they were destined to lose, and Musial could cherish the first dent he put in the right-field screen at St. Louis' rickety Sportsman's Park.

"Yeah," he says, "I hit pretty well after that."

He hit so well that he became the first person you think of now that his old ball club is closing out the Phillies and closing in on the Eastern Division championship. It doesn't matter that he is almost sixty-two, no longer lives and dies with the Cardinals, spends more time joshing with his restaurant's customers than attending the team's board of directors meetings, and really doesn't get out to see that many games. Stanley Frank Musial loomed so large in his twenty-two years as a Cardinal that he cast a shadow that will never disappear. There will always be his 3,630 hits—1,815 at home and 1,815 on the road—and his history-making five home runs in a doubleheader against the New York Giants. If you listen closely, you may even hear the raucous crowd in Brooklyn praising him by chanting, "Stan the Man! Stan the Man!"

It's hard to imagine in an era when ballplayers, the great as well as the not so great, bounce from team to team in search of big money, but Stan Musial was more than a star with a life-time .331 batting average. He was the Cardinals the same way Ernie Banks was the Cubs and Ted Williams the Red Sox and Joe DiMaggio the Yankees. He was something special to the team, the town, and even the nation.

When everything around him was going up in smoke, The Man kept swinging sweetly. He was reliable that way, spectacularly so. "After I was in the big leagues three or four years, I knew before the season I was going to hit .330 or .340 or .350," he says. "You can call that confidence or conceit or anything you want, but it's a hell of a good feeling."

In the beginning, the Cardinals made him feel the same way because they were always on top, always one step ahead of Leo Durocher's feisty Dodgers. The first four full seasons Musial played in St. Louis, his team won four pennants and three World Series and made it blissfully easy to climb out of the dirt after one of Durocher's hired guns had sent him sprawling with a fastball aimed at his ear. "We'd get knocked down and then it was our turn to knock them down," he says. "We really didn't think much about it." But even he has to admit that forgetting was easier when he was catching a fly ball for the last out in the pennant-clinching game in 1942 or breaking the Dodgers' hearts in the 1946 play-offs, the first playoffs the big leagues ever saw.

"I guess I was spoiled by so much success that early," Musial says. His words are hardly the product of haste, for he has had a lot of time to think about them. In the last seventeen years of his career, the Cardinals never won another pennant. They traded away siege guns Johnny Mize and Walker Cooper, which Musial didn't like, and they moved him to first base, which he wasn't so crazy about, either. And they never came closer to glory than second place.

The best shots they had were in '57, when he batted .351 with a cracked shoulder blade, and '63, when he announced that he would retire at season's end and prayed for the best. He was forty-two that year, still capable of banging out two hits in his farewell game, still strong enough to light up the Dodgers' esteemed Johnny Podres with his 475th and final home run. But there was nothing he could do to stop a Dodger rookie named Dick Nen from hitting the homer that finished the Cards.

"I had to realize that you can't achieve everything you want," Musial says. "I didn't have any time left in me anyway. I could still get around on the fastballs that guys like Sandy Koufax and Don Drysdale were throwing, but my concentration at the plate kept wandering. There wasn't anything I could do about it. It was just age. And the Cardinals were better off the next year with Lou Brock out in left field. They won the World Series and they never would have done that with me out there."

He says it with a smile, too, a man comfortable in his own skin, a man who became a hero on the baseball diamond and realized that honesty was part of the deal. A man who will always be Stan the Man.

Reggie Jackson
The Ego Is a Lonely Hunter

Chicago Sun-Times
October 13, 1978

NEW YORK—Hitting a baseball is a solitary existence, a job for a loner. Yet the men with the least need for someone to lean on at the plate attract the most glad-handers away from it. Ergo Reggie Jackson.

He is a creation of his own egomania, an athletic thespian who has convinced himself that he must turn every World Series into his personal Oktoberfest if he is to be loved. The process seems simple, just a straight shot from Point A to Point B. But nothing is as it seems, not even Reggie Jackson's magic.

The evidence shows up everywhere, from ballparks to the hotel lobbies through which Jackson so often wanders alone. He wears a vague, almost dazed look on his rapidly aging face. It is as if he can't believe that the rest of the Yankees have left him to find out just how much of himself he can stand.

But Jackson knows. Of course he does. He can hear Thurman Munson and Graig Nettles down at the other end of the Yankees' clubhouse, talking about their preference for strong, silent ballplayers. Jackson is strong, but he is not silent; by his teammates' standards, he is to be distrusted and disliked. Rapprochement is out of the question.

You would think it would be different when there is a big game to be played, for big games are when Jackson is all that he so desperately wants to be. But the Yankees cut him no slack even then.

Think back to their American League championship series against Kansas City. Jackson and Bucky Dent were running in the outfield before a game when Dent pulled up to greet a relief pitcher on his way to the bullpen. The pitcher said something and Dent doubled up with laughter. An instant later, Jackson joined them. The pitcher turned and walked away.

The scene was the perfect preamble for the lunch Jackson had with Steve Garvey the day before the World Series began. You can only speculate about whether they discussed Jackson's simmering feud with Munson or the Texas Death Match that Garvey and Don Sutton had in the Dodgers' clubhouse two months ago. But there is no doubt that they couldn't keep their toil and trouble off their minds.

"Steve and I have to talk to each other," Jackson said. "Nobody on our own teams will talk to us."

Still, Jackson is never without an audience. As the closest thing baseball has to Muhammad Ali, he will always find reporters clustered in front of his locker. Other Yankees seldom tread there, but according to Jackson's idea of democracy, that is probably just as well. They might take up space a writer could put to better use. Jackson is building his own legend, his own myth, and there is no better way to do it than through the obliging media.

Unfortunately, he has never played for a team on which everybody could see the practicality of his strategy. In Oakland one thing led to another and finally little Bill North leaped up and fetched him a rap on the snout. In Baltimore Jim Palmer watched him preen at the plate and pop sunflower seeds in the outfield until he could stand it no more. "Reggie is the biggest hot dog I've ever seen," Palmer said. "There isn't enough mustard in the whole world to cover him."

The Yankees, of course, have been the least hospitable of all, which explains in part why Jackson celebrated their playoff victory over Boston by waltzing into the Red Sox' clubhouse and commiserating with George Scott. The rest of the explanation lies in the armada of TV crews that followed Jackson there to document his compassion.

"That's weak, that's really weak," said Bill Lee, Boston's radically chic lefthander. "Everything that guy does is staged."

It certainly looked that way when Jackson celebrated his game-winning home run against the Red Sox by shaking hands with Yankee owner George Steinbrenner before he accepted the congratulations of his teammates. That's known as sending a message.

The message was that he doesn't need them. He is Steinbrenner's prize. He hobnobs with celebrities and big shots, and he doesn't buy anything less than the top of the line. LeRoy Neiman, who is to art what Ripple is to wine, paints pictures of him relentlessly. And Jackson is always ready to open his arms to anybody else he thinks might do him some good.

Case in point: A New York sportswriter made the mistake of asking Jackson about the merits of a certain car this summer. Jackson said he would speak to the president of the company that manufactures the car. They were friends, naturally.

The next day, Jackson reported that the president wanted to know more about the writer. "I told him that you had covered baseball for a long time," Jackson said, "but he wanted to know if you were a friend." There was a long pause. "I told him I thought you could be a friend." Suddenly the writer wasn't interested in the car anymore. He was wondering what Jackson's definition of a friend is.

Maybe Jackson doesn't have one. Maybe he thinks he doesn't need one. At least it looked that way after he struck out against neophyte Bob Welch in that marvelous ninth inning Wednesday night, besmirching his reputation and burying the Yankees a little deeper in this World Series. Jackson scowled, cursed, and threw his bat not once but twice. When manager Bob Lemon tried to console him, Jackson jerked away angrily.

He didn't need anybody's help. He was going to answer each of the press's embarrassing questions by himself. "The man beat me," he said. "I'm not proud. I admit it. The man beat me." And he kept on confessing as long as there was somebody around to confess to.

It was the same as when he hits a homer to win a game. He was all alone in a crowd.

Pete Rose
Pete Belongs in Cooperstown

GQ
September 1995

For those of you keeping score at home, baseball waited little more than a heartbeat after the strike to disgrace itself again. This time shame came in the form of Darryl Strawberry, who has been so busy drinking, snorting coke, cheating the IRS, and getting run in for beating his wife that he has scarcely had a spare moment to devote to hitting home runs the past three seasons. None of that, however, was enough to stop the New York Yankees from signing him to an $850,000 contract. It was an ugly bit of business, and yet it begged a question that could have a happy answer: If Strawberry is allowed to play, how can the guardians of the game's would-be morality keep Pete Rose locked out of the Hall of Fame any longer?

Rose belongs there, you know. He belongs there as surely as there are stitches on a baseball. But instead of hanging his bronze likeness in Cooperstown, the pooh-bahs hanged the man himself. His crime was gambling, and he paid for it with a lifetime suspension that cost him his job managing his hometown Cincinnati Reds and erased his name from the Hall of Fame ballot. A special investigation and *Sports Illustrated* both reported that he had bet on baseball, but even the possibility that a confession might open the Hall's doors to him couldn't convince Rose to talk. No surprise there. Anyone who ever saw him play knew he wasn't going to beg, and anyone who had an ounce of sense knew that a little thing like a bet would never have stopped him from busting his hump.

He was the most single-minded competitor in baseball since Jackie Robinson, and the blind men with the power refused to factor that into the death sentence they gave his dream. It was as if Rose had never been the ignition switch for World Series champions in Cincinnati and Philadelphia. As if there had been no integrity in every step he took on the diamond. As if he weren't the game's all-time leader in hustle as well as hits. And it wouldn't fly. For you would never catch Rose saying, "It's tough getting up for day games," the way the feckless Strawberry did after rolling in late for the New York Mets one too many times. What you would hear was Rose saying, "I'd run through hell in a gasoline suit to play baseball." And meaning it.

The passion he brought to the game is only hinted it in the 4,256 hits he bashed from both sides of the plate. Far more indicative of the forces that drove him was the way he crouched at the plate, a bulldog ready to bite the first good pitch he saw. And from that flowed the style that defined him, sprinting to first base on walks, bowling over catchers, forever forcing the issue, as if anything less would have meant exile to a lifetime of digging ditches. In twenty-four seasons that saw Rose bounce to five different positions and become an all-star at each of them, the only thing phony about him was the dye he used on his hair. But that could be forgiven, for he was the rarest of treasures: He was an icon who played the way mere mortals thought they would if they had been out there.

One of the wonders of his greatness was that he was not a genetic marvel like Willie Mays, who was there are the beginning of Rose's career, or Mike Schmidt, who was there are the end. Everything Peter Edward Rose achieved was through the sweat of his labors. Honest toil was what bonded him to the factory guys who punched out at four o'clock, fueled up on boilermakers until the ballpark gates opened, and roared when they watched him slide headfirst as he turned a single into a double. This was a workingman, pure and simple. A workingman who made himself so much more than that.

And Rose, bless his brash soul, never had a moment's doubt about his place in baseball history, never hid behind pretense or false modesty. So after he lashed a double for his 4,000th hit, his eyebrows went up like window shades when he heard a sportswriter describe what surely awaited him as if it were subject to debate. "Hey, pal," said Rose, "I ain't no potential Hall of Famer." He made "potential" sound as though each letter had been soaked in vinegar. And why not? In those days, eleven years ago, he was a sure thing.

How quickly it all unraveled. The gambling scandal broke in 1989, and by 1992, the year Rose should have been swept into the Hall his first time on the ballot, he was a non-person as far as baseball was concerned. He was also an ex-convict whose tax beef had cost him five months in a federal prison camp and no doubt proved to the game's bluenoses that he was an irredeemable lowlife. But if you look behind the plaques hanging in Cooperstown, you will find virtue in short supply among the drunks, adulterers, and worse (see Ty Cobb) who have been welcomed there. Nary a one of them was morally superior to Rose, as if morality is an issue once the first pitch is thrown.

The game is what matters, and Rose did nothing but honor it when he was between its white lines. He played with a purity that Darryl Strawberry has never been able to fathom as he fritters away the talent that could have made him someone special. Yet baseball has welcomed Strawberry back while it continues to treat Rose like a virus who would infect the Hall of Fame. And that is a bigger sin by far than any Rose ever committed.

Nolan Ryan
On Second Thought

The National Sports Daily
July 3, 1990

I'm guilty. I think we should establish that right away. At a time I can't quite pin down in my previous life as a newspaper sports columnist, I did indeed write that Nolan Ryan had "a heart like a blister." O infamy. O ignominy. Oh, what a dummy.

Don't ask me why I did it. I haven't the slightest idea. To be honest, I didn't even remember sticking it to Ryan until the day after he painted his latest no-hit masterpiece. I had worked my way to the bottom of a package of chocolate chip cookies, and there, waiting for me amid the crumbs, was a Nolan Ryan base- ball card. Ever so briefly, the joy of serendipity overpowered my craving for more cookies.

Then it hit me: *Heart like a blister.* It must have been '78 or '79 when I, the sports columnist, advertised my stupidity with that little beauty. If I couldn't figure out how wrong I was about Ryan then, I certainly can now. The man has more than five thousand strikeouts, he's going to win three hundred games, he has splashed six no-hitters across three decades, and at forty-three he's nearly as ancient as I am. Heart like a warrior would be more like it.

You may not believe this—at the moment I'm finding it a little difficult myself—but I never thought I was a ripper when I was a columnist. I never figured I had to draw blood to get an audi- ence. The pieces I liked doing best were about prizefighters bob- bing and weaving with their dreams and the simple pleasures of baseball, from watching Mike Schmidt pickle a home run to listening to Bill Veeck's flights of fancy. But writing a daily column ultimately brings everything out of you, the sour as well as the sweet. And I had some sour in me, along with a multitude of opinions and a capacity for raising hell.

Now that I'm safely ensconced in Hollywood, I like to think all that is behind me. But every once in a while, the words I spewed for nearly a decade—first in Chicago, then Philadelphia—find their way out of the past to haunt me. There was, for example, the former reader who saw my name flicker across his TV screen and wrote to remind me that I once called television "the twenty-one most wasted inches in your living room." Just kidding, folks.

But that's not to say I've turned my back on every harsh thought that ever appeared under my byline. To tell the truth, I'm proud of being the guy who called Billy Martin "a mouse studying to be a rat." In fact it's one of the few lines that readily springs to mind, for I have a memory as full of holes as the Dodgers' infield. Fortunately—or unfortunately, as the case may be—old friends are only too happy to help me out. "Vermin attract vermin." Are you sure I said that about baseball's team owners and their hirelings? "John Thompson doesn't coach. He contaminates." That was me, too, huh? All right, I'll drop my pose as a sensitive wordsmith.

Looking back, maybe the most amazing aspect of my career is that I never got my lights punched out. The likeliest candidate to do the honors was Dave Kingman, whose gonzo stare had me wondering if he was the mutant spawn of the Addams family. But Kingman never laid a glove on me, most likely because he wasn't any better at confrontations than he was at fielding. Bob Arum wanted a piece of me that cooler heads wouldn't let him take. Herman Franks, when he was managing the Cubs, actually challenged me to meet him under the grandstand. I respectfully declined because Herman was thirty years my senior and normally never did anything more strenuous than light cigars and throw his dirty underwear at the clubhouse man.

All Nolan Ryan has ever thrown are baseballs. He has done so harder and longer than anybody the game is likely to see again. And I reacted as though I had a brain like a bunion. I hope he didn't read what I wrote. Not that it matters, you understand. Either way, I was wrong. I'm sorry and—easy for me to say now—I'll never do it again.

Strange, isn't it? I plow through a package of chocolate chip cookies and end up apologizing for something I hadn't thought about in years. In a sense, I feel a kinship with Marcel Proust, who wolfed down his madeleines and went on to write three volumes of remembrances. Myself, I think I'll call it quits here by telling Nolan Ryan that of all my confirmed hits, he is the only one I feel bad about. The rest of the bums deserved it.

Johnny Bench
Old Too Young

Chicago Sun-Times
August 24, 1983

He was the first proof a lot of us had that time waits for no one. We were graduate students then, trapped in the dim corners of a library that is now past tense, unnerved by the possibility that a war might gobble us up before the real world could, and Johnny Bench was hitting home runs in Cincinnati. He couldn't have been more than nineteen or twenty, and we ignored books, papers, and professors to marvel at the future that lay ahead of this precocious catcher from Binger, Oklahoma. He was what we had all yearned to be before curveballs straightened us out, and the only problem we had with his being the chosen one was that it was hard to have a hero younger than we were.

Lo these many years later, it is equally strange to watch Johnny Bench ambling toward retirement at thirty-five. Just as we are figuring out where our lives are taking us, he is leaving the game that has made him a millionaire, a celebrity, and a museum piece. "I'll be old when I play for the last time October 2," he says. "October 3 I'll be young again."

And yet, until his last hurrah on a Sunday in Houston, Johnny Bench must be haunted by a photograph taken when he was still a teenager, a simple portrait of him in a Buffalo Bisons uniform that now fetches $10.50 wherever nostalgia carries a price tag. "I know that's exactly what they're charging if it has my autograph," he tells a stranger who has just placed a copy of the picture beside him, "so I just won't sign it." The collector will have to make do with the BENCH, JOHNNY that someone has carefully printed on the back of the photo.

"Didn't they know who you were?" Reds reliever Tom Hume asks with feigned innocence when he notices the ID.

"Not back then," Johnny Bench says.

That's hard to imagine when you hear the early arrivals at Wrigley Field start buzzing as soon as they see the 5 on his broad back. In these final days, on his last trip to Chicago as a player, Johnny Bench's presence is something special—a chance to take pictures with your camera or your mind and an opportunity to let him provide the captions with his own words.

He tells you about the havoc he never wreaked on the downtrodden Cubs: "Tony Perez was the guy who always hit well for us here. I didn't do much for some reason. Maybe it was because the background was so busy. Maybe it was because every game we played here was four hours. Every time you went into the ninth inning with a five-run lead, you always knew somebody was going to score three, four, or six runs." And he tells you about the sentiment that his friendly enemies in Pittsburgh showered on him when he made his farewell appearance there: "They gave me a golf cart, and when Willie Stargell drove me around the field, the people were standing and clapping and clapping and clapping. It was like everything I ever tried to do had paid off."

He can't tell you much more than that. It would only belabor what the record book already proves: Johnny Bench is the greatest catcher in history, a bright and shining light in an era that also produced Carlton Fisk and Thurman Munson. The three of them made glamorous a position besieged by dirt, sweat, and pain, and each did it with a sense of style and a load of passion.

Fisk remains the patrician craftsman who never backs away from a scrap. Munson was the clutch-hitting sweathog in Yankee pinstripes who died before his time. And Johnny Bench is the icon they pushed to greatness they could never achieve themselves. He is the slugger who has bashed an unsurpassed 324 homers as a catcher, the workhorse who tied Bill Dickey's record by catching a hundred or more games in fifteen consecutive seasons, the thoroughbred who never saw a base stealer he couldn't throw out or a pitching staff he couldn't hold together. "Catching made me what I am," he says. But there are four National League pennants and two World Series championship trophies that wouldn't be decorating Cincinnati's Riverfront Stadium if it weren't for him.

The Hall of Fame awaits his arrival, and Johnny Bench will get there as soon as he is eligible to pass through its portals. He will travel on the legs that hurt more and more every time he squatted behind the plate, the legs that are the reason he is retiring long before the age at which retirement is fashionable these days.

"If I'd caught a year or two longer," he says, "I wouldn't have been able to do the things I wanted to do when I was through with baseball." But baseball was his life, and he tried to keep it that way by playing third base and first base and pinch-hitting. He tried, only to discover what he had always suspected about himself and the position he loved. "The game wasn't fun unless I could control it," he says. "As soon as I gave that up, I didn't enjoy coming to the ballpark anymore."

To Johnny Bench's credit, he admitted it. Two months into the season, he announced that he was retiring and gave the Reds a chance to plan for his absence. "I couldn't torture myself," he says, "and I couldn't torture the team."

His honesty is one more reason to appreciate him, even as he delivers a pre-game monologue about golf. "I play with a lot of different styles," he says as he lounges in the dugout. "I've got a little Lee Trevino, a little Miller Barber, a little Jack Nicklaus. If I could get a little of Ben Crenshaw's putting, I'd be in business." It is a dream for a summer day, and it is not interrupted until the cries of autograph seekers finally bring him back out into the sunshine.

"Johnny, Johnny, are you going to play today?" cries a kid waving a bubblegum card of the catcher who used to be.

"No," Johnny Bench says softly.

Nothing can make his answer sound right.

Earl Weaver
The Earl of Baltimore

Chicago Sun-Times
August 16, 1981

BALTIMORE—Based on the available evidence, it is easy to assume that Earl Weaver perfected managerial sin. After all, the profane potentate of the Orioles has spent the past thirteen seasons kicking dirt on home plate, tearing up rule books under umpires' noses, and generally behaving as if he were renting his soul to the devil with an option to buy. Yet here it is the middle of August and he has only been kicked out of one game. Reputations have been ruined for less.

Understandably, Weaver is not pleased to hear that his dark star appears to be fading. In his corner of Memorial Stadium's third base dugout, he looks up from a pregame meal of a sandwich and a cigarette and searches the horizon for an explanation. "Musta been the foggin' strike," he says at last. "Guys like me, I coulda got tossed five foggin' times in the time we were off. I'm streaky that way."

Satisfied, he resumes dining only to be interrupted moments later by Jim Palmer, the noted pitcher and underwear model. With a mischievous smile, Palmer raises his voice in a song that suggests one more reason why his fearless leader has been wont to raise hell with umpires: "Happy Birthday."

"Oh," Weaver says, "you remembered."

"Of course," Palmer says.

"I know why you remembered, too," Weaver tells his favorite rascal. "You know that at my age, it's gotta hurt."

He has turned fifty-one on this gray Friday, but there will be no party for him. The Orioles will play the White Sox, and then Earl Weaver, the owner of a full head of hair and none of his own teeth, will go home to be with his wife and his prized tomato plants. He will go home to rest, to savor his stature as the winningest manager in the big leagues, and to get away from all the insufferable questions about how the White Sox are pretending to be a new and improved version of the Black Sox.

They have been quoted anonymously in the press as saying they would throw games at the end of this split season if it would help them get into the playoffs. The mere suggestion of such chicanery has horrified the lords of baseball and forced the team's management to talk faster than a married politician photographed in the arms of a Las Vegas strumpet. To Weaver, who once marched his team off the field in Toronto to save his bone-weary pitching staff, the Sox's scheme sounds like the work of dummies.

"What the fog," he says. "The White Sox better not lose too many foggin' games deliberately or they're not gonna be in it. The simplest thing for them to do is win as many games as they can and root like hell for foggin' Oakland. Look at us, we're in the same boat. We gotta hope New York beats every-foggin'-body except us. Ain't that something? I gotta root for them damn pinstripes."

Nobody said the split season would honor tradition. Indeed, there are those who believe that cutting the season in half smacks more of the old Georgia-Florida League than it does of the American or the National. "Oh, no you don't," says Weaver, who spent his playing career in towns where two cars on Main Street constituted a traffic jam. "I don't want no foggin' headline sayin' WEAVER CALLS SPLIT SEASON BUSH." As a matter of fact, if he had his way, every season would have two chapters, strike or no. "If you start bad," he says, "it's nice to be reborn again." When was the last time Bowie Kuhn addressed any issue so eloquently?

The next thing you know, Weaver will find himself running for commissioner when all he really wants to do is figure out a better way to handicap horse races. That's the way baseball works: What's dumb gets done. So lest the game's kingmakers get the wrong impression from his bleats about old age and his apparent flirtation with respectability, Weaver tries to erase some of the points he has scored with the establishment. The best way to do that is to discuss the fine art of making umpires look like donkeys.

He remembers hearing how a minor league manager named Grover Resinger responded to being given five minutes to get off the field and out of the ballpark. "He asked if he could see the umpire's watch," Weaver says, "and when the dumb fogger handed it to him, Resinger threw it over the top of the foggin' grandstand."

Then there is Frank Lucchesi, an old sparring partner from the Eastern League. Once, Lucchesi sat on home plate until the police came and carried him into the dugout. Another time, after being ordered off the premises, he climbed the flagpole behind the outfield fence and flashed signals to his team from there. But what Lucchesi did best was drive Weaver to heights of creative genius.

"I forget what the foggin' call was," Weaver says, "but the umpire blew it, so I went out and talked like a Dutch uncle and they changed it back. Then Lucchesi comes out and he talks like a Dutch uncle and they change it back. I'm standing there on the mound talking to my pitcher, and when I see them do this, I grab my foggin' heart and fall on my face. Right there on the mound.

"One of my players comes runnin' out and rolls me over and starts fannin' me with his cap. The umpire is right there with him. He says, 'Weaver, if you even open one eye, you're out of this game.' Well, hell, by then, I couldn't resist, and you know what I saw? There was Lucchesi with one of them old Brownie box cameras. He told me later it was the greatest foggin' thing he'd ever seen."

A mischievous smile creases Weaver's face.

"Hey," he says, "maybe I oughta do that again."

It could save his reputation.

Gene Mauch
The Toughest Loss of All

Philadelphia Daily News
March 8, 1985

MESA, Arizona—The words come slowly, the cigarettes quickly. There are long pauses when Gene Mauch is turning ideas into sentences, and he fills them by lighting one smoke after another, cupping each in his right hand the way prisoners and baseball managers do. In a sense, he fits both descriptions. He is trapped by the game that has lured him back to the California Angels' dugout and the emotions that locked him in a private hell for the past two seasons.

"I don't spend that much time thinking about Gene Mauch, I really don't," he says as a fresh cigarette warms him in the morning chill. "I've lived my whole life by the seat of my pants. I've been flattened several times, but only one of them really put me down."

Then he grows silent again.

All you can hear is an occasional shout from one spring training diamond to another and the thump of baseballs in gloves.

This is Gene Mauch's world, but he has been carried out of it, however briefly, by love and sadness. His melancholia has nothing to do with the 1964 Phillies, for that was just a team that lost a pennant it should have won. The loss that consumes Gene Mauch now, for just a moment, in the place where he has taken refuge, is the loss of his wife.

"I'm not gonna talk about Nina," he says, his words choked, half whispered. "Never gonna. Too tough."

It was that way even before cancer killed Nina Lee Mauch in 1983. When her husband walked away from the Angels the year before, he uttered not a word about her agony or his torment. Never mind that he was in a situation where he could have used a little sympathy.

His team had just blown the American League playoffs to the Milwaukee Brewers, and everywhere Gene Mauch turned, there were critics laying the blame on him. Even California's usually benevolent owner, Gene Autry, was second-guessing his pitching Tommy John on three days' rest and leaving right-handed reliever Luis Sanchez in against Cecil Cooper, the left-handed-hitting slugger who wound up clipping the Angels' wings. Both moves captured Gene Mauch's spirit—proud, defiant, stubborn. If he was going to win, if he was finally going to end the quest for a pennant that began in 1960, he was going to do it his way. And he failed. And that, too, was typical of Gene Mauch.

But in the sweet used-to-be, whether he was operating out of Philadelphia, Montreal, or Minnesota, he would have said the hell with everybody else's opinion. In 1982 he said good-bye. Someone else could manage the Angels. He was going home to be with his wife. When she died, he must have wondered if he might not just as well be buried with her.

"I was deep into indifference," Gene Mauch says. "It was so bad, I was indifferent about being indifferent. You know what I mean? I didn't give a spit or a damn or a darn. I didn't care about anything. I wasn't analyzing myself. I just didn't care."

He tried to boost his spirits with the games retirees play, for he had always been happy scrambling for a ten-dollar Nassau on a golf course or bidding four spades when he should have bid two. But it was no use. "Recreation is what you want to do when you want to do it, not when you have to do it," he says. The realization made his case of the blues that much worse.

So Gene Mauch returned to baseball through the back door last season as the Angels' director of player personnel. And still the numbness in his soul persisted. "I didn't know if I'd ever get excited about anything again," he says. He was watching games every day, managing both teams in his mind the way he had since the Brooklyn Dodgers shipped him to Durham, North Carolina, in 1943, but it was no good. He was just a robot.

Everything about him was mechanical and methodical until he chanced upon what passed for a pennant race in the American League West. To dispassionate observers, the Angels, Kansas City Royals, and Minnesota Twins looked like three teams of drunks as they staggered down the stretch, but where Gene Mauch was concerned, they were on a mission of mercy.

"The last two or three weeks of the season, I started feeling things going on inside me again," he says. "Things that got me excited."

"Were you surprised?" someone asks.

"I wasn't looking to be surprised. I wasn't looking for anything."

Maybe that is why the story of how Gene Mauch rediscovered himself at age fifty-nine is so appealing. He wasn't put on earth to sleepwalk through life, and when he was in ballparks where no sleepwalking was tolerated, he woke up. The process was painful, for the Angels never caught Kansas City. But it was also productive, for Gene Mauch decided he would return to managing if the opportunity ever arose.

Now he is back in the job that John McNamara forsook after last year's disappointment, and already the naysayers are after him. They call his team too old and his pitching staff inadequate and his own skills suspect, but Gene Mauch can't hear them. "I haven't felt like this since I took over the Philadelphia ball club in '60," he says. It doesn't matter that he has never managed a pennant winner in twenty-three seasons. The heat is what he needs.

Once again, Gene Mauch has become a silver-haired general, bowing to no one, expecting the best from everybody. He is preparing to get lost in the pursuit of victory, and there is something soothing about that. "You go into a baseball vacuum in February and you don't come out until the season's over," he says. The outside world will never catch up with him in there. Maybe his memories won't, either.

Dick Allen
More a Ghost Than a Legend

Chicago Sun-Times
February 8, 1982

Wandering seemed to suit Dick Allen, who stormed through the
big leagues and never really found a port. After he swung from
the heels one last time, he drifted off to become the mysterious
figure he had always fancied himself.

He worked the racetrack, had some horses of his own. That
was all anyone professed to know about his new life. It sounded
like a fitting second career for the amateur philosopher who gave
us our most astute assessment of artificial turf: "If a horse can't
eat it, I don't want to play on it."

The form chart said you could find Allen on the East Coast,
but he kept turning up on the other side of the country. He blew
through Turf Paradise in Phoenix two autumns ago, talking about
claiming horses and doing public relations for the track. "I was
floored by the PR thing," an Arizona handicapper says. "I thought
he didn't kiss anybody's *tuchas*." Before the Turf Paradise regu-
lars could find out for sure, Allen was gone. And nobody out west
caught sight of him again until he materialized in Santa Anita's
morning mist last fall.

He didn't talk much about horses, though. The Dodgers were
winning the World Series on the other side of the San Rafael
Hills, and they were one of his old teams. Besides, there wasn't
anyone in the workout crowd with the sand to ask him about
the fire that had ravaged his stable back in Pennsylvania. "He

was just hanging around," one of his fellow kibitzers says. "He didn't have anything running. In fact, I never even asked him what he was doing here."

That has always been for Allen to know and for everybody else to find out. So it was when the Texas Rangers announced last week that they had hired him as their spring training batting coach. There was no windy explanation, just a terse message from general manager Eddie Robinson that he admired Allen's brainpower. He would have done well to add that his newest employee isn't bad at keeping secrets, either.

"What's that you say?" Allen's mother asked thirty-six hours after the Rangers hired him. "Dick got a job? Well, I always knew he was a good ballplayer."

Maybe a ballplayer is what Allen should still be. He won't turn forty for another month, and with his statistics—.292 lifetime batting average, .534 career slugging percentage, 351 homers in fourteen seasons—he could be earning diamonds and rubies by the bucket. But there are the tendons he severed in his right wrist when he was carrying the Phillies, tendons that would betray him when cold weather set in years later. And there are the bridges he burned in Philadelphia, St. Louis, Los Angeles, Chicago, and Oakland, bridges burned seemingly beyond repair.

When you tote up the damage, you can't help thinking that Dick Allen would be better off mucking stalls at a racetrack in the middle of nowhere. But he wouldn't—and that is one more twist in the mystery he is living. Despite baseball's well-earned reputation for holding grudges, Allen found three friends waving his banner when the Rangers came calling.

Pat Corrales, the Phillies' new manager, was a running mate from their bush league days. Pittsburgh's Chuck Tanner nursed Allen through three seasons with the White Sox and got his reward every time the bespectacled first baseman launched another rocket to the upper deck. Roland Hemond, the Sox's general manager, thinks his team wouldn't have stayed in Chicago if it hadn't been for Allen. "We were 56-106 a couple years before we got Dick from the Dodgers," Hemond says, "and the first year we had him, we took Oakland into the last week of the season." Allen steered the ship without any help, whacking thirty-seven homers, becoming the American League's most valuable player, and snuffing any complaints about his lack of zeal in batting practice.

"It would be May 22 and he'd say he finally had his timing down," Hemond says. "From then on, he wasn't going to hit against anything except major league stuff. In a way, I always thought that Caruso must have been like that. He probably never tinkered with his fine-tuning once his voice was right. He was an artist. So was Dick Allen. Dick would sit in the dugout while everybody else was taking hitting and he'd say, 'So-and-so is pitching against us tonight and he'll start me away, then he'll come inside.' It was like Dick knew exactly what was going to happen. And after the first inning, we'd be ahead 3–0."

Unfortunately, the good that Allen did between the white lines has been obscured by his personal excesses as well as by the sands of time. He is readily remembered for his endless feud with Philadelphia's grandstand vultures and the BOO! he wrote in the infield dirt with his toe. He drank too much and missed too many games, embittered the Dodgers' venerable Walter Alston, and bid adieu to the White Sox by calling them quitters.

His vitriol kept people intimidated and off-balance. Maybe that was his goal all along. Maybe he didn't want them getting close enough to see how he had been scarred by playing in pre-integration Little Rock or how badly he strayed after the Phillies traded Corrales away from his side. It was better—or should that be safer?—to cloak himself in mystery, but now he is back in a role that threatens his guise.

The Rangers' hitters will be watching everything their new coach does, and old admirers and critics alike will be waiting to see if the devil is done with him. For all we know, Allen may even examine himself once he has a uniform on again and can pause to remember how he looked chasing his fortune at the racetrack. With luck, he will realize that there are some things you can't escape in this life. One of them is who you are.

Frank Robinson
Hard Game, Hard Man

Chicago Sun-Times
August 1, 1982

I don't see anyone playing in the major leagues today who combines the talent and intensity that I had. —FRANK ROBINSON, before he stopped talking about his election to the Hall of Fame

The home runs are where you start the story. There were 586 of them—enough to make you forget his dead throwing arm, enough to make you forget that his 200 pounds were carried on matchstick legs, enough to make you forget that his greatness was fashioned with much more than his bat. But Frank Robinson made such beautiful music with it that you would have to be cursed with a deaf ear not to think of it first.

In those dizzy days when the Cincinnati Reds were called the Redlegs lest anyone accuse them of being godless commies, maestro Birdie Tebbetts used to turn his back on batting practice and try to match the tunes with the tunesmiths.

Craaaack!

"Right-handed or left-handed?" Birdie would ask.

"Right-handed," someone would say.

"Got to be Robinson."

He was twenty years old in 1956, breaking into a lineup that featured such prime beef as Ted Kluszewksi, Gus Bell, and Wally Post, but nobody fretted about his youth. Instead, they claimed he would have been there at nineteen if he hadn't ruined his right shoulder diving in the outfield, for he seemingly had been born to raise hell at the plate. "When he hit the ball, the sound was distinctive," says Jim Brosnan, the author and erstwhile Reds right-hander. "It was the kind of sound that drove pitchers into deep depression."

The pitchers, being a testier sort than the gentle souls we find on the mound now, sought therapy by knocking Robinson on his dime. It was just what he wanted, just what he begged for by hanging over the plate with his elbows stuck in the strike zone like matched targets. "Every time he came up, you knew you were going to war," Don Drysdale says. The metaphor is no exaggeration. More than a few of the pitches Big D sidearmed for the Dodgers served the same purpose as hand grenades, and Robinson did not look kindly at shrapnel.

One night in the Los Angeles Coliseum, when the Brooklyn expatriates were cowering in front of a left-field screen only 251 feet from home plate, Drysdale warmed up for his duel with Robinson by conking Vada Pinson in the head with a curve. His next pitch was a fastball behind Robinson, a message meant to emphasize Drysdale's ill humor.

"I'm sure," Brosnan says, "that Don was out there thinking, Okay, I just popped Robinson's buddy and I just flattened Robinson—now I ought to be able to get a fastball by him. So he tried and Robinson must have hit it forty-five rows over the screen."

In retrospect, why he homered has as much to do with his enshrinement in the Hall of Fame Sunday as the fact that he homered at all. For twenty-one seasons, Frank Robinson was the ultimate competitor, a warrior who absolutely refused to rely on his natural gifts alone, a hardnose who squeezed as much from his talent as he possibly could. He is the only man to be the most valuable player in both the National and American leagues. He batted over .300 nine times and drove in more than a hundred runs six times. He was the majors' first black manager. And all those accomplishments were built on the foundation he laid with his own true grit.

"If you want to talk about the players who never let up, you have to talk about Robinson first," says Harry Dalton, the front-office wizard who twice traded to get him on his side. When Robinson joined Dalton's Orioles in 1966, labeled "an old thirty" by his former employers in Cincinnati, he responded by winning the triple crown and taking Baltimore to a World Series championship. When Dalton's Angels got him from the Dodgers seven years later, beat up and bedraggled, he hit thirty homers swinging one-handed and saved a floundering franchise. He never let up and his toughness never let him down.

It didn't win him friends in enemy dugouts, but Robinson wished a pox on the enemy anyway. He never joshed with them around the batting cage, the way today's glad-handers do, and after Maury Wills belittled the Orioles before the '66 Series, Robinson took out his bench jockey's stiletto and peeled the Dodger sprinter like a grape.

He was fierce, relentless, and proud. He never cried about playing in an era when Willie Mays, Hank Aaron, and Roberto Clemente got more publicity than he did, and he never bellyached about a contract once he signed it. But when he negotiated in that pre-agent era, a time when a hundred thousand dollars a year defined stardom the way a million dollars a year does now, he came in cleats high. And he went out determined to prove that he was as good as the money he got.

It wasn't simply a matter of knocking down fences, either. If there was a double play to be broken up, Robinson broke it up. Two nights in a row at old Yankee Stadium, he tumbled into the bleacher seats as he turned sure home runs into outs. He refused to be just another slugger; he played to leave his mark on every game. "You'd watch him sometimes," says Davey Johnson, the former Oriole second baseman, "and you'd swear he was writing the script for the ending."

He would beat out a bunt to start a midsummer night's rally or hobble around the bases on sore legs to keep the Orioles alive in the World Series. It's easy to forget such moments at times like these, when we look for easy explanations of greatness. But those 586 homers aren't the only reason Frank Robinson will see his bronzed likeness hung in Cooperstown. He will be honored for his heart and his courage and what he gave to the game.

What he gave to the game was everything he had.

Brooks Robinson
Honored To Be a Hero

Chicago Sun-Times
July 31, 1983

BALTIMORE—What a strange and quirky city this is, with its aging preppies flaunting their pedigrees in Roland Park and its east side grandmas scrubbing their white marble stoops. The summer heat drapes over everyone and everything like a thick, wet wool blanket, and sometimes you wonder if the street peddlers hawking their melons and tomatoes aren't really bellowing prayers for cool breezes.

For every newcomer who praises the wonders of the hanging-plant bars in Harbor Place, there are a dozen old boys who still think the Bromo-Seltzer tower is a work of art and preserve the native patois by calling their city "Bawlmer." Time was, in fact, the only thing an outlander could understand in their monologues was that they nurtured a passion for Brooks Robinson.

Brooks Robinson had a name that couldn't be mispronounced and a style at third base that couldn't be forgotten, and he came to represent this town of sailors and tarts and well-fed bankers in a way that baseball shall never see again. He joined the Orioles too early to board the grand old game's gravy train, the one that carries big star after big star to the highest bidder, so he had to settle for payment in Baltimore's love. Even now, after he has endured financial turmoil and seen players who couldn't have oiled his glove making four and five and even six times what he did at his peak, there is no denying that the deal left him wealthy in ways almost forgotten.

"Did you hear they're giving me another Brooks Robinson Day?" he asks with the eager, helpful innocence that becomes him as much at forty-six as it did at twenty-six. "Yeah, they had one in '76, when I didn't know I was coming back in '77, and they did it again in September of '78, when I really was finished. And now they're going to try again." The big day is August 15. "The players can't believe it. They don't think they'll ever get rid of me."

He laughs, knowing full well that he will be forgiven the Orioles' excesses. He laughs, for by the time his No. 5 is run up Memorial Stadium's flagpole again, he will be what his admirers have always described him as—a Hall of Famer.

They will make it official at Cooperstown Sunday, memorializing Brooks Robinson in bronze for revolutionizing defense at third base and pounding one line drive after another in the clutch. Much ado will deservedly be made of his sixteen Gold Gloves and the most valuable player award he won in 1964 with 28 home runs, 118 RBI, and a .317 batting average. And yet there is more to his story than numbers and yellowed press clippings. There is the humanity that moved him to welcome Frank Robinson in '66 when their egos could have collided and to step aside for Rick Dempsey in '78 when he, the greatest Oriole of them all, was the most expendable man on the roster. There is all that, and there is also the simple decency that established Brooks Robinson as a true hero in a city that disdains phonies as readily as it does bad crab cakes.

He could mock himself when his teammates caught him wearing one black sock and one brown, but he never mocked a scorer who charged him with an error. Likewise, he refused to get nasty with a writer who detailed the decline of his batting average, and eight years later he went out of his way to greet the ink-stained wretch at the all-star game.

Malice never played an inning in Brooks Robinson's soul. He was just plain folks. The difference was that, unlike the rest of his kind, he got asked to cut the ribbon at supermarket openings.

"It wasn't a bother, it was an honor," Brooks Robinson says. "Being a hero, if that's what I really turned out to be, is something you dream about when you're a kid, and I got to live my dream. I came here a couple years after the team moved from St. Louis and I kind of grew up with the Orioles—lived through the bad years and played in four World Series. I signed autographs and I went everywhere the people wanted me. I worked at being Brooks Robinson, but I loved it. It's just the way I was."

Fittingly, the blue-collar crowd at Memorial Stadium had the privilege of letting him know how high he was soaring. The message, however, wasn't printed in a newspaper or splashed across a gaudy electronic message board. It was hummed in delicious rumors and hymned in cheers that carried forever and ever.

"There was just something different about the way people sounded after I had that good Series in 1970," Brooks Robinson says. "They made me realize the Hall of Fame was a possibility."

Perhaps it was then that he began to understand how all memories, good or bad, serve a purpose. If he was ever goaded, it was by his recollection of the way the Orioles shipped him back to the minors in 1959, when he thought third base in Baltimore belonged to him. If anything in his past ever comforted him, it was the good feeling that emanated from that magical 1970 World Series against Cincinnati. He got more for being the MVP and moved the Reds' Johnny Bench to grumble, "I wish we'd known Brooks wanted the car that badly. We would have passed the hat and bought him one."

How many times will Brooks Robinson hear that in the next few days? How often will he be asked about the September battles against the Yankees and the last homer he hit, his only one in '77 but one that still paid off in victory? The memories are vivid now, and if that is a blessing, it is not without a touch that smacks of old Baltimore's sense of heroic propriety.

Though he does the color on the Orioles' road telecasts, Brooks Robinson strives to stay away from Memorial Stadium when the team is home. He even talked his way out of a pregame gig on the six o'clock news to avoid the place he made synonymous with diving catches and off-balance throws. And he will not venture inside its walls again until the Orioles are honoring him and proving beyond a doubt what he decided long ago.

"I don't mean to sound rude," Brooks Robinson says, "but I've already done everything I can here."

Ernie Banks
Mr. Cub Remembers

Chicago Daily News
August 5, 1977

He works in an office now. How that must hurt, even though the office is at Wrigley Field. When he dreamed as a young man, there was probably never a hint that he would have to stop playing the game that was, and is, his life.

But he did, and now he finds himself growing more and more apart from the new breed of Cubs. He has visited their clubhouse only once in this delicious season. The rest of the time, he has done nothing more than watch the players through his window as they leave the ballpark.

Ernie Banks says he doesn't mind.

He is the Cubs' group sales manager and their unofficial host, and he insists that he has all he can do to take care of those jobs. But he still leaves the impression that he would love to have someone tell him the clubhouse isn't the same without him.

"When I walk in there," Banks was saying Friday, "I think of where Billy Williams used to sit, and where Ron Santo used to sit, and where Glenn Beckert used to sit. It's a real emotional jolt for me."

In less than twenty-four hours, Banks would be playing in the Cubs' first old-timers' game with the men who populate his happy memories and the happy memories of fans who go back four decades and more. "It's hard to believe I'm an old-timer," he said.

He has already begun a campaign to make Saturday's crowd forget that he is forty-seven years old and that his final game as an active player was in 1971. On Tuesday, he jogged a mile in Wrigley Field, sweated through a set of calisthenics, and stirred a breeze by swinging a bat big enough to fell an ox.

"Fifty-four inches, forty-eight ounces," he said. "They don't allow any bigger bats in professional ball. You swing this one—just swing it—and you'll build up the muscles in your forearms."

Banks followed his self-prescribed regimen until Friday. Then he pronounced himself almost ready to face live pitching for the first time since he smacked a home run in an old-timers' game in Los Angeles a year ago. What he had to do before that, though, was confer with Lew Fonseca, the attending physician for the Cubs' hitters.

"Lew Fonseca told me a very important thing," Banks said. He picked up a thirty-five-inch bat bearing his name from against a file cabinet and took his stance behind his desk. "Lew Fonseca told me not to swing the way I used to. I've got to get set when the pitcher takes his sign. Hey, I tried it. It worked beautiful."

So Banks had the safeguard he was looking for. While he is as courtly as he has been painted, he is also unrepentantly proud of his 512 career homers and his membership in the Hall of Fame. "I want people to remember me the way I was," he said, "not as somebody who couldn't pick up a grounder or hit the ball out of the infield."

It is easy to see him as a man-child who may never be able to accept a role in the world outside the white lines of a baseball diamond. After all, he was so bewildered by retirement that he almost left the Cubs organization and returned to Dallas, where he was born. But P. K. Wrigley, the team's reclusive owner, wouldn't let that happen. He stepped in and saw to the invention of a job where Banks would spend half his time hustling tickets and the other half wandering around the ballpark, charming the customers.

It was a splendid idea with one possible flaw: The public might see Banks as the Chicago equivalent of wasted old Joe Louis greeting round-the-clock gamblers in a Las Vegas casino. Banks would have none of it Friday, however, as he signed autographs with one hand and guided a camera crew from ABC-TV news on a tour of the bleachers. The best word for his every move was dignified.

"It shouldn't be any other way," he said. "The fans respect me and I respect them back."

Dignity does not translate into stiffness where Banks is concerned. After the Cubs stymied the Mets 5–0, he told everyone who approached his office, "It was Ladies Day and we made all the ladies happy." When he discovered that Dave Lamont, who occupies the desk next to his, had a prospective ticket buyer on the line from Webster, Iowa, Banks shouted, "Tell him we want all of Webster to get behind the Cubs."

The office litany continued until Banks remembered something more important. "I better hang up my uniform for the old-timers' game," he said. "Don't want any wrinkles in it."

He reached into a well-worn duffel bag with a peeling identification tag and pulled out his uniform. "These people up in Milwaukee made it for me special," he said. "It's just like the one I wore when I broke into the big leagues in 1953."

He held it high and turned around to look at the blue 14 on the back. Then he stood and pulled the top on over his white shirt and striped tie. When he had zipped it up all the way, he spun slowly, modeling it for everybody in the office and wishing perhaps that he could go back to the time when the feel of a big league uniform was brand-new.

Bill Veeck
"Bionic Man I'm Not"

Sport SCORE
May 9, 1979

The phone wouldn't stop ringing and Bill Veeck wouldn't stop answering it, which may be all the proof anybody needs that he is still baseball's reigning revolutionary. The day before, in front of 41,043 witnesses, his Chicago White Sox, gracing Comiskey Park for the first time in 1979, had been thoroughly disgraced by the Toronto Blue Jays. Now Veeck, the only team president in captivity who has no secretary to fend off unfriendly voices, was taking the consequences right in the ear.

"Halloo," he said. "This is he. . . . I'm a little battered and very bloody, thank you. . . . I can't very well make any excuses for twelve bases on balls or a 10–2 score, can I? . . . We just stunk out the joint."

Basic Veeck: If you can't give the folks a winner, at least you can give them charm.

In half a century of trying to keep the customers satisfied, however, there have been times when even charm was beyond Veeck's means. Take the first team he ever called his own, the 1941 Milwaukee Brewers of the American Association. He spent money he didn't have sprucing up their nine-thousand-seat ball-park, and when fifteen thousand trusting souls sardined their way into it on opening day, he figured his gamble had paid off. And it would have if a rainstorm hadn't washed the game into oblivion in the fourth inning. Veeck took cover in a saloon across the street. It would be just as easy to hand out rain checks there, he reasoned, and, besides, maybe everybody who wanted one wouldn't find him.

Times and methods change.

"You have my apologies," Veeck was telling Caller No. 162. "Why don't you come tomorrow as my guest? And if you have friends who were with you at the game, tell them to come back, too . . . [pause] . . . Everybody is invited back. . . . You can look in the newspaper and see where I said it. I want everybody to find out that we aren't as bad as we looked . . . [long pause] . . . Honestly."

He sells hope now, Bill Veeck does. The question, of course, is whether Chicago will buy it. Veeck already knows there is a market for a winner in this city that has overdosed on defeat. In 1977, when he had Richie Zisk and a shot at the pennant, 1.7 million people paid to see the White Sox. The count was down only two hundred thousand last year, even though Zisk was gone and the Sox were DOA, proving that good memories sell tickets. But now the memories are bad and Veeck is searching for a way to erase them. Ergo hope.

It stays with him even though only a thousand of the opening-day shock victims accepted his invitation to return. It stays with him even though the returnees saw the Sox piddle away a five-run lead and lose to Toronto again. It stays with him even though the Sox's lone weekend series with the Yankees fell on Easter and drew forty thousand fewer fans than it should have. It stays with him, one suspects, because nothing else seems quite so natural.

Remember, Veeck is the peg-legged wreck who considered Chicago's brutal winter a splendid one because there wasn't a doctor in town who could find enough wrong with him to merit his thirty-third operation. "I know this doesn't sound very gracious," he says, "but I think Illinois Masonic Hospital finally had a year when they didn't need me to finish in the black." He would have gone willingly, though, if the hospital had smuggled in the unparalleled artificial knee that the Russians have developed and the United State has banned. Never mind that his diet of beer and cigarettes is corroding his plumbing. Never mind that his hearing is beyond salvation. William Veeck Jr., sixty-five years old and trying to forget it, wants the Russian knee so he can play tennis again. No pessimist, he.

Let somebody else talk about the psychedelic trips the White Sox outfielders take in search of fly balls. Veeck would rather tout Chet Lemon as baseball's next great center fielder. His strategy is the same when right-hander Francisco Barrios' million-dollar arm and ten-cent brain come up for discussion. Veeck thinks positive and, when the subject is Harry Chappas, big.

Not big physically, you understand. Veeck liked the rookie shortstop right where he was, which, with knees bent, is five foot three. That made him the smallest major leaguer since Bill You-Know-Who unveiled his pinch-hitting midget. Keeping Chappas in the majors, however, proved a good deal tougher than measuring him.

He was trying to make the long jump from Class A to Chicago, and the change in altitude was too much for him. "He lost a little bit of his reckless abandon," Veeck allows grudgingly. Chappas was batting .059 and failing to throw the ball to first base with any regularity when the White Sox dropped him back in the minor leagues. Yet Veeck talks as if becoming a magazine cover boy had given Chappas more trouble than the curve or the play in the hole. "People acted like he planned it," Veeck says. "He didn't. What he did do was win the shortstop job this spring."

Maybe yes, maybe no. There are members of the White Sox family who contend that Chappas will never handle the position with the consummate grace of his thirty-six-year-old playing manager, Don Kessinger. Indeed, by the second week of the season, Kessinger had inserted himself at shortstop. "I just need the exercise," he said. Far be it from him to spoil a gate attraction. Far be it from him to spoil the dreams of his boss, the last hustler in baseball.

"I think I would rather be called a promoter," Veeck says. "That's what you are when you deal in dreams and hope and the ephemeral idea called fun."

For years, however, the lords of baseball acted as if they would sooner have the Boston Strangler as a houseguest than admit Veeck to their lodge. He was a boogeyman because he wasn't afraid to live by his wits, his imagination, his guile. He was a freak because the fans, not the almighty dollar, came first.

When he announced his intention to repurchase the White Sox in 1975, he ran into roadblocks set by old foes as well as people from whom he expected an ounce of loyalty. "You don't belong here," said Bud Selig, the president of the Brewers, who a decade earlier enlisted Veeck in the futile fight to keep Milwaukee in the National League. "The game has passed you by." Now, four years later, the yapping has stopped. Skeptics attribute the silence to the power elite's conviction that it has been proven right.

"There's no point in trying to create the impression that I'm a wizard," Veeck says. "I've made a lot of mistakes."

He stocked the world champion Yankees with Bucky Dent, Jim Spencer, and the manager who tamed the Bronx Zoo, Bob Lemon. He let Zisk and Oscar Gamble, the siege guns of '77, ride out of town as free agents and received nothing in return. He swung a major trade for Bobby Bonds, then peddled away the peripatetic slugger two months into the 1978 season. But his most infamous deal may have been the one involving Ron Blomberg, the former Yankee monologist and designated hitter. After coming to bat just twice in two seasons, the oft-injured Blomberg was healed by a fat four-year contract from the supposedly penniless White Sox. In turn, everybody who watched him limp and swing and miss got sick. This spring, after exactly one season in the Sox's employ, Blomberg was released with full pay. It was the only cure possible.

"I still think he can hit," Veeck says. "I'll always think he can hit. But he wouldn't give himself a chance. His pride wouldn't allow him to go to the Instructional League last winter or down to the minors to get his timing back. I don't know. . . ."

He sighs in exasperation.

The enemy is watching silently, maybe even contentedly.

"That never occurs to me," Veeck says. "I just go ahead and do what I think is right."

In other words, he hustles.

Who else would have sent three-foot-eight Eddie Gaedel up to bat for the St. Louis Browns? Or passed off Jack Soo, of TV's *Barney Miller*, as an American Indian chief turned crooner? Or loaded a scoreboard with fireworks and a recording of *The Hallelujah Chorus*? Or had Nellie Fox pause from his duties as the American League's most valuable player to milk a cow during National Dairy Week? Or offered live squid as a door prize? Or let a section of fans manage a game with cue cards?

Who but Veeck?

"I don't deal in larceny," he says. "The people pay a buck to see a ball game and I try to give them 110 cents' worth of enjoyment with the fireworks and what have you. There's no larceny in that."

And there is only a little in the rest of what he does.

Exhibit A for the prosecution is the way Veeck snookered the *Chicago Tribune* last summer. To set the stage for you, the White Sox lost nineteen of their first twenty-one games, which made them about as popular as lice. Then, for some perverse reason, they came back to win eighteen of twenty-two games and put Veeck in the mood for a little fun. Apparently the handiest fall guy was the *Tribune*'s beat reporter, who found him in the middle of his usual pregame meal, Schlitz and Salem Longs.

The reporter told Veeck the Sox could use a lovable clown like the San Diego Chicken. Veeck said he already had a lovable clown in lop-eared, rubber-necked Max Patkin. Better yet, he said, Max

Patkin used to pitch in the big leagues. If the Chicken ever pitched anywhere outside a public park, he'd get de-feathered.

The reporter said he was just trying to think of something to get the fans out to Comiskey Park. Veeck said better coverage might help. He was on a roll now. He said the Cubs got more ink than the Sox. He said he had measured it himself. He said the disparity would be reason enough to move the Sox out of town if he didn't care so much about the South Side's kind hearts and gentle people. (Hustler's Rule No. 357: Always leave yourself an out.) He said he was sinking fast.

To be sure, he resurfaced immediately. The reporter's story about Veeck's outburst was splashed across the top of the *Trib*'s sports page. Other reporters from other newspapers hastened to the scene. Radio guys hauled their tape recorders to Comiskey at record speed. For the first time all season, the smell of TV sportscasters' hairspray wafted through the park. Two days later, the sports editor of the *Tribune* announced that he had measured the coverage of the Sox and the Cubs in his paper and the Sox had come out on top.

"That's odd," Veeck said, and a sly smile flickered across the face that looks like it belongs on a woodcarver's doll.

Veeck makes a beguiling monument to the art of hustling—all fuzz and wrinkles and twinkles. "When he wears a tie," says his wife of twenty-nine years, Mary Frances Veeck, "he looks like he's forgotten his pants." So he leaves his collar open and makes sure he has his wits with him instead of a tie.

The solution has worked ever since Veeck came home from World War II with his right leg full of shrapnel. Eventually a series of amputations would leave him with a stump only a few inches long. But at the time, his leg was in a cast and the infection that festered in there smelled like a cesspool. Maybe the cologne he sprinkled through the holes in his cast killed the stench. Or maybe nobody could tell the difference in Cleveland, which wasn't known for its fragrance even then. Whatever, he walked into one of the city's most prestigious banks and asked for a million-dollar loan to buy the Indians. And he got it.

Then the fun began. The Indians broke the American League's color barrier and won a World Series. Veeck moved to St. Louis in hopes of saving the Browns, a venture that went down like the Hindenburg. Life improved briefly but joyously when he bought the White Sox for the first time as he installed his exploding scoreboard and, in 1959, won the last pennant Chicago has seen. Then he sold the Sox and waited to find out if his notoriously poor health was going to kill him.

He survived only in a manner of speaking, for he had no baseball team to run. The club owners in the majors, the ones who had always feared his willingness to swim against the tide, saw to that. He lived in exile in a sprawling manse on the Eastern Shore of Maryland, surrounded by 10,000 daffodils and the manuscripts for his first two books, *Veeck—As In Wreck* and *The Hustler's Handbook*. In the late sixties, he had a brief interlude running Suffolk Downs race track in Boston, but all that really did was give him the inspiration for another book, *Thirty Tons a Day*. Better to be in baseball, where a man doesn't run the risk of wearing his mistakes on his shoes.

But how to get back? The Baltimore Orioles were dangled in front of Veeck, then jerked away rudely. While he was still fuming over that affront in late 1975, an appeal came from Chicago to save the White Sox. They were in danger of being deported to Seattle. Veeck, a knight in battered armor, couldn't let that happen.

He sold his Maryland home and invested every cent he had in a fight with the American League. "No other owner would have taken such a risk," he says with pride. He put the touch on old cronies, quickly moved to total strangers, and finally found himself at the door of the greatest White Sox fan of all, Richard J. Daley. The mayor of Chicago leaned on the right people, made sure the necessary cash was in hand—and then listened to how Veeck had still stolen the show.

He had been in the Continental Bank of Illinois talking some tightwad out of half a million dollars. In mid-pitch he leaped to his feet to make a point and the hinged knee of his wooden leg came undone. Nuts, springs, and pinions skittered every which way. Down there on the floor with them was Veeck, face first.

Very calmly, very quietly, he asked for a pair of pliers to put himself back together.

"Bionic Man I'm not," he said.

He has tried to be everything else, though, and Chicago, which is used to a slower, stodgier kind of sports executive, has had to adjust to him all over again. Even at dawn, when he is soaking the stump of his right leg, he is busy reading newspapers, magazines, and great chunks of the four books he devours every week. His home phone is listed. He thinks nothing of waking somebody at two in the morning if that is when a question occurs to him. He invited Bob Lemon up for drinks the night after firing him as the Sox's manager—an invitation that was accepted, one hastens to add. He waves to his public from seat 18 in the press box and, at least once, he has gimped into the grandstand to take a punch in the nose while breaking up a fight.

He won't let up because he can't.

"I am not a person of high ideals," he says, "and to let anybody labor under that impression would be quite wrong. If I ever want to sell, I want something that somebody else wants to buy."

He had it in '77 and then it was gone last season, carried away by the winds of free agency. The change left him with a team preoccupied by throwing to the wrong base and bickering in the clubhouse. If any one player captured the essence of those Sox, it was Claudell Washington, who took five days to report after being traded from Texas. His explanation: "I overslept."

Because Veeck is a tolerant man, Washington is back this season. Larry Doby is, too, but as a batting coach, not a manager. He was a loyal lieutenant for three decades after Veeck made him the American League's first black player in 1948. After canning Lemon, Veeck made Doby his manager, out of loyalty if nothing else. Alas, the story had no happy ending. The Sox performed wretchedly for Doby, who antagonized umpires to the point of outright hatred, and, by season's end, it was certain he was out. Doby cried foul, and civil rights leader Jesse Jackson took up his cause. "I can't help that," Veeck says. "Their feelings have to be secondary to mine. That's one of the unfortunate things about this game."

So, at last, the manager's job belongs to Kessinger. It is easy to wonder whether he will be able to lift the Sox above their limitations, because he wouldn't say birdseed if he had a mouth full of it. Veeck, however, turns off his hearing aid at the first sound of criticism. "Maybe I could accuse myself of senility," he says, "but I'm still more excited and curious about this season than any I've ever been involved in."

As spring training drew to a close, he gathered his manager and coaches in his Florida motel room and asked each of them to write down the names of the twenty-five players they thought should go north. "I said 'should go,'" Veeck says, "not 'will go.'" Ron Blomberg's name didn't appear on a single ballot. "I told them he was my problem, not theirs," Veeck says. "I was the one who made a stupid deal."

A sigh of relief swept through the room, and after the meeting, a coach—Veeck won't say which one—came up and stammered his thanks.

"I told him I knew what he'd been thinking," Veeck says. "He'd been thinking, Watch this old whore."

Now only one question remains. It is about Harry Chappas and why *he* was brought north. But before it can be asked, Veeck has hurried off to do business on his favorite corner, under his favorite streetlight. Just watch him.

Carl Yastrzemski
Family Tradition

Chicago Sun-Times
August 28, 1983

It was the old man's last season. Baseball had never taken him any farther than the semipro games they played beside the potato fields on New York's Long Island, yet he could look over from second base and know there was hope. His shortstop was his son.

They had been out there together since the boy was fifteen, saving their best shots for barnstorming juggernauts like the Homestead Grays and Indianapolis Clowns and imagining what it would be like to worry about the Yankees and Tigers instead. Now the boy's eighteenth birthday was history and the scouts from Boston were flashing the hundred-thousand-dollar bonus that eventually lured him out of Notre Dame. When the money was spent, however, the Red Sox's great thinkers took one look at the statistics the kid and his heavier-hitting old man had rung up that summer. "Are you sure we signed the right one?" they asked. Carl Michael Yastrzemski Sr. was forty-four.

Carl Michael Yastrzemski Jr. celebrated the same birthday the other night by bashing a double that sundered a tie, and then he gave a slice of his birthday cake to his late boss' wife. Family means something in the Yastrzemski clan. So does tradition. The men do their utmost to fight the clock and ignore the passing years. They don't just hang on, though; they persevere with grace and style. But as it went with the old man, so it goes with his son. Forty-four is when the game gets called.

Yaz resisted admitting it for as long as he could. A few weeks ago, his average was up to .330 and his sights were on Atlanta if the Red Sox had no more use for him. Then came an 0-for-19 cold snap that forced him to acknowledge both his age and the presence of Chris Chambliss and Gerald Perry in the Braves' power structure.

"It wasn't me who said anything about playing another year anyway," Yastrzemski says. "That was just a lot of speculation on everybody else's part."

Even now, though, he can't bring himself to announce that his last game will be October 2 in Boston. He prefers conversational circles, talking about going full-time with the meat company he works for in the off-season and spending next spring with the Red Sox's fledgling sluggers. He does no farewell grandstanding and asks for no parties as he bids adieu to city after city.

The golf carts and silver-plated shotguns can be saved until somebody else retires. Carl Yastrzemski has already received his greatest gifts. "I came here early this season after I'd just spent nine days in traction with a bad back," he says, staring out at Comiskey Park's greensward. "I asked the White Sox people if I could have the field to take some extra hitting and they told me, 'Sure.' I got the field all three days I was here. And it's been like that everywhere since I came to the big leagues. So why should I get something extra now? I've had twenty-three years of the best treatment you could ask for. That's thanks enough."

Yaz earned everything he ever got by making himself far bigger than five feet eleven and 185 pounds when he was at the plate. He cocked his bat high behind his head with the same lethal authority he might have used with a pistol, and he swung with a ferocity that drove baseballs out of sight and pitchers to drink. In the days before he was a first baseman and designated hitter, he roamed left field in Fenway Park with a con man's flair. Balls would ricochet off the Green Monster and he would play the carom perfectly, wheel, and unleash a throw that would turn a potential double into an out. All things considered, the word to describe him was consummate.

"Maybe I wasn't the greatest hitter going, but I wasn't too bad," Yastrzemski says. "Maybe I wasn't the best guy in the world for hitting home runs, but I still did all right. Maybe I wasn't the best defensive player in the world, but I was pretty good. I guess the best thing I had going for me was, I was a hell of a competitor. I made things happen."

So it is that admirers judge him on more than his .286 career average, his 451 homers, or his 3,401 hits. They focus instead on the way he has grown since he was a twenty-year-old rookie burdened by the load of replacing Ted Williams and perplexed by the fractious, ineffective Red Sox team on which he found himself. In the seasons that followed, he was called a pouter, a loafer, a backstabber. Then he became a winner.

The catalyst for the transition was the 1967 pennant race, a four-team donnybrook featuring the Red Sox, Tigers, Twins, and White Sox. "Everybody kept talking about pressure," Yastrzemski says, "but I told them, 'Hell, this is the most fun I've ever had in my life.'" He proved it, too. In the last two games of the season, when Boston finally took the pennant home, he had seven hits in eight at-bats, drove in six runs, and wrapped up the triple crown. The only other time Yaz gained as much attention was when he popped up eleven years later.

He had already homered and singled and driven in two runs. "But all anybody remembers is that pop-up," he says. It came against Goose Gossage with two outs and two runners on base in the ninth inning, and it sealed the Red Sox's casket in their sudden-death playoff with the Yankees.

The amazing thing was that Boston's prickly, contentious, opinionated fans didn't hold it against him. Instead, there was an outpouring of sympathy for the suddenly fragile, undeniably graying figure who slumped in front of his locker in the Red Sox's clubhouse. Carl Yastrzemski had lampblack under his eyes and tears in them, and you knew what was going through his mind: Sooner or later, it was going to be this old man's last season, too.

Bill Lee
Spaceman

Chicago Sun-Times
April 9, 1978

Once upon a time, Bill Lee wished aloud that the Boston Red Sox would issue him No. 337 because, upside down, it spelled his last name. Once upon a time, Bill Lee was banned from shagging fly balls in batting practice because, in his manic devotion to duty, he stopped only when he collided with the outfield wall. There is no once upon a time, however, when Bill Lee is described as the ultimate left-hander. The role is his for eternity.

Word of Lee's eccentric ways has traveled as far as the hideaways where Ted Williams fishes. When Williams surrendered his privacy to tutor the Red Sox's hitters this spring, he made a point of avoiding Lee. The reason, he said, was that he doesn't trust college men. "But, Ted, I'm like you," said Lee (USC, class of '68). "I hate hair dryers, too."

Williams hates them because they sound like power mowers and blow out the clubhouse lights. Lee hates them because they represent another extravagance that saps the earth of its energy. "What's good for the earth should be good enough for the people on the earth," he says. "It never works out that way, though." Ted Williams wouldn't understand.

Now Lee must worry about gaining his wife's understanding instead of Williams's. He will meet the good Mrs. Lee in Cleveland twenty-four hours after he pitches against the White Sox at Comiskey Park Sunday afternoon. By then he will have gone a week without shaving or, as he would have it, a week without wasting soap, water, and razor blades. Unfortunately, the kindest thing that can be said of his hirsute mug is that he looks like a nighthawk at a diner.

"I know, I know," Lee says as he tries to come up with an explanation stronger than conservation. He opts at last for what may be construed as a putdown of Samson: "I had a beard last year and did bad. I wanted to try one again this year and see if I do good. That way I'll know my beard doesn't have any power over me."

Such curlicue thinking earned Lee the nickname "Spaceman" soon after he descended on the American League eight years ago. "It was supposed to be derogatory, I guess," he says. He wasn't offended, though. He was delighted, and still is. "The only thing I wish they would do now," he says, "is expand my title a little bit. I think they ought to call me Space and Time Man. You know, because I can go through a day just exploring things. I'm free floating."

Lee alights to throw his sinkerball, unburden himself of sundry opinions, and have a good time, not necessarily in that order. When the Red Sox began limbering up for opening day at Comiskey, for example, he paused in mid-wind sprint to look up an old friend in the left field stands. The old friend handed Lee a coonskin cap that inspired him to do his imitation of Davy Crockett.

"I've known the guy for three years, ever since he gave me a gas mask to use while I took ground balls at third base," Lee said.

"What's the guy's name?" someone asked.

"Beats me. All I know is he always sits next to a girl of mammary distinction."

After Lee finished gazing at her and waving his cap by the tail, he began doing what he does best—talking. "I don't know what to think about the White Sox's new white uniforms," he said. "The guys look thinner in them, but there are definitely going to be laundry problems." Of course, those problems will be nothing compared to the ones he sees in baseball, starting with the designated hitter rule. "It doesn't let managers manage," he said. He also frets over the absence of blue-collar fans at the World Series. "You look up in the stands," he said, "and the only collars you see are white." But he wasn't going to say anything about the hated Yankees—"Billy Martin's Brown Shirts," he called them last year—until he learned that Martin had broken their tacit ceasefire.

"He said you bend your lip too much," a Boston writer reported.

"It's better," Lee said, "to be quick with your lip than to be a violent sucker-puncher."

The Yankees entered his personal hall of infamy after his left shoulder was ravaged in a 1976 brawl with them. The injury snuffed out his chances of a fourth straight seventeen-victory season. It almost snuffed out his career as well. There was a pleasant pause in the trauma early last year when he spent an afternoon drinking in a Greenwich Village bistro and then went out and beat the Yanks. But most of the season was devoted to coping with rumors that the Red Sox wanted to get rid of him.

"They were playing games with my mind," he said. "Mainly Zimmer." Don Zimmer, who, given a can of spinach to hold, would be a dead ringer for Popeye, manages the Red Sox. "He had a one-year contract, just like he does now," Lee said, "so I could understand his low tolerance for non-achieving. But I had a screwed-up elbow along with my screwed-up shoulder. I needed time to recover." He lucked his way into getting it, and by dint of five victories late last season and a strong spring training this year, he now stands as the third starter in Zimmer's four-man rotation.

If Zimmer were to list his favorites among the Red Sox, however, Lee would rank considerably lower than third. That was guaranteed last week after they traded right-hander Jim Willoughby to the Cubs. "I went in and lit a candle on Zimmer's desk," Lee said. "It was a novena for my friend."

There was never a thought about what the candle would do to his relationship with Zimmer. "He's at the point where I don't exist in his mind," Lee said. "I'll be talking to him and I'll pick up on something he says and try to throw it back to him. But all he does is look away and talk about something completely different. I can't possibly communicate with him. Maybe all communication is useless anyway. You know, you take things to the nth degree and they don't make any sense."

"Does that mean you're going to stop talking?" someone asked.

"Are you kidding?" Bill Lee said.

Mark Fidrych
Bird with a Broken Wing

Chicago Sun-Times
April 26, 1978

Two days of rain have reduced Comiskey Park's outfield to the consistency of overcooked oatmeal. Now, with the emerald green puddles reflecting the stadium lights, all but one of the Detroit Tigers' pitchers are tiptoeing through their wind sprints. The exception is Mark Fidrych. He's making waves.

He splashes and laughs and the other pitchers jump and cuss. He does it again and again, until the shirt tail hanging outside his pants is dripping with muddy water. He knows he'll be making an extra contribution to the team's laundry hamper, but it doesn't stop him. This is his game and he's going to play it, because he doesn't know when he will have his next chance to play a more important game—baseball.

The problem is Fidrych's right shoulder, which, unfortunately, is attached to his pitching arm. "It's inflamed in there," he says, offering a diagnosis that has yet to be improved on. "The doctors have got to cool it down."

Fidrych felt the fire in his arm a week ago in Detroit. He herky-jerked his way through four innings against the White Sox, and then Ralph Houk, acting like a worried parent as much as a hard-bitten leader of men, gently escorted him off the field. Houk told himself the kid would be all right after a few days' rest. The kid wasn't. The moment he began warming up to pitch against Texas Saturday, the pain sizzled through his shoulder again.

Now there is no telling when Fidrych will charge back out to the mound, smooth the dirt with his bare hands, explain his diabolical plans to the ball, and send it darting toward a perplexed hitter. Now there seem to be legitimate questions about whether the phenomenon known as The Bird has become an endangered species at twenty-three.

"This is the first time I've ever had a hurt arm," Fidrych says. He is taking liberties with the truth and he knows it. "Well," he says a moment later, "except for last year."

Last year must have been choreographed by the Marquis de Sade in conjunction with the American Medical Association. In spring training, The Bird tried to imitate a majestic golden condor as he leaped for a fly ball. When he landed, he unmajestically tore the cartilage in his knee. The episode cost him the first fifty-two days of the season, an unbearably harsh penalty for one of the world's foremost bundles of energy.

When he could pitch again, he chewed through hitters as if they were fingernails. There was never a doubt that he was the same Mark Fidrych who became the American League's 1976 rookie of the year by winning nineteen games and putting an average of thirty-one thousand fannies in the seats every time he pitched. The chief difference in the 1977 Fidrych was his staying power, or lack thereof. By July 20 he was on the disabled list, gone for the rest of the season. The diagnosis was tendonitis. Fidrych accepted it as manfully as possible, never thinking that his shoulder would be wracked by the same devastating pain this season.

Coping is harder the second time around. There is no smile beneath the pale blond mustache Fidrych has cultivated. His eyes only light up when he talks about the Grateful Dead, his favorite band, or when an older, wiser teammate details the non-athletic plans for the night ahead. The games? "The games are a drag," Fidrych says. "I just sit there and wait for them to get over."

So far, nobody has suggested that he be given a ticket home.

"If that happens, I'll just take the summer off," he says. "Getting hurt and having bad breaks and stuff like that is just part of the game, just part of life." The philosophy serves as a shield. After showing us so much of himself in past seasons, Fidrych isn't going to let us peek at his fears. Somebody else will have to worry that his bright future may no longer exist.

"You wonder if he's having trouble because we played in snow in Toronto and Detroit," Ralph Houk says, punctuating his sentence with a period made of tobacco juice. "You don't know, though. You can't pinpoint anything. He's such a great kid. It would be a tragedy if baseball lost him."

"Everybody should pray for him," says Rusty Staub, the Tigers' aging siege gun. "The fans, the club owners, the players on the other teams—everybody. And maybe they should let him have some time to himself, too."

Left to his own devices this spring, the most eccentric thing Fidrych has done is barbecue a chicken in front of his apartment. When he has to pitch, he does it with eight hours' sleep. More often than not, the sartorial disaster of seasons past has shown up at the ballpark wearing a suit, albeit with his favorite Fleetwood Diner T-shirt peeking from under his open-necked sports shirt. There are even rumors afloat that he has grown up, that he has been scared into being serious about his livelihood.

"I've never been not serious," he says, digging through his locker in search of a dry undershirt. "I know what ball gave me. If I wasn't here, I'd be back home working in a gas station."

Yet even escaping the reality of Northboro, Massachusetts, has not satisfied him. He seems no happier when he talks about the high-rent pleasures of the Detroit suburb where he lives now. "When a man doesn't have anything to go home to," Mark Fidrych says, "he doesn't want to go home."

He leans against his locker and stares off into space. The clubhouse TV is on, but he doesn't see it. A stereo is playing in the background, but he doesn't hear it. He wants to keep running, and he knows he can't do it on empty.

It would seem that Fidrych never caught another break. He was gone from baseball at twenty-nine and dead at fifty-four, killed in an accident while working on his dump truck back home in Massachusetts. But he had a wife who loved him, a 107-acre farm that he could call his own, and friends who embraced him for reasons that had nothing to do with that one magical summer in the big leagues. He was, they said, "a hell of a guy." Would that we could all be remembered that way.

Steve Bilko
The Slugging Seraph

from the book *Cult Baseball Players*
1990

In that summer I fell in love with baseball, I celebrated by practicing a form of heresy then common to boys throughout Los Angeles: I ignored the triple crown that Mickey Mantle was fashioning
for himself. It was surprisingly easy to do. New York and Yankee Stadium seemed too far away to fathom; indeed, for many
of us who were blissfully ignorant of Walter O'Malley's lust for
the West Coast, the very idea of the major leagues was exotic,
remote, maybe even unnecessary. After all, we had the L.A. Angels and the Hollywood Stars of the Pacific Coast League. Better yet, we had Steve Bilko.

He was the first fat guy my friends and I ever had for a hero,
the first fat guy we ever wanted to grow up to be. If he had been
some anonymous tub of guts loaded down with beer and salami
at the grocery store, we would have snickered behind his back.
If he had been one of those unfortunate fifth-grade blimps, we
would have made his days a nightmare. Unless the poor kid could
hit like Stout Steve of the Angels. And Stout Steve hit what he
must have weighed—a ton.

The 55 home runs, those 164 runs batted in, that .360 batting
average. Mantle couldn't match any of them. Of course, less im-
pressionable observers would have conceded that Bilko beat up
on minor league cunny-thumbers in Wrigley Field, L.A.'s band-
box replica of the home of the Cubs. But that meant nothing to

the kids who marveled at his power, and it probably meant even less to Bilko. For here was a coalminer's son who hit twenty-one homers in his rookie season with the St. Louis Cardinals, only to be chased off first base the following year by Joe Cunningham. Here was a vagabond slugger who couldn't earn steady employment with the perpetually forlorn Cubs and actually asked to be demoted to L.A. And now he was the biggest man in town in a way that had nothing to do with the Angels' plea that he tip the scales at no more than 230 pounds—fat chance—or the headline that claimed NOT EVEN MRS. BILKO KNOWS HIS WEIGHT. He was bigger than John Wayne, bigger than Jimmy Stewart, bigger than any matinee idol you can think of, and he had the press clippings to prove it. "There wasn't a movie star who could touch him," George Goodale, who was the Angels' publicist, told me. "I know. I kept count myself."

The adulation didn't stop with that, however. Neil Simon was in the throes of creating a TV show called *You'll Never Get Rich* and he needed a name for the conniving Army sergeant Phil Silvers was going to play in it. Simon went through a multitude of possibilities, but there was one name he couldn't get out of his mind, the name he read every day on the sports page, the name that almost chose itself: Bilko. Nothing like that ever happened to Mickey Mantle.

Still, it took me a while to fess up to the hold Bilko had on me. The problem was my parents' loyalty to the Hollywood Stars. Owned by the founder of the Brown Derby, haunted by the memory of the time they played in short pants, the Stars weren't much to look at in 1956 once you got past two fallen bonus babies, Paul Pettit and Jim Baumer, and a cadaverous second baseman named Spook Jacobs. The Angels, on the other hand, were a work of art featuring Gene Mauch, Bob Speake, and George Freese as well as Stout Steve. But my mother and father cared not. Gilmore Field, the home of the Stars, was in a better neighborhood that Wrigley, so that was that.

Ever the obedient only child, I did my best to root for the Stars, but I could feel myself backsliding, being lured astray by the thunder in Bilko's bat. I thought I might be saved the next season when the Stars imported Dick Stuart, who was fresh from a sixty-six-homer campaign in Lincoln, Nebraska, that prompted him to dot the i in his first name with a star. Then Stuart bashed five home runs in the Stars' first four games and I was sure he could turn me around. At last the Stars had someone getting the royal treatment that had heretofore been reserved solely for Bilko.

One of Stuart's first stops was Twentieth Century Fox, where he found himself posing for a picture with the bounteously endowed Jayne Mansfield and having his fancy tickled by a question he must have been waiting for all his life.

"How come you're getting the headlines and I'm not?" La Mansfield asked.

"Because I'm hitting the long ball," Stuart replied.

Bilko was speechless. Talking wasn't his game, hitting was. So he stuck to his strength while the new kid in town flapped his jaw, neglected his swing, and wound up suffering exactly the fate you might imagine. Soon afterward, he was dispatched to Atlanta, and from there back to Lincoln. Bilko, meanwhile, was piling up 56 more homers for the Angels. That made 111 in two seasons, establishing him as a legend of sorts and teaching me about the insight that baseball can provide into the men who play it.

To my way of thinking, there is no other sport that reveals so much about its performers as human beings. Baseball players aren't hidden by helmets and shoulder pads, nor are they separated from the rest of society by their runaway pituitary glands. Give or take the stray Dave Parker or Eddie Gaedel, they resemble everyday people and they function in a setting where you can follow their every move, talk to them, yell at them, maybe even reach out and touch them. Watch ten games in person in a season—really study them from batting practice to the final out—and you should be able to identify the loafers, the brooders, the pranksters, the head cases, and the just plain good guys.

Steve Bilko was just a plain good guy. I imagined as much when I was eleven years old, and twenty-two years later, when I was a sports columnist for the *Chicago Sun-Times*, I learned it for a fact. Death had taken Bilko by surprise at forty-nine and I wanted to write a farewell, but I had never gotten any closer to him than the stands were to the diamond. So I started calling his old friends, and slowly there began to emerge a picture of a gentle galoot who always got a breaking ball instead of the break he needed. One erstwhile Angel remembered how deeply touched Bilko was that a team executive was at the airport to greet him when he blew into town. Another recalled Stout Steve trying to repent for a night of beer drinking by locking himself in the bathroom, padding the cracks around the door with towels, and turning the place into a steam bath. And everybody agreed that it was too bad he didn't hit his prime a little later, when the majors were expanding and pitching was thinning out. "If Steve had come along in the sixties, he would have been a hell of a big league player," said Bob Scheffing, his manager during the glory years on the West Coast. Instead, Bilko came to symbolize a breed that is now extinct.

All those home runs he hit for the Angels signaled the beginning of the end for an era when a big lug could drag his Louisville Slugger from one minor league outpost to another and make a living. As the majors were growing, the minors were shrinking, changing, chasing kids back to the real world before they had a chance to grow old swinging from the heels. Never again could there be a Joe Hauser in Minneapolis, a Howitzer Howie Moss in Baltimore, a Joe Bauman in Roswell, New Mexico. It was twilight for those long-ball gods, and only two of their spiritual descendants, Randy Bass and Moe Hill, would survive into the seventies and eighties. But neither of them ever matched what Bilko accomplished in the two best seasons of his career. Hardly anybody did. And I'll tell you something else that set him apart from the pack: When he went back to the big show, in 1958, he took a pay cut.

Things didn't get any better on the field. Bilko started the season in Cincinnati, then got a return ticket to L.A., which had stepped up in class with the Dodgers. In both uniforms, he looked lost, and he had the statistics to prove it. No wonder he was back in the bushes the next year. I got to see him play there because my family had moved to Salt Lake City and he passed through town with the Spokane Indians. But somehow his presence didn't mean as much anymore. I was getting older and my horizons were expanding, my requirements for my heroes getting stricter. Maybe I even thought of Bilko as a mirage. He wasn't, of course. He was the real thing. I would learn just how real after he died.

The news shook loose memories of how Bilko hung on to do honorable work for the L.A. Angels of the expanded American League, and how he hit twenty homers in the first of his two seasons with them. I seemed to recall also that he got to play in Wrigley Field West again. Yes, but only in 1961, an old teammate told me. I started to say that was too bad, because Wrigley was where I would always picture him, and then I was silenced by a bit of history that made everything right. On the last day of the '61 season, in the last game played in his old launching pad, Stout Steve Bilko said thanks for the memories the only way he could: He hit the last home run in the park's history. It was one of those rare moments when justice is poetic.

George Brett
Lipstick on a .407 Batting Average

Chicago Sun-Times
August 29, 1980

MILWAUKEE—They are not mere scoreboards anymore. In this era of gimmicks and gadgetry, they are message boards. A bit of grandiose nonsense perhaps, but without the one in County Stadium, George Brett never would have faced the sweet temptation he thought he had left backstage at a burlesque house.

Brett gets invited to such exotic places because of the way he swings a bat for the Kansas City Royals, and now he appeared to have punched his ticket again. On a sticky, mosquito-bitten night, he perched on first base with his fifth straight hit while the enemy crowd changed its jeers to cheers and the message board flickered enticingly. THAT MAKES .407 FOR BRETT, it said, but he didn't want to look. Looking wouldn't have been professional.

Likewise, Brett didn't think looking would be gentlemanly when he went to visit Miss Morganna Roberts lo those many months ago. Miss Roberts is a stripper with a sixty-inch chest and a fondness for kissing ballplayers. Because Brett kisses back, he has become her favorite, a status he didn't want to jeopardize by gawking at the undraped female forms on parade backstage.

"But, man," he says, "she talked and I looked."

So it was in Milwaukee, with the crowd on its feet for a full minute and the message board glowing brighter and brighter and Brett telling himself he would only put pressure on himself if he caved in to temptation. But, really, what could he do?

"I peeked," he said.

Up there in lights, waiting for him to savor it, was a batting average that belies the modern player's pained bleats about jet lag and the dread slider. Not since 1941 has a big-league hitter flown so high so late in the season. The star of the show back then, of course, was Ted Williams, who finished at .406 and became the man whose shadow Brett chases with a mixture of ardor and reluctance. "How do I know I'm gonna be the next .400 hitter?" Brett says. "I've got forty games left. I might go 0-for-160 and then you writers will be coming around to see if I'm gonna hit .300."

It would be easier to believe him if he hadn't been so entranced by the sight of that message board. But the fact that he fell under the board's spell, and admitted it, speaks volumes. This is no complex character we are dealing with here, no apprentice tycoon who just happens to wear a jockstrap for a living. Brett may have had a fancy-schmancy dentist close the gap between his two front teeth, but that is as uptown as he has gone.

The bright lights and big cities are for Reggie Jackson, with whom he is certain to run one-two in the most valuable player balloting. George Howard Brett, on the other hand, will gladly stay in Kansas City for the requisite million dollars a year, drinking beer at the Granfallon, hunting in the hills outside of town, and seldom looking backward.

"There's really no point in that," he says. "If I hadn't made it in baseball, I'd just be working for my brother John's construction company. Really, there probably isn't anything else I could do except hammer some nails for him."

And yet there are times when the laboring life doesn't seem so terrible to Brett. They'll come to him when he isn't at third base or surrounded by teammates or squirreled away in his home. In the clubhouse, trapped in front of his locker, he cannot escape the unpleasant residue of his own brilliance—reporters. "Why don't you guys just reword what the other guys write?" he says plaintively. But that is not the way the newspaper game is played, and Brett, a gamesman if there ever was one, understands, and consents, and cooperates. There is just one stipulation: "I want you to know this isn't any fun."

Brett is an expert on fun, the way all kids from Southern California seem to be. And, yes, even at twenty-seven, with six full seasons and one American League batting championship behind him, he still qualifies as a kid.

Maybe it is because he reminisces so vividly about body surfing, about scrounging around his parents' home for hamburger money, about getting tossed in jail the night before Thanksgiving 1974 after a bar fight with his biggest, baddest brother, Bob. Or maybe it is simply because when he can't find anyone to run with in Kansas City, he'll hop a plane to the coast as nonchalantly as he used to hitch a ride to the beach.

Only when Brett has a bat in his hands does he seem fully grown and dangerous. He swings left-handed with a vengeance born of the days when he was hitting .200 and warming up pitchers in the bullpen. "I thought that was where I was gonna stay," he says, but the possibility turned into a burr under his saddle. He sought out Charlie Lau, then the Royals' batting coach, and the rebuilding process began. Brett learned to spray line drives everywhere, think along with pitchers, and block out all distractions. Even when Detroit's Milt Wilcox knocked him down with two straight pitches earlier this season, Brett finished his business at the plate before attempting to pound knobs on Wilcox's head.

It was a perfect example of putting first things first, and an indirect admission that Brett is aware of what he is on the verge of. For the most part, he opts for humility, claiming that .360 would be a lofty enough average for his taste. But there are other times when he just can't contain himself, when the breaks he needs to make history come so fast he can't begin to count them. One night it's a single up the middle that the pitcher should have flagged down. The next night it's a home run with a broken bat.

"I'm not kidding—a broken bat," Brett says. "Tell me I'm not hot."

The message board wouldn't dare.

Brett finished the season at .390. He led the league, though, and he was still number one in Morganna's heart.

Willie Stargell
The Pirates' Patriarch

Chicago Sun-Times
October 18, 1979

BALTIMORE—The tears would come later. They would flow like the California white wine that Willie Stargell was drinking in great gulps now from a pale green bottle. All around him, the rest of the Pittsburgh Pirates were woofing and shouting, shucking and jiving, but Willie Stargell moved through their midst quietly, almost somberly. It was as if he wanted to get used to his role as one of baseball's newly crowned champions, wanted to find out what the boundaries of propriety are.

In the days and weeks and months ahead, unfortunately, his amazing grace will be forgotten and his sheer brute strength will be put on a pedestal. The adoring throngs will think only of what happened Wednesday night in the seventh game of the World Series, in the whirlpool of noise that was Memorial Stadium.

They will think only of Willie Stargell driving the ball into the right field bullpen for the home run that sent the Baltimore Orioles stumbling toward a 4–1 defeat and oblivion. For that, for the way he resuscitated the Pirates after they were one game from extinction, the public and the opinion makers will hail Willie Stargell for making it happen. It will be true, of course, but never forget that he is so much more than that. He is the reason the Pirates can call themselves The Family.

"We don't do it to be sassy or nasty or anything like that," he said. "We just think it typifies our ball club. We've worked hard, we've overcome and scratched and fought. I wish the rest of the world could share the feeling I have just from being part of it."

It was only fitting that Willie Stargell would flinch noticeably when someone clapped him on the shoulder and shouted that he had been named the most valuable player in the classic that turned into an endurance test. "I appreciate it, I'm flattered," said the man with the .400 batting average, "but couldn't they cut up whatever they're going to give me and let everybody on the ball club have a slice?"

He has style, and a little thing like success was not going to change him. He would not crow that the 1971 World Series had been the late Roberto Clemente's show and the 1979 Series was his. No, he would talk about how Clemente was never far from his mind. "Roberto showed us how to win, how to drive, how to grind it out," he said.

The way the Pirates' patriarch moved and spoke in this, the finest moment in his noble career had to touch everyone who came in contact with him, from President Carter to the clubhouse kid wondering when he was going to get a chance to start cleaning the champions' spiked shoes. Even when he broke away from the mob of reporters surrounding him, shouting, "I got to get me a bottle of wine," Willie Stargell still managed to do it with a touch of class. "I'll be back," he said. And he kept his word.

There was so much to talk about, so many memories to bronze for the trophy case of the mind, that Wllie Stargell quite frankly didn't know where to begin. The bottle of Imperial Royal that he wrapped his paw around became a security blanket.

"Willie, Willie," yelled a reporter wedged behind a TV camera. "Did you ever have a greater thrill than this?"

"Only once," Willie Stargell said. "When I signed a contract in 1959 and they gave me a $1,500 bonus and $175 a month." A long drink of wine. "Then and now . . . it's hard to find the words I feel."

He would try, though, for trying is part of his style. He would think back to the morning and how he couldn't wait to get to the ballpark, how he could almost feel that he was going to get four hits. And then, another long drink of wine later, he would recall how he didn't feel right when he walked to the plate in the sixth inning. Forget that he had already collected a single and the first of his two doubles. Forget that he was on his way to a Series record of seven extra-base hits. Willie Stargell was not comfortable.

He was worried about the Orioles' 1–0 lead and the curve ball that lefthander Scott McGregor had been using to hogtie the Pirates. Down at first base, Bill Robinson, who had just singled, was waiting to be driven in. He was someone else for Willie Stargell to worry about.

"Usually all I do when I go up there is be hackin'," Willie Stargell said, "but now I was trying to think a little. I'd been seeing that slow curve, so I moved up in the box really sneaky-like."

McGregor didn't notice, which was a fatal mistake. He threw the curve, and when it crossed the plate knee-high, Willie Stargell put the wood to it, up to a point. "I didn't hit it real good," he said. But it was good enough. It sailed and sailed, and when it finally landed in the Pittsburgh bullpen, the Pirates had the lead they would never surrender.

All they had to do afterward was protect it. Fittingly, Kent Tekulve marched out of the bullpen with one out in the eighth to participate in the proceedings. Willie Stargell was waiting for him on the mound. "I said, 'Tek, show the people why you're the best in the National League. And if you don't think you can do that, then you play first base and I'll pitch.'"

Perfect. In the gut-wrenching pressure, The Family's grand old man was lightening everybody else's load. It was his party, the one he had produced himself, and he was going to see it through to the end, laughing all the way.

The laughter would begin when the Orioles' Rick Dempsey hit the last fly ball of the night to Omar Moreno in center field. "I saw Tim Foli start jumping over at shortstop," Willie Stargell said, "and I couldn't help myself. I had to start jumping, too." He would not stop until the last bottle of champagne had been emptied, and the last hand had been shaken, and the last dance had been danced. Then, in the quiet, Willie Stargell would cry tears of joy.

Fernando Valenzuela
And a Rookie Shall Lead Them

Chicago Sun-Times
October 23, 1981

LOS ANGELES—In a year when baseball almost died by its own hand, Fernando Valenzuela restored sanity with the most ironic of pitches—a screwball. He threw it and threw it until he had done far more than win his first eight games for the Dodgers and capture the country's imagination. There was something intoxicating about this Mexican farm boy with the Babe Ruth belly and the birth certificate nobody believed, and when people searched for a way to describe his magic, they decided it was because Valenzuela is an original. Wonderful as that sentiment is, though, it does not quite serve the truth, for there have been plenty of ballplayers like him. The catch is, they all lived in books.

If you read Bernard Malamud's *The Natural* or any of John R. Tunis's deceptively sophisticated studies of life on the diamond, if you believe that reality and mythology don't necessarily have to follow separate paths, then you were prepared for Valenzuela and his magical left arm to be delivered to the doorstep of Dodger Stadium. You knew the only place he could call home was the sun-baked communal farm of Navajoa, where the roads are dirt, running water is a yet-to-be-experienced luxury, the first power line went up four years ago, and little children stare at cars the way their big-city counterparts would flying saucers.

Anything else would have leavened Valenzuela's saga and stolen the poetry from the derring-do the Dodgers expect of him now. They are two games from extinction in the World Series, two games from being swept to oblivion by the Yankees, and Friday night the rookie who never pitches his age must begin saving them. In the home park that has become a shrine for this city's vast Mexican population and a gold mine for a ticket scalper named Scooby-Doo, he faces the only challenge anyone in his position could have. For he is a story—baseball's biggest—and the rules of narrative structure cry for an ending like this.

What makes the moment even richer is that Valenzuela appears to treat the Series no more reverently than he would the second game of a midseason doubleheader against the Cubs. At twenty, he already possesses a veteran's nonchalance, and if his heart beats faster at the sight of the Yankees, nobody knows it. In truth, nobody knows anything about him except the bare essentials, and the information gap created by his Spanish vocabulary makes him all the more mysterious, all the more appealing.

It matters not that Valenzuela has a translator. A lot gets lost in translation. His words reach us sounding flat and lifeless—"I feel glad to have reached the major leagues"—but his dark eyes advertise mischief and suggest the good times that are both his creation and his reward. Let a chorus of twentieth-century foxes serenade him by chanting, "Fernando, we love you," and the smile on his moon face tells you that he knows enough English to get along very nicely. Let someone ask who is pitching when his own number has been called, the way a reporter did in Montreal four long days ago, and he will prove that his sense of the ridiculous is bilingual.

"Beckwith," he told his inquisitor from behind a sly smile.

The answer prompted a look of dismay. Joe Beckwith isn't on the Dodgers' roster anymore. "C'mon, Fernando," the reporter said. "Aren't you going to pitch?"

"No," Valenzuela said, his smile turning big and bold. "Sutcliffe."

Rick Sutcliffe isn't pitching for the Dodgers these days either, but that isn't the point. The point is that Fernando Valenzuela knows the hour is his. He can laugh and the world will laugh with him. Whether he cries is something else again. Outsiders will never know about it because he doesn't let them in and probably wouldn't know how if he wanted to. In Navajoa, you don't call someone up and make an appointment. There is only one phone in town and the use of it remains a blissful mystery to Valenzuela. Or so the story goes.

It is a lot easier to find the truth in how Valenzuela is on the verge of losing his innocence. Already there is an agent on the scene complaining that his client's $42,500 salary is a disgrace and predicting that the sky will be the limit come negotiating time. But until Valenzuela gets tangled up in the web of high finance, he has the purity to restore a doubting public's faith in baseball.

When he looks toward the heavens in the middle of his delivery and then mystifies the best of hitters with his smorgasbord of pitches, he erases memories of a strike that had nothing to do with home plate. He makes every other sport in this overloaded autumn—football, basketball, hockey, all of them—seem unnecessary for the simplest of reasons: When he is on the mound, he matters and the hitter matters, and you can forget about everybody else on the face of the earth.

To see Valenzuela at work is to luxuriate in the memories baseball really doesn't deserve this year. They begin with his 13-7 record and the screwball he used to reduce Montreal's fence-denting Gary Carter to ashes Monday, but that is just the beginning of the parade. What about the claims that Valenzuela is really thirty, a late bloomer with a shady past? And what happened to the bartenders who refused to serve him after the *Los Angeles Times* ran a photo of the birth certificate that proved he was born November 1, 1960 and therefore not quite drinking age? The incidents are savored with the same zest as the sale of Fernando Valenzuela medallions for $19.95 apiece, his being named one of *Playgirl* magazine's ten sexiest men, and Dodger catcher Mike Scioscia's observations that "Freddie thinks it's still spring training."

What a wonderful world Valenzuela lives in, everything still fresh and exciting, every hitter no more threatening that the village smithies he bowled over in Mexico. It has been this way since he lucked into pitching the Dodgers' season opener. Jerry Reuss and Burt Hooton, the leading candidates for the assignment, wound up in sickbay, so Valenzuela was asked to forget that he had thrown batting practice the day before. When he shut out Houston, the reaction was giddy surprise. It would take a while before he was recognized as a hero fit for the pens of Malamud and Tunis, before he made the point that saved baseball. Some people write fiction. Fernando Valenzuela lives it.

Jim Palmer
Good-bye Doesn't Come Easy

Chicago Sun-Times
May 21, 1984

BALTIMORE—By the time there was no more room for him in the only big league home he has known, it seemed that everyone had forgotten what Jim Palmer really was, Jim Palmer included. Perhaps this should have been shrugged off as understandable, for Palmer had stood around in his underwear and been paid instead of arrested because he was part of an advertising campaign. He became a sex symbol and a celebrity when he was no longer a great pitcher for the Orioles, and the transition was a troubled one. When his fastball was gone, it was replaced by a ball of confusion.

All the logic and insight that Palmer had displayed in the past was forgotten as paranoia overwhelmed him. He was playing in the right ballpark, spacious Memorial Stadium, and he was playing for the right team, a gang of sluggers that could erase his gopher-ball sins, but he convinced himself there was no hope. Before the current season was scarcely a month old, he had blamed a shelling in Minneapolis on a hard hotel pillow and waved the white flag of surrender in Chicago after claiming to have pulled a muscle in his neck while checking a runner at first base.

Hypochondria had always been part of his repertoire, but now Palmer was taking it to uncharted heights. The hardest he threw the ball all spring was eighty-one miles an hour, and he would have had the Orioles believe that it was because his cap raised a blister on his forehead if manager Joe Altobelli hadn't shot down that excuse a year ago.

The closest Palmer came to the truth about his tattered confidence may have been on a team bus ride that featured a conversation about pitching to Jim Rice with the bases loaded. "I'd walk him," Palmer announced.

"But what if you went 3-and-0 on the next guy?" a teammate asked.

"I'd grab my arm," Palmer said. "Milt Pappas taught me that."

Presumably his response was meant as a joke. Altobelli might well have interpreted it another way, though. The Jim Palmer he watched through his first year and one month as the world champions' leader wasn't the one who won 268 games for the Orioles, owned eight twenty-victory seasons, and stood with Tom Seaver as the standard of excellence for their generation's right-handers. The Jim Palmer inflicted on Altobelli was the one with a 9.17 earned run average and nineteen walks in 17.3 innings. He was a wise guy who seemed more intent on belittling the retired Earl Weaver than he did on finishing any game he started, and finally Altobelli decided that Palmer would never start another one for Baltimore.

Only once after that did Palmer take the mound. It was to mop up a sloppy 12–2 loss to Oakland, and when he was finished, he found Altobelli waiting to apologize. "You don't deserve that," the manager said. Even if he had never seen a trace of proof, even if his patience had been pushed to the limit, Altobelli knew what thirty-eight-year-old James Alvin Palmer had meant to his game, his team, and his town.

But Palmer didn't remember it until he was at the press conference last week where the Orioles granted him the unconditional release he had been campaigning for. He held on to his reserve for as long as he could, standing tall and handsome in a blue blazer and white shirt while general manager Hank Peters became a study in undisguised misery. "These are not happy days," Peters said, and his eyes proved it. At the side of the dais, you could see Palmer's eyes welling with tears, too.

"Maybe I'll come back in about ten minutes when they're a little clearer," he said once the stage was his. He has lived his life in the limelight, beating Sandy Koufax in the World Series at age nineteen, working for ABC-TV when the Orioles weren't making October theirs, and providing the beefcake for Jockey shorts, but now Jim Palmer longed for the shadows. After he managed to get out the message he came to deliver—"I still think I can pitch"—there was no hope. "I'm going to leave," he said, his head bowed. "Thank you very much." And he ran for the privacy of a waiting car with the same elegant stride he had always used to leave the mound.

At last Jim Palmer had realized that history would remember him as a baseball player above everything else. He realized that he loved that sense of identity, and the feel of his uniform, and the demand to put his stamp on a game every five days. But there was no guarantee he would ever have any of it again.

"I don't think it hit him like an ax until walking in here put him up against the harsh reality," his agent, Ron Shapiro, said. "I think what he did is something a human being has to do. The macho image of an athlete is that you're not supposed to have emotion, but Jim had to break loose. This was the end of something."

The underwear ads should survive, at least until Palmer stops looking a decade younger than he is, and surely there is a place for his quick wit on television. But never again will you see the pitching motion that flowed from an artist's sensitivity, the ball hidden by glove, foot, and guile. Never again will you see the Jim Palmer who used to get every call in every big game, who used to pitch his best against the best teams, who used to flap his arms like an angry stork while sawed-off Earl Weaver wagged a finger at him. O, the moments he gave Baltimore.

They all seemed to come back to the early arrivals at Memorial Stadium the night after Palmer was released. He wasn't scheduled to wear No. 22 again, but there he was pitching batting practice, carrying on with his former teammates, seeking something that was beyond him. He hadn't been a local hero at the end, and Baltimore, which boos no one except Reggie Jackson, had made an exception by booing him, too. There was none of that now, though. There were only cheers and applause, a rousing thank-you for the golden past, and Jim Palmer soaked it up one last time. If he had to say good-bye, this was the way to do it.

Oscar Charleston
A One-Way Ticket to Obscurity

Sports Illustrated
September 5, 2005

There were some hard miles on that bus, and harder ones on the man behind the wheel. His name was Oscar Charleston, which probably means nothing to you, as wrong as that is. He was managing the Philadelphia Stars then, trying to sustain the dignity of the Negro leagues in the late 1940s as black ballplayers left daily for the moneyed embrace of the white teams that had disdained them for so long. Part of his job was hard-nosing the kids who remained into playing the game right, and part of it was passing down the lore of the line drives he'd bashed, the catches he'd made, and the night he'd spent rattling the cell door in a Cuban jail. His players called him Charlie, and when it was his turn to drive the team's red, white, and blue bus, it was like having Ty Cobb at the wheel. Of course the players never said so, because sportswriters and white folks were always calling him the black Ty Cobb and Charlie hated it.

While Cobb counted the millions he'd made on Coca-Cola stock, Charlie bounced around on cramped, stinking buses until he, like their engines, burned out. The Stars would play in Chicago on Sunday afternoon, then hightail it back to Philly so they could use Shibe Park on Monday, when the big leaguers were off. So they drove through the long night, with Charlie peering at the rain and lightning, wondering which was louder, the thunder or the racket his players were making.

When he could take no more, he glanced back at Wilmer Harris and Stanley Glenn, a pitcher and a catcher, earnest young men who always stayed close to him, eager to absorb whatever lessons he dispensed. "Watch this," he said, yanking the lever that opened the bus door. Then he leaned as far as he could toward the cacophonous darkness, one hand barely on the wheel, and glowered the way only he could glower.

"Hey, you up there!" he shouted. "Quit making so damn much noise!"

The bus turned as quiet as a tomb. "I bet there wasn't one player hardly breathing," Glenn says. The Stars were a strait-laced bunch—"the Saints," some called them with a sneer—and they weren't inclined to test whatever higher power might be in charge. But Charlie was different from them, and everybody else for that matter. And when the thunder boomed louder still in response to his demand, he proclaimed his defiance with a laugh. If it didn't kill him, it couldn't stop him.

On my plaque they said I was versatile. They said I "hit well over .300 most years." Most years. Like saying Joe Louis was a pretty good fighter. —OSCAR CHARLESTON in *Cobb*, a play by Lee Blessing

The words are the product of a writer's imagination, but the inspiration for them was as real as the bile Charleston must have choked on every time his skin color was held against him, every time he was told he couldn't play where he belonged. Bigotry handed him a one-way ticket to obscurity. Even when he went into the Hall of Fame, in 1976, he was overlooked. How could it have been otherwise when there were big names, *white* names—Bob Lemon, Robin Roberts—going in with him? Besides, the general public had been conditioned to think only of Satchel Paige and Josh Gibson, if it thought of Negro leaguers at all.

Satch and Josh had swept into Cooperstown after its walls of intolerance crumbled five years earlier, and a myth sprang up around them that made it impossible to imagine anyone having paved the way for them. But Oscar Charleston did. He played so long ago that even Double Duty Radcliffe, who was 103 when he died in 2005, said, "He was before my time."

Double Duty exaggerated, of course, for the two of them were teammates on the 1932 Pittsburgh Crawfords. Yet by then Charleston had spent most of two decades as the reigning icon in black baseball. No matter what he did for the Grays—and he played first base, batted third, and managed what became the greatest Negro leagues team ever—there was always an old-timer around to say you should have seen him when he was *really* Oscar Charleston.

Starting in 1915 he turned centerfield into an art gallery on behalf of the Indianapolis ABCs, New York Lincoln Stars, Hilldale Daisies, and three kinds of Giants: Chicago American, St. Louis, and Harrisburg. His vagabond life was inspired by the disposable nature of the era's contracts and the wisdom of another black baseball pioneer, Pop Lloyd, who said, famously: "Wherever the money was, I was." At every stop, including Cuba in the winter, Charleston hung great catches as if they were paintings. He played shallow the way Tris Speaker did and Willie Mays would, but when he went back for a ball, legend says he performed acrobatics that have eluded everyone else in the position's history, leaping, spinning, making catches behind his back. Yet his showmanship was founded on fundamentals that compensated for what was, at best, an ordinary throwing arm. Never would artistry interfere with winning.

And never, until Charleston moved on to the Homestead Grays in 1930 and declared himself too old and slow for the position, would a team of his put anyone else in center. Fellow centerfielder Cool Papa Bell, mesmerized by the sight of Charleston playing so close that he could almost shake hands with the second baseman, imitated the icon who became his manager on the Craw-fords. And Gentleman Dave Malarcher, who patrolled the outfield with Charleston in Indianapolis, once said, "People asked me, 'Why are you playing so close to the right field foul line?' What they didn't know was that Oscar played all three fields. I just made sure of the balls down the line, and all the foul ones too."

But when Charleston broke in with Indianapolis, he thought he was a pitcher. Maybe it was symptomatic of what Stanley Glen says, affectionately: "Oscar was left-handed, and he acted like a left-hander. You know, a little crazy." Charleston was an Indianapolis kid, the seventh of eleven children born to an African American woman and a Sioux father who was a construction worker and, the story goes, a jockey. Oscar had enlisted in the Army at the end of the eighth grade, at age fifteen, and now, after four years and an infantry tour in the Philippines, he was playing for the team that once employed him as a batboy.

Maybe his days as a pitcher were done as soon as the ABCs saw him track a fly ball, just lower his head and not look up again until his internal radar had guided him to the spot where it came down. Or maybe the end came when the ABCs saw him booming baseballs to faraway places. It was a time when every team, black or white, was hunting for its own Babe Ruth, and here was another reformed southpaw pitcher who had the bat and the build: a hair under six feet tall, 190 pounds and getting bigger, with spindly legs and a chest-o'-drawers torso.

If, as historian James A. Riley suggests, Charleston never matched the Babe's power, he was easily the black equivalent of Rogers Hornsby, who batted over .400 three times in one four-year stretch. Of course, he was faster than Hornsby and almost anyone else—the Army clocked him at 23 seconds in the 220-yard dash—and he was capable of dragging a bunt, stealing a base, and cutting the glove off your hand with his spikes if a throw happened to beat him. However you choose to look at Charleston, slugger or slasher, he raised enough hell with his bat to launch a thousand stories.

He hit the triple that gave the ABCs black baseball's unofficial championship in 1916. He won, or tied for, five home run titles. In his best year, 1921, *The Baseball Encyclopedia* says he batted .434 with fourteen doubles, eleven triples, fifteen homers, and thirty-four stolen bases in sixty league games. That fall he had five homers in five games against a team of major league (i.e., white) barnstormers. Then he roared off to Cuba, where he batted .471. Even when he was calling himself an antique, he rang up a .372 average for the Crawfords in 1933, as if to remind the future Hall of Famers he was managing—Josh and Satch, Cool Papa and Judy Johnson—that he was made of the same stuff they were.

Teammates and opponents stampeded to proclaim his greatness. One of the few still standing, Buck O'Neil, the eternal flame of the Negro leagues, testifies that, as Double Duty Radcliffe put it, "a better player never drew breath." Of the departed, Newt Allen, the Kansas City Monarchs' second baseman, swore that Charleston hit the ball so hard, "he'd knock the glove off you." Dizzy Dean, who faced him while barnstorming in the 1930s, described pitching to Charleston as a throw-it-and-duck proposition. Ted Page, a splendid Crawfords outfielder, told historian John B. Holway that Charleston introduced himself to the great Walter Johnson before an exhibition game by saying, "Mr. Johnson, I've done heard about your fast ball, and I'm gonna hit it out of here." In Page's account, which may qualify as legend become fact, a home run was indeed what Charleston hit. To win the game, naturally.

But all that is mere preamble to the proclamation that John McGraw issued from the game's intellectual mountaintop: "If Oscar Charleston isn't the greatest baseball player in the world, then I'm no judge of baseball talent."

Decades later Bill James could hear the echo of McGraw's endorsement as he set to work on his engaging, argumentative *Historical Baseball Abstract*. Swept up in the list-making orgy that defines contemporary culture, James wanted to rate the top hundred players ever. If he generated controversy by including a player who was a mystery to "a lot of very knowledgeable baseball fans," he says, so much the better.

Numbers had to be crunched—James without statistics would be like Hendrix without his guitar—and other people's lists had to be studied. But when it came to Negro leaguers, everything changed, because there weren't always game stories and box scores to substantiate the players' greatness. "When we went to New York, Chicago, Washington DC, they'd write up our games in the newspapers," says ninety-three-year-old Andrew Porter, a victim of Charleston's terrible swift bat when he pitched for the Baltimore Elite Giants. "But during the week we'd be out playing in small places, and you wouldn't know nothing about it."

So the list became for James a matter of the heart and the gut. "You wind up making a lot of assumptions," he says. But at every turn, he found more praise for Charleston from men who had seen him play, men who knew his greatness to be the cold, hard truth. "There was a scout for the Cardinals, I think his name was Bohlen—he'd scouted for them for many years—and at the end of his career he said the three greatest players he'd ever seen were Cobb, Ruth, and Charleston," James says. "He wasn't hyping Charleston, he was just looking back, and he seemed so reasonable, so straightforward, that I said, 'I'm willing to believe.'"

Thus did James anoint Charleston the fourth greatest player ever. Only the Babe, Honus Wagner, and Willie Mays are ahead of him, in that order. And—how Charlie would have loved this—Cobb is one place behind him. Then you have Mickey Mantle, Ted Williams, Walter Johnson, Josh Gibson, and Stan Musial. James expected at least one roaring good argument about Charleston's presence in such august company. Instead, all he got was this: "stunned silence."

Oscar Charleston deserves better.

Even when he was horsing around, you could sense the brute in him, the anger lurking just beneath the surface. It was there when he wrestled Gibson before games, supposedly for fun, two powerful men sweating and grunting and tossing each other around on the ball fields that both served and betrayed them.

Charleston was past his physical prime by this point, and he was giving away fifteen years to Josh, but damned if he'd let it show. "Must have been like two water buffaloes hooking up," says Hall of Famer Monte Irvin, who heard all about it when he was a young Newark Eagle. A decade or more later, when Gibson was dead and Charlie was still full of the devil, he would playfully snatch up Stanley Glenn—"and I was six foot two and weighed 225 pounds," Glenn says. The louder his young catcher squawked, the more Charlie laughed. It wasn't always a pleasant sound. "You never knew when he was angry," says Mahlon Duckett, the Philadelphia Stars' second baseman throughout the forties. "They tell me in the old days, he could be laughing and knock you out."

Maybe that's why the Crawfords' Ted Page paid attention to Charleston's eyes; he knew they wouldn't deceive him. "Vicious eyes, steel-gray, like a cat," Page said in Holway's book *Blackball Stars*. To look into them was to see a man worth steering clear of in a fight, "a cold-blooded son of a gun."

Charleston used his fists on everybody who crossed him regardless of pigmentation, on the field or off, as if breaking a nose or knocking out teeth gave him not just satisfaction but also sustenance. The smart ones backed down, the way professional wrestler Jim Londos, the Stone Cold Steve Austin of his day, did when

Charleston threatened to throw him off a train for making too much noise. But at least one Ku Klux Klansman failed to get the message about discretion being the better part of valor, and, according to Cool Papa Bell, Charleston yanked the hood off his head and made him run like a scalded dog.

Laughing all the way, Charleston teed off on opponents, teammates, umpires, even the owner of the Hilldale Daisies. In all the accounts of Charleston's battles, the closest thing to a recorded loss is when Oliver Marcelle, the Atlantic City Bacharach Giants' hyper-violent third baseman, supposedly clubbed him over the head with a bat. That is one story, however, that Buck O'Neil is quick to shoot down in his autobiography, *I Was Right on Time*. "Oscar," he says, "had a stoplight nailed to his chest."

Still, Charleston was the fastest gun in the West, and challengers came from every direction, even the grandstand. One Saturday afternoon in Havana in 1924, Charleston was playing for the powerhouse Santa Clara team when he stole third base and carved up a Cuban infielder with one of his spikes-high slides. As the poor devil lay bleeding in the dirt like a Hemingway bullfighter, a uniformed Cuban soldier charged out of the stands and jumped Charleston from behind. Charleston shook off the cheap shot, then used the soldier for a punching bag until the cops showed up. They dragged Charleston off to the *calabozo* for the cell-door-rattling night he told his young Philadelphia Stars about a quarter century later.

"Jim Murray had a line about Frank Robinson and how he played the game the way the great ones played it, out of hate," Bill James says. "I don't know that Oscar was filled with hate, but there was a lot of anger in him."

Charleston might have been scarred by the racism in his boyhood Indianapolis. "At that time," says Riley, the historian, "there was more Klan activity in Indiana than there was in the South." Something ugly might have happened in the Army too. But no anger-management specialist is needed to track down the most likely source of what drove him: Here was a proud man confronted daily by the fact that the world beyond the Negro leagues would never know just how great he was. He would never face Ty Cobb on the diamond, never find out once and for all if Cobb shouldn't have been called the white Oscar Charleston.

The only reported instance of Cobb's playing against blacks comes from the autumn of 1910, when he toured Cuba with the Detroit Tigers. He batted .370—he also got thrown out stealing by a Negro leagues catcher named Bruce Petway—and then he swore off interracial ball. So it took playwright Lee Blessing to conjure up a meeting between that snapping-turtle racist and Charleston, in *Cobb*. "Were you any good?" Cobb asks, as if word never reached him. "Better'n you," Charleston replies.

It's the only possible answer, for Charleston was locked in eternal competition with a legend who was his mirror image in everything except race and fame: played center field, batted left-handed, took no prisoners on the bases, even managed, and did it all furiously. Forever overlooked, Charleston had the right to be angry. But the Negro leaguers still with us hesitate to say so. And those who do say so are quickly negated by testimony that follows O'Neil's benevolent template: "Charlie? No, Charlie wasn't angry."

Yet one afternoon in 2003, as O'Neil walked among the life-sized statues in Kansas City's soulful Negro Leagues Baseball Museum, the awe he felt all those years ago returned to lower his guard. Double Duty Radcliffe, traveling by wheelchair, had joined him, and their eyes settled on Charleston's defiant bronze presence.

"Look at that neck," O'Neil said, and smiled appreciatively at what its thickness portended. "He'd knock you out the way." And Duty said, "I seen him knock two fellas out in Indianapolis. Knocked 'em cold."

They made the violence seem matter-of-fact, gave it the same ritual quality as a ballplayer's knocking dirt from his spikes with a bat. But anger as ritual becomes something deeper, more profound. Better, perhaps, to call what drove Charleston an abiding rage.

★ ★ ★

The scrapbook's yellowed pages are crumbling around the edges. The museum provides white cotton gloves for handling the book on those rare occasions that it comes out from under lock and key, but the gloves do only so much. The rest is left to fate, like the legacy of the man who kept the book.

Charleston gathered his clippings with little regard for their dates or the names of the newspapers they appeared in. His overriding interest, it seems, lay in stories that proclaimed him CHARLESTON THE GREAT in the States and *EL FAMOSO PLAYER CHARLESTON* in Cuba. But here and there are glimpses of something deeper than vanity. His obsession with Cobb surfaces repeatedly; one story wonders how much Charleston is worth if the Georgia Peach makes thirty thousand dollars a year. In an engagingly literate if disingenuous letter to the *Pittsburgh Courier's* sports editor, Charleston writes about "[elevating] Negro Athletics to the place we would have them be" while claiming that umpires jobbed his Harrisburg team. And he takes special care to chronicle the way his brawl in Havana inspired cartoons, essays apologizing for the Cuban soldier's "wicked attack," and a public collection to buy him a gold watch (price: $82.50).

In the midst of all that, one clipping seems almost as if it came from somebody else: "Miss Jane B. Howard of Harrisburg, Pa., was quietly married to Oscar Charleston Thursday noon at the residence of Mr. and Mrs. Percy Richards, 3305 Lawton Ave."

The story goes on to say that Charleston would be playing for St. Louis come spring, so the year must have been 1921. His wife was an elementary school teacher and the daughter of Harrisburg's most prominent African Methodist minister, Martin Luther Blalock. She was well-read, knew much about culture and travel, and in time—she lived until a few weeks past her hundredth birthday in 1993—she became the Blalock family's cornerstone. All of which makes her marriage to a divorced, brawling ballplayer three years her junior that much more puzzling. But Janie never did any explaining. "She was from an age," says her niece Elizabeth Overton, "when you didn't tell your business."

It was no secret, however, that she had known tragedy before she met Charleston. Her first husband had died on their honeymoon, the victim of a flu that swept Cuba. "Our Janie was a widow," Overton says. "Maybe that's why she considered Charleston more than she would have."

They made a striking couple, especially in photos in which they are dressed for winter, Oscar in a topcoat and fedora, Janie with a cloche pulled snug over her ears. She was pretty and petite, barely five feet tall but hardly shy. "She'd set anybody straight," Overton says. One of the few secrets Janie shared was that she took Oscar to Sunday school, much to the amusement of his teammates. Not that they saw much of her. "She didn't mix well," Double Duty Radcliffe said. But she was with Charleston in Harrisburg for four seasons, and she accompanied him to Philadelphia, Pittsburgh, Cuba, and even a managing job in Toledo, until her father died in 1942 and she went home to care for her mother, home for good.

Janie never had children, and once she returned to Harrisburg, though she and Oscar didn't divorce, there was no husband by her side. How much she saw of him thereafter is lost to time, but when he died of a heart attack in Philadelphia on October 5, 1954, nine days shy of fifty-eight, there was one last sign that he never stopped loving her: He willed her all his earthly possessions. And she turned right around and gave them to his sister, who had cared for him at the end.

It was an act of integrity, just as Oscar's had been. To think anything else would be as wrong as to assume the worst because Janie never set out pictures of him. "You want pictures to last," her niece says, "you keep them in the dark."

☆ ☆ ☆

Restless, always restless. At the plate he kept wagging that big bat until he found a pitch to demolish. Everywhere else he just kept moving. He worked security at Philadelphia's Quartermaster Depot during World War II and ran the depot's mixed-race ball club. He helped Branch Rickey seek out black talent for the Brooklyn Dodgers, and legend says it was Charleston who steered Roy Campanella their way. He tossed baggage for the Pennsylvania Railroad, and he umpired too. Unable or maybe plain unwilling to slow down, he signed up for a second season of managing the Indianapolis Clowns weeks before he died. When the guys who had played for him on the Philadelphia Stars went to his viewing in South Philly's biggest hall, what they saw, Stanley Glenn says, was pure Charlie: "He looked like he was going to jump out of there and say hello to you."

To this day, the last of the Stars can hear him barking at their best left-hander for throwing a "balloony pitch" and bitching at hitters who didn't take every extra base in sight. They remember, too, a morning departure for a road trip when Charlie ordered whoever was driving the bus to pull out just as the left-hander ambled around the corner.

"But you said we were leaving at eight," the players said. "It's only five till."

"Next time he'll be early," Charlie said.

There was only one way in Charlie's world: his way. Time and again he let the Stars know it, but never so memorably as the night he picked up a bat to pinch-hit in an exhibition game. He was past fifty and the lights in the park barely deserved the name, but he still bludgeoned a shot to right-center field. "It would have been [an inside-the-park] home run for anybody else," Mahlon Duckett says. "Charlie fell out at third base." And there the Stars assumed he would stay until somebody got a hit. But when the next batter flied to center, Charlie tagged up and broke for home, just the way he had in the old days. "I said, 'What's he doing?'" Duckett recalls.

He was doing what he always did when a throw beat him by ten feet. He was lowering his head and plowing into the catcher, and he wasn't worrying that the catcher still had his mask on. Hell, Charlie probably relished it, even when his head hit the mask. The catcher dropped as if he'd been shot, and the ball skittered away, and the man who had risked his bull neck for a single run in a game that meant nothing left a message for all who would follow unaware: Tell them Oscar Charleston was here.

3

Hoops and Horses and Everything in Between

Pete Maravich
The Pistol's Parting Shot

Chicago Sun-Times
September 24, 1980

Boston Garden creaks with age and smells of mankind's excesses, yet Pete Maravich always thought of it as his salvation. To call it home was to be a Celtic and to be a Celtic was to be a winner, and there was no seeing beyond such idealism until Maravich was out on the old dump's hallowed parquet floor at last. Only then did he realize that once you are haunted, you are haunted for keeps.

Even when he was under the thirteen NBA championship banners that hang from the Garden's rafters, Maravich couldn't free himself from the specter of his father. Press Maravich, a vagabond college coach, had molded his son to superstar specifications and undone himself in the process. "His life ages a man before his time," the *wunderkind* called Pistol Pete once said. But it was harder by far on the woman who bore Press Maravich his famous son.

She couldn't stand the days and nights alone and the crank calls meant to harass the coach and prodigy who spent too few hours under the same roof with her. She paid the cost of other peoples' fame for as long as she could, and then she ran out of psychological currency. One suicide later, Pete Maravich was without a mother.

The whole sad story was etched on his face, a visage so devoid of joy that a stranger seeing it for the first time would never believe how much happiness Maravich created with his phantas-magoric shooting and psychedelic passing. He belonged to the same breed of irrepressible showmen as Earl Monroe and Julius Erving, yet his small, pinched mouth wasn't made for smiling. Greatness, quite simply, was not a commodity to be enjoyed when you looked at it through Maravich's deceptively innocent eyes. The circles beneath them and the worry lines above them told you that, and if you still didn't believe it, he would tell you in his own words.

"I'm in a cold business," he said midway through the journey that took him to four NBA cities but never to a jewelry store for the championship ring he coveted. "I don't like the conniving, the flesh-peddling, all the dirty things."

So it was no surprise to hear that Maravich called it a career at thirty-one the other day. He was in Boston, the would-be promised land he found his way to last season. The Celtics were still saying they needed his savvy and his sniper's eye in their backcourt, but he would have none of it. He was leaving and not coming back, and the reason should have been obvious: His innocence had finally succumbed to his disillusionment.

The battle had raged inside Maravich for each of his ten years as a professional, leaving him weary and suspicious of everyone, maybe even himself. He disliked dressing rooms for considering serious questions, and on those occasions when he found a quieter setting for an interview, he would tell the reporter, "It was better this way, wasn't it?" It was better, but for Maravich, it wasn't the best.

The best was when he had a basketball in his hands and nothing on his mind except drawing mobs of kids into steaming high school gyms with the wizardry no one else has equaled. "I can dribble six balls at one time, juggle three, and spin two on my finger," he used to say. His lessons in showmanship began when he was four years old, and from then on, basketball would be as much showbiz to him as it was sweat. But not everybody appreciated it.

"If you're lucky," Maravich once said, "50 percent of the people will love your act."

And the others?

"I guess they hate you."

The truth hit Pistol Pete at Louisiana State. He was pulling up his floppy gray socks, dancing to the music of John Fred and the Playboy Band, and short-circuiting scoreboards by averaging 44.2 points a game for his college career. The bad feelings had something to do with the behind-the-back passes he heaved into the third row and something to do with his being his father's robot.

And the bad feelings only got worse in the NBA. In Atlanta a sweet team turned sour because its underpaid black star begrudged Maravich his fat paycheck. "Nobody wanted anything to do with the rich little white boy," he said afterward. The longer he stayed in the league, bouncing from Atlanta to New Orleans to Utah, the stronger the suspicions became that the rich little white boy was a loser. "I have this reputation, this stigma," he would say, thinking all the while that the Celtics were the cure.

Maybe they would have been ten years ago, or even five. But by the time Maravich showed up in Boston last season, his brilliance was a memory. A surgically repaired right knee had cost him precious steps and a stretch in Utah's doghouse had coated his jump shot with rust. In a career fraught with frustration, perhaps that was the biggest frustration of all: He was in the company of winners and he couldn't contribute the way he wanted to.

It was a cruel indignity, yet one that an abundance of high-salaried athletes are willing to endure. Maravich was better than that. "I've shot too many baskets," he told the Celtics the other day, and then he left. His exit was quiet and tasteful, marred only by the familiar voice of his star-making father. Press Maravich used the occasion to say his son should still be what he was raised to be—a general manager, a big shot, someone special. God's mercy on Pistol Pete.

There was no happy ending for Maravich. His heart gave out in 1988 while he was playing in a pick-up game in a church gymnasium. He was forty. Bob Dylan, musing about him years later, provided the perfect epitaph: "He could have played blind."

Julius Erving
Sky King

Chicago Sun-Times
April 18, 1983

BOSTON—What is there to say about dignity and the dunk shot? That they belong to different levels of the game called life? That they are as poorly matched as a hand-carved mahogany walking stick and the flapping soles on a pair of worn-out Converse All-Stars? Every question seems to build a case for just how improbable this coupling is, and then you see Julius Erving play and all bets are off. When the Philadelphia 76ers' renowned Doctor J goes sky-walking, he might as well be wearing a top hat and tails.

High in the NBA stratosphere, Erving examines his options with style and serenity, flicking defenders away as if they were lint on a suit and punctuating his trips to the basket with dunks that prove the deception of appearances. His knees may ache with tendonitis and his hang time may not be what it once was, but Erving's regal bearing never betrays him. Every time he returns to earth, he is ready to straighten his tie and meet the rest of his obligations, whether they are the product of crisis or celebrity.

Dig up 76er general manager Pat Williams' tribute to him as "the Babe Ruth of basketball," for example, and Erving won't hide behind false modesty. He is what he is—the biggest man in a sport in which his six feet, six inches are hardly worthy of notice until he is airborne. "All I try to do," he says, "is make sure I'm never guilty of anything that makes me look small."

It is a goal you might not think of unless you saw him Sunday when his dignity suddenly overshadowed his final dunk shot. The occasion was the 76ers' regular-season finale with Boston, a silly little 114–101 defeat that found the league's biggest winners minus Moses Malone, who was back in Philly nursing his aching body. The last five men on the roster played the fourth quarter, but coach Billy Cunningham refused to go along with the joke.

Everything was all right until the Celtics' Tiny Archibald bounced the ball off the head of an overzealous reserve guard named Franklin Edwards and woke up Cunningham. Suddenly, he realized that Boston had outscored his troops 11–4 in four minutes. To show his displeasure, he started screaming about expletive-deleted fouls, picked up a technical, and would have had a second if Erving hadn't restrained him and, wearing a white towel around his neck like an ascot, strolled onto Boston Garden's parquet floor.

"Tell me, Bob," the captain of the Sixers said to the referee in the middle of the contretemps. "What seems to be the problem?"

Just like that, there wasn't one.

A statesman in short pants, a diplomat in a world of thoughtlessness, Julius Erving strives to say the right thing. If he didn't, he could have put a new crack in the Liberty Bell this season when the 76ers brought Malone to Philadelphia for two million dollars a year, or approximately what it costs to keep Erving in jersey No. 6. Maybe Harold Katz, the team owner who keeps his payroll fat with money from the diet business, consoled the Doctor with an infusion of extra cash. Surely the board-pounding Malone eased the transition by saying, "This is still Doc's team—I'm just here to help." Above all, however, Erving refused to sully his dignity, or anyone else's, by bellyaching.

He considered his thirty-third birthday and the load Malone would share with him, and from that came the kind of self-analysis that was on display Sunday.

"I don't think my role is to dominate anymore," he said. "I don't have to take the ball and beat somebody all the time. I just have to be part of the heart and soul of the team. No, that doesn't bother me. I'm only being realistic. I'm not as strong as I used to be, and my first step isn't as quick as it used to be, either."

He paused, making sure the message had registered on his dressing-room audience. Then he smiled.

"Of course, I'm certainly not an average player."

Dignity again. Dignity and pride and everything else that had driven Erving to burn the Celtics for twenty points, eight rebounds, and four blocked shots in twenty-three minutes. When he could have been marking time, he was snatching missed shots one-handed or whirling between Larry Bird and Robert Parish for lay-ups or sneaking up to stuff Parish's jumper from behind. It was one of those performances that left you wondering how many otherwise woebegone games Julius Erving has saved artistically, if not on the scoreboard. But it was also one of those golden solos that left you dreading the possibility he will never win a championship ring.

The record book dismisses such fears as irrational. Bonded by Erving and Malone, Maurice Cheeks and Andrew Toney, the 76ers made a 65–17 wreckage of the regular season and started everybody dreaming despite the scars of past playoffs. Even Erving can be heard saying, "I think we're the team to beat. I don't think anybody in the league can beat us four times in a seven-game series." History, alas, refuses to be rewritten.

You remember how the Lakers throttled Philadelphia without Kareem Abdul-Jabbar last year, how the Sixers collapsed against Portland in 1977, how they have always picked the worst moments to wilt like roses under a desert sun. And Erving does, too. "The only thing that matters now is what's ahead of us," he says. It is nothing he hasn't said before and won't say again. The public expects such matter-of-factness from its heroes. What he doesn't talk about, however, is the fluttering stomach he must conquer, the uneasiness his own son once warned him about as he put basketball aside and prepared to speak to an arena full of admirers.

"Daddy, don't get a butterfly," Julius Erving Jr. said.

"If you don't get a butterfly," Julius Erving told him, "you're not doing it right."

The Doctor got his championship ring that season as the 76ers ripped through the playoffs, winning twelve of thirteen games. It was only fitting that he put the ribbon on the package with a three-point play that sealed their sweep of the Lakers in the finals.

Larry Bird
The Ultimate Celtic

Chicago Sun-Times
April 26, 1982

BOSTON—This is when the ghosts begin to stir. They have been up in Boston Garden's rafters all winter, dozing among the heating ducts, girders, and catwalks, and now a spring breeze reminds them of their place in history. It's the next best thing to smelling the smoke from Red Auerbach's cigar, and if they look up, they'll see the Celtics' championship banners flapping. Ghosts they may be, but when the NBA finally gets around to the playoffs, they know where they belong.

So down they swoop: Cousy, who can still dribble behind his back, and Havlicek, who stole the ball, stole the ball, stole the ball to beat Philly in '65, and Russell, who still has the proud bearing of an eagle but rarely pauses to sign an autograph. They were champions in April and they were champions in May, and you can bet they'll be grousing about a season when the Celtics may not wrap things up until June 10. You might even think that these ghosts are no different than any other old-timers if those of us who believe in them couldn't see what happens when they alight on the Garden's parquet floor.

Back where they earned the right to live in peoples' imaginations, they become strangely reverent about the one representative of the present they believe could have cut it in the past. His name is Larry Bird, and his only apparent shortcoming is that he can't see the Celtics' ghosts. Can't see them and doesn't believe in them.

"I didn't know nothing about pro basketball before I came here, so why should I?" he says. "Just because I play for the Celtics don't mean I play any harder or less hard. If I was playing for anybody else, I'd still be trying my best. A team really shouldn't matter, should it? Shouldn't it really be what's inside of you?"

The sentiment is precisely why Larry Bird, at twenty-five, in just his third season in Boston, has become the ultimate Celtic. He has a heart that beats for what he does, a sense of purity that has him diving into the press table for loose balls whether the title is on the line or it's just the last waltz of the regular season. The defending champions have always been rightfully famous for their pedal-to-the-metal style, and Bird picked up on it as soon as he arrived at the hellhole the Celtics call their training camp.

"You fight for survival up there," says K. C. Jones, who would be a backcourt ghost if he weren't a very visible assistant coach. "There are mosquitoes everywhere and you shower outdoors and the rookies sleep in bunks and the courts are asphalt. Some guys walk in there and they say, 'I thought this was the big leagues,' but when Larry was a rookie, he went out there and whipped that place. First loose ball there was, he got it—the hell with the asphalt. That surprised me. Since then, nothing he's done has surprised me."

Bird has scored as many as forty-five points in a game, grabbed as many as twenty-one rebounds, dished out as many as twelve assists. "Watch him rebounding," Jones says. "He works his butt off on the offensive board and then he hustles down and takes care of business on the defensive board. It can be the forty-sixth minute of a game and he's still out there grinding." He triggers the Celtics' fast break and clogs up the opposition's passing lanes when the break goes the other way, no small feat for someone whose greatest liability is a lack of foot speed. But when it comes to basketball, his is a higher form of intelligence. He knows the angles, he knows the percentages, he knows things that only his greatest rival, Magic Johnson, of all the other players in the NBA, may know.

Bill Fitch, the Celtics' reigning whipcracker, marvels at how Bird remembers everything in a game, from the time on the clock when he cranked up a second-quarter jump shot to the color of a banner flapping in the upper deck. When he hears Jones call Bird "a basketball computer," Fitch can only nod and let his assistant resume testifying. Jones seizes the moment to list the forty-karat performers he played against in his time—Oscar Robertson and Jerry West, Elgin Baylor and Wilt Chamberlain, forces of nature, every one of them. And then he hits you with his Sunday punch: "None of them could fill as many categories as Bird. Bird's the best."

Tell it to the man himself, though, and he looks at you like you're a ghost, for he has no more faith in words than he does in the supernatural. "I don't think nothing about that," he says, "and I don't say nothing about that."

All he does is play the way he has since basketball was a break from working on a garbage truck in French Lick, Indiana. Even when he was a kid with no apparent future—a dropout from Indiana University who had yet to realize that salvation awaited him at Indiana State—he knew nothing but high gear on the court. "Why should I change now, when people are paying me good money?" Bird says. It is another of those questions that tip his hand, that make you realize that behind the stock answers lies something more than a six-foot-nine hayseed.

Bird has the selfless wisdom to have told Fitch that reserve center Rick Robey should shoot a technical foul in the regular-season finale to pump up his sagging confidence. And Bird has the mother wit to have zapped the very same Robey after seeing him with his old college coach: "First time I ever saw you shake a hand from Kentucky without no money in it." And when the Celtics' ghosts hear about that while they are watching him bank in an off-balance runner, they know he is someone who will be joining them in the rafters someday.

The signs are everywhere, especially in the eyes of the teams that think Larry Bird doesn't deserve to be so special. They tell themselves that he doesn't jump any better than he runs, that he'll never have his No. 33 retired, that he won't even bring another championship to Boston. And they almost talk themselves into it. They almost drag him back to the company of mortals. But just when they think they've got him, he vanishes once more—a ghost before his time, whether he believes in ghosts or not.

Big House Gaines
No Way to Treat a Legend

Chicago Sun-Times
December 7, 1979

The travel money was still a long-distance promise, and Big House Gaines was trying to pretend that it didn't matter. There were little jokes about how even thirty-four years of coaching college basketball couldn't prevent a fellow from walking into an occasional surprise. And there were gentle warnings not to be too quick to write off the promoter of the tournament up in Chicago as a thoroughgoing fraud. But the longer he waited, the more Big House Gaines worried that his athletes weren't going to fly halfway across the country unless they sprouted wings.

Patience, he kept telling himself. This was one trip that could do him some good, could lift him from the backwater of North Carolina and drop him in the middle of a prime spawning ground for leapers and shooters. True, the tournament would be played in a nondescript high school gym on the South Side and the Chicago papers would likely ignore it the way they did the last time he was in town, four or five years ago. But he couldn't think of that, or of his 640 victories, or of the fact that he is the winningest coach in the college game.

"Do you think your life would be different if . . . if . . ."

The man on the phone from Chicago was stuck for the right words.

"If I was a Caucasian, you mean?" Big House Gaines said.

★ ★ ★

He is already a legend at Winston-Salem State University. The proof lies in the C. E. Gaines Athletic Complex. "They've named it, but they haven't dedicated it," he says. "I guess they're waiting for me to go to the great beyond." Or for the school's 2,200 scholars to realize that C. E. Gaines and Big House Gaines are one in the same.

"Some of 'em even call me Mr. House," he says. "They don't know who the hell I am."

The leg he pulls is his listener's.

Of course the kids know him. How could they miss him? At fifty-six, he stands six foot five and weighs 285 pounds, not far from the load he was carrying when he climbed into his Ford coupe and left Paducah, Kentucky, in 1942 with fifty dollars in his pocket. When the student manager of Morgan State University's football team saw him roll into Baltimore, he said, "The only thing I ever saw bigger is a house." And a nickname was born.

It lasted through his tour of duty as a two-way tackle and a rough-hewn basketball center. And it traveled well when he set out for Winston-Salem, where he thought he would be coaching football and wound up coaching basketball, too. He proved he could win at both, taking a football team that was 0-8 the year before he arrived and making it a champion three years into his five-year regime. It was basketball, however, that best suited his chess master's intellect. He created an offense so deceptively intricate that losers never realized what was happening until it was too late. And yet nobody in the outside world seemed to notice. Or was it just that nobody was paying attention to black schools?

"Let me tell you a story," says Jerry Krause, the erstwhile NBA talent hunter. "It's the NCAA finals in '75 or '76 and the passing game has suddenly become the rage. So two thousand coaches show up for this clinic and Bobby Knight gives a rousing speech on the passing game. Then Jerry Hale, the guy from Oral Roberts, gets up and, sure enough, he talks about the passing game, too. Well, House is the third coach to talk, and the first thing he wants everybody to know is how wonderful it is that these great young coaches are trying to sell such a great offense. You know, the offense that black schools have been using for thirty years."

Big House Gaines has carved his place in basketball history despite a bare-bones budget that only recently was fattened up to $210,000 a year. The money, it should be pointed out, is for all of Winston-Salem's sports, not just basketball. "With a situation like that," he says, "you take all the help you can get."

Every once in a while, an old grad will stumble across a stock clerk with a nose for the basket, Earl Monroe (class of '67) being the classic example. But more often than not, the young men who arrive at Winston-Salem are longer on dreams than they are on talent. Big House is ready for them. "They've got to realize that not everybody is gonna be an Earl the Pearl and make a million bucks," he says. "It's my job to knock that out of them and get them ready to go out in society." With that, he wades into a list of names that never cracked a big city sports page. The names belong to former players who made something of themselves in Los Angeles and Atlanta and Cincinnati. They are teachers and bankers and politicians and, yes, basketball coaches.

"You know," Jerry Krause says, "House used to call me to see if I'd draft a kid in one of the low rounds because the kid had a chance for a coaching job. You bet I did it. I did it in a minute. How many other coaches look out for their kids like that?"

It was night now and the phone in Big House Gaines's office was ringing with the wrong kind of calls. "We were supposed to leave for Chicago at seven in the morning," he said. "Now I guess we're not going." There was no use putting stock in the tournament promoter's week-old promise that a benevolent corporation would come through with travel money. Winston-Salem would stay at

home and its proud coach would wonder about the potential recruits whose paths he never got a chance to cross.

He didn't know the half of it. In a South Side printing plant lay
the programs for the tournament that was never to be.

They were dedicated to Big House Gaines.

Al McGuire
Sunday's Jester

Chicago Sun-Times
February 15, 1981

Any time a guy puts a flower in my lapel, I add forty-five minutes to the banquet.
—AL MCGUIRE

MILWAUKEE—You look at Sunday's Jester and figure life has always been his very own tire swing. He perches courtside at the college game he used to coach so well, the eternal wise guy cloaked in the respectability of an NBC blazer, and he plays bumper pool with the clichés that clutter television sportscasting. He blurts out the first thought that pops into his mind, laughs unashamedly at his own wit, and takes home enough money each year to bankroll an emerging nation. From all appearances, Sunday's Jester has no problems. Only other people do.

They didn't know what to make of him when he was vice chairman of Medalist Industries, didn't know whether to call him Coach or Al or Mr. McGuire or crazy. Even when he was turned out in what he disdained as his "sincere suit," he kept them guessing. He would climb aboard the motorbike that symbolized his low regard for conformity, and when he reached the highway near his Milwaukee home, he would throw himself at the mercy of his spiritual needs.

"If I went left, I went straight to Medalist, where everybody wore a tie and knew how to work the Xerox machine," Al McGuire says. "If I went right, I headed out to the countryside, out to Pewaukee and Oconomowoc, where they had cold cans of beer and sawdust on the floor."

Once a month, McGuire headed in the direction that provided him with the plain-folks sustenance he yearned for. He would have gone out there more often, but not until he was shed of his corporate trappings did he have the freedom to do what his heart told him. Not until he realized he was attempting the unthinkable did he feel comfortable with the old sweet urge to run until he ran out of road.

"Why don't you let me do the driving?" McGuire says to the man at the wheel of the car. "You can just sit back and ask me questions."

He has all his answers ready—about the fight with Bill Sharman in his NBA days, about strolling into the middle of the Harlem riots to recruit a center known as "The Evil Dr. Blackheart," about leaving Marquette with the 1977 NCAA championship as something to remember him by. Spun with craftsman precision, the stories are supposed to represent the essential McGuire. It isn't until he ceases telling them, however, that a lasting impression of him begins to form.

The brashness is replaced by sensitivity, the street smarts are tempered by a world-weary fragility. The differences begin to shine through as McGuire hunts up a friend on Oconomowoc's main drag, an amiable Notre Dame grad who runs a clothing store. In no time at all, you realize that their friendship has absolutely nothing to do with basketball. They met because they both collect toy soldiers by mining the antique shops that dot Wisconsin's country roads, and now their mutual interest has evolved into unshakable trust. "You ought to see this guy's house," McGuire says. Fifteen minutes later, he is driving onto the island where it sits with a perpetually unlocked door. "Quiet, huh?" he says once he is inside. "I like to come out here by myself and just think."

It is a strange way to imagine the volatile New Yorker who never shied from laying hands on wayward players and whose penchant for technical fouls seemed the product of a career death wish. The memories haunt him no matter how quietly he slips into a roadside tavern for a beer and some pickled eggplant. "You guys know who this is?" the old farmer behind the bar asks his 2:00 p.m. customers. There are whoops of recognition, not-so-subtle digs at a non-believer hiding behind his Stroh's bottle, and silence when McGuire asks if anyone has any toy soldiers for sale.

"Nothing like that," one of the afternoon drinkers says at last. "But I bought my daughter a toy fire engine, oh, must be thirty years ago."

"Bring it around, why don'tcha?" McGuire says. "Next time I get out this way, I'll take a look and tell the bartender here how much I can offer. How about it?"

The drinkers stare in blank disbelief. McGuire understands. It was the same way last year when Marquette inducted him into its hall of fame. School officials kept asking if he was going to show up. "I coached there thirteen years, you know," he says. "It wasn't like I ever missed a game." But what could he do besides be there on time? He climbs into the car and throws it into gear, hoping the drinker with the toy fire engine will take him at his word.

It is a strange world Al McGuire inhabits. He wonders how many people realize it. He wonders if his public would be surprised to know he has never seen the Milwaukee Bucks play or that he has yet to watch his first big-league baseball game. He wonders if the pipe-smokers on Marquette's faculty ever understood how much he despised them, or if the TV moguls who made him Sunday's Jester know that their racket drives him crazy. "If I had a steady diet of television," he says, "I'd wind up like Ray Milland in *Lost Weekend* or Olivia de Havilland in *Snake Pit*."

He saw enough of such characters when he was serving the all-nighters at his mother's saloon in Rockaway Beach, New York.

"I'd be there with the winos and a couple broads with one eye," he says, "and I'd say, 'Hey, God, is this what life's going to be?'"

Now McGuire knows better. He understands what he is and how he became that way, and yet his subconscious tells him he still hasn't finished this long strange trip.

"I can't speak and I have a problem reading," he says. "Now and then, I'll dream I'm back in college and I can't copy off anybody else's test. It's a fear, I guess, huh?"

The hum of the engine fills the car.

Ben Wilson
Only the Good Die Young

Philadelphia Daily News
December 7, 1984

CHICAGO—The news was like death itself. Someone ran up and said Ben Wilson had been shot, and the next thing Bob Hambric knew, he was racing out the door and down the street, not quite believing that any of this was happening.

Hambric was Ben's coach, the surrogate father who had overseen the growth of a skinny, clumsy freshman into the nation's foremost high school basketball player, and every step he took jumbled his emotions a little more. "I was in a fog," he says, "but then I saw the school policeman hustling out there, too, and I knew there was trouble. He's used to panic."

So Hambric moved even faster, increasing the distance between himself and the elementary school students he had been introducing to the wonders of Simeon Vocational, the students who were supposed to hear Ben Wilson speak next.

And Ben Wilson lay on the gritty sidewalk half a block north of Simeon, felled by two bullets from a .22-caliber Ruger revolver and numbed by shock.

He was propped against the wire fence next to the A&A Store, where he had come on his lunch hour with two girls to wander amid the video games and school jackets. Simeon's football coach was giving Ben first aid by the time Hambric reached his side, and inside the A&A a student was describing how it happened, Ben bumping a stranger and saying, "Excuse me," and the stranger telling the kid with him to shoot Ben. It was the Tuesday before Thanksgiving and a dream had been shattered.

Now the school policeman was trying to hold back the crowd that was spilling onto Vincennes Avenue. A crowd—how ironic. Ben Wilson always drew a crowd. He was seventeen years old, and what he could do with a basketball meant that he was forever surrounded by teammates, admirers, and recruiters. They filled his ears with the sound of adoration, but in these tortured minutes, he couldn't hear a thing.

Maybe it was just as well. The air was flooded with the wailing of sirens and grief. "The kids were crying," says John Everett, the pro football official who flexes his muscles as an assistant principal at Simeon. "I broke down, too." But Bob Hambric held his ground, refusing to let the tears inside him fall, waiting for his world to stop spinning out of control.

He looked for a pool of blood, saw none, and took heart. The wound that was visible in Ben's side seemed almost harmless, just a puncture in his windbreaker. "I was thinking the kids he played with would have to learn to get along without him for a while," Hambric says. They could start that very afternoon, in fact, when a photographer from USA Today was scheduled to take their picture as the No. 1 high school team in the country. There were plenty of pictures of Ben that could be sent along later.

That was the only consolation Hambric could find as he watched Ben being placed in an ambulance. The attendants worked with the practiced haste of men steeled by the random cruelty on Chicago's South Side, and yet they overlooked one thing, Ben's blue-and-white stocking cap.

Hambric picked it off the sidewalk, flicked the dirt off it, and put it in his pocket. He figured Ben would need the cap when he came home from the hospital.

☆ ☆ ☆

They say this city has never seen a funeral to equal it. More people turned out when Mayor Richard J. Daley died, and the same was true of the passing of Cardinal Cody, the archbishop of Chicago. But Ben Wilson was a kid.

He wasn't a politician who built an empire by trading jobs for votes, and he wasn't a religious leader who weathered controversy by showering his flock with blessings. Ben Wilson was a black basketball player with a golden future. He was someone for his people to rally around in a city where not being white can still get you chased from your home, chased into the bitter night.

So they came to say good-bye to Ben Wilson, both the family and friends who had known him as "Benji" and the strangers who had merely seen his name light up the sports page. There may have been as many as eight thousand of them at his wake in Simeon's six-hundred-seat gym. "They were three deep for something like six hours," John Everett says. "At one time the line stretched for two blocks. It was unbelievable." And the funeral itself was even more so—perhaps ten thousand mourners crowding inside and outside the headquarters of Operation PUSH, the civil rights organization, before Ben Wilson was laid to rest.

The swell of emotion was as startling and heart-tugging as his mother's courage. Five hours after her son died at dawn on November 21, Mary Wilson stood before a student assembly at Simeon and said, "I know hatred can never return good. I'm just sad. I don't feel hate for anyone."

Whatever chance there was for hatred must have been eliminated by sorrow when Mary Wilson listened to the doctors telling her how badly her son was hurt. She is a nurse, which means she has listened to those droning, unemotional voices before, but now the wounds she was hearing about were her son's. One of them was in his groin—no problem. But the other bullet had struck his aorta. "When they told Mrs. Wilson that," Bob Hambric says, "I'm sure she knew right away how serious it was."

It was serious and it was wrong, the way every senseless shooting is. But there was something that made the killing of Ben Wilson worse yet, because it violated one of the unwritten rules of inner-city life: Athletes are off limits to violence. They are the ones who have a ticket to better places, and they are not to be deterred by either gangs or freelancing thugs.

Simple geography should have reinforced that premise at Simeon, for the school is surrounded by a steel mill, a 7-Up bottling plant, and an assortment of warehouses. There is no neighborhood for a gang to call its turf, and when homes finally do come into view, they are clean and solid, a proud statement that the rules of decency are meant to be obeyed.

But every time Coach Hambric's friend, Mike Washington, thinks of the two sixteen-year-olds charged with Ben Wilson's murder, he knows how little all of that meant. "Those guys," says Washington, "broke the rules.

And they ended a story that shimmered with happiness.

☆ ☆ ☆

In the beginning, Ben Wilson was a project. He came to Simeon on the coattails of a better player, a player who was stronger and faster but couldn't live up to the academic and athletic demands that Bob Hambric put on him. He flunked out, but Ben Wilson stayed.

He wasn't just skinny then, he was short, too. Somehow, though, Hambric saw beyond those five feet eleven inches. "I'd always wanted a big guard," the coach says, "and I thought Ben could be it." Nobody else understood why when they saw Ben flopping around as the last man on the freshman-sophomore team.

"He didn't even start a game, and Coach Hambric was always talking about how great the kid was going to be," John Everett says. "I just shook my head and said, 'Good luck, Coach.'"

But luck didn't make Ben Wilson the player Indiana, DePaul, Illinois, Georgetown, Iowa, and Michigan were fighting over—

unless, that is, you think it was the fates that kicked his pituitary gland into overdrive. He was six foot three by his sopho-
more season, and six seven as a junior, and six eight going on
six nine this year. "You could almost see him growing when he
was walking down the hall," Hambric says. But the measuring
tape didn't shoot a hundred jump shots a day for Ben, nor did it
jump rope for hours, run mile after mile, or soak up everything
his coach told him.

"Ben was special," Hambric says, "and I felt I was special because I was chosen to guide and train him. There was a natural
attraction between us. We did things together, went to shows,
played basketball Sunday mornings with the old guys I usually
run with. Ben did all his studying in my office at school, and if
he wasn't studying, we'd talk about things. I'll probably never
have another player like that."

The reasons for Hambric's pessimism are as obvious as the
Illinois state championship that Simeon won last March, and
as obscure as the day Ben Wilson discovered what he could be.
Hambric had the varsity practicing at one end of the gym and he
wanted to make a point to a senior guard who was loafing. "So
I looked down to the other end of the gym and hollered, 'Ben,
come here,'" Hambric says. "Ben came down, got a couple baskets, did what I wanted him to do. I thought it would make the
senior angry, but he just laid down right there. I asked Ben, 'You
want to stay here?' and he said, 'Yeah, yeah.'" He didn't leave
until he had no choice.

By then, he had laid the foundation for Simeon's thirty-four-
game winning streak and convinced the prestigious Athletes for
a Better Education to name him the premier player in the nation.
Chicago had never produced one of those before. A lot of great
ones had come out of the city's high schools—Isiah Thomas,
Mark Aguirre, Terry Cummings—but now Ben Wilson was up
where his footprints were the first.

If anyone doubted that he deserved to be there, they needed only watch how much of the court he covered by himself. When fouls hog-tied Simeon's center, Ben would move into the middle and throw his 185 pounds around as recklessly as he could. If there was trouble against the press, he would bring the ball up court, using his height to see over the defense. The next thing anybody knew, though, he was making you forget about his size.

"He was always able to maintain the ability of a small person," Hambric says. "He could drive to the basket and fold his body up. There wasn't a crack he couldn't get through if he needed to."

And yet the way to remember him is standing tall. Think of the game he played against Corliss High School last season when Hambric benched two starters for missing practice and Simeon trailed in the first half by as many as ten points. "Ben just rose up over everybody else," Hambric says. The deficit shrank to three points, and then to one as Ben dunked an offensive rebound. A heartbeat later, he was blocking a shot at the other end of the floor and taking the ball back to where he could unleash the last-second jumper that won the game.

That was Ben Wilson as he seemed destined to be forever—unstoppable.

★ ★ ★

He was buried in his traveling uniform. His mother will hang the new home uniform he never wore in his closet. His coach gets the ski cap and the game films from last season that he didn't think he'd have the courage to watch.

"I thought at one point I would just erase them," Bob Hambric says. "I guess I'll have to buy a new case of tape instead."

That way, he can always have Ben Wilson.

It is something everybody in Chicago is trying to do now. They will retire Ben's No. 25 at Simeon in the spring, and when the school builds a new gym, it will be named after him. Money is coming in from around the country for a memorial fund to aid

Ben's family and the two-month-old child he fathered out of wedlock. Scarcely a day passes when a newspaper story doesn't point out that Ben was just one of ninety young people Chicago has lost to gunfire this year, and in City Hall politicians of every persuasion are grinding their axes on the tragedy. So much tumult, so much shouting, but some things never change.

In front of Simeon Vocational, its doors locked by a city teachers strike, a kid dribbles a basketball. How old can he be, eleven, twelve? He feints and whirls, even flicks the ball between his legs as he works his way past the school and toward the spot where two bullets ended Ben Wilson's dream.

Surely the kid knew who Ben was. Maybe he is even imagining himself as Ben at the height of his powers. But you will never get anyone to believe that he can hear Ben's coach saying, "Tomorrow isn't promised to you," or that he understands he is traveling on a street of broken dreams. And that is as it should be.

Wayne Gretzky
Borderline Case

Chicago Sun-Times
February 6, 1981

It is the time of year when Wayne Gretzky must be a man, and the job is never as easy as when he is wearing skates. Once they are off and he is on equal footing with the mere mortals who supply the hairy chests for the National Hockey League's image, he is left to fend for himself with instincts that aren't really there yet. Just last summer, he dwelled in a teenager's world where all he needed to get by was a ready smile and a couple of bucks in his pocket. Now he travels an adult path where a thick hide is as important as a suitcase.

In Canada they utter Wayne Gretzky's name in the reverent tones normally reserved for Howe, Hull, and Orr—bake him cakes, beg for his autograph, buy every blessed product he endorses. In the United States he gets jerked back to reality, playing in half-empty arenas for a half-bad team called the Edmonton Oilers. And yet it makes no difference that he plays as well as any kid two weeks past his twentieth birthday ever did.

The most frequent sound he hears is that of his own footsteps as he walks away from another loss, waiting for the darkness to swallow him. He is a star nobody south of the border sees, a tourist who knows little of the American cities he visits, a stranger in the night.

The challenge under the circumstances is to keep up appearances. Wayne Gretzky does what he can. "We don't see much of any place and no place sees much of us," he says. "We don't go to Chicago to visit Wrigley Field or the Playboy Mansion. We go to Chicago to do a job. We're professionals." It is a recurring theme in Wayne Gretzky's conversations, this business about being a pro, and the reason behind it is as obvious as the 94 points he has rung up already this season: A pro is what he was born to be.

"Other people have what it takes for being plumbers or doctors," he says. "I was different. I guess my family figured that out right away."

They had him on skates when he was two, had him wobbling around the Grand River's icy crust in Brantford, Ontario, as soon as they were sure the winter wind wouldn't blow him away. Legend has it that at five he was on a hockey all-star team for boys eight and older, but Wayne Gretzky is careful to undo the myth. "I was six," he says. He can afford to be honest, for when he was eight, he was tearing up fourteen-year-olds, and when he was fourteen, he hit the road with his brilliance, and when he was sixteen, his 70 goals and 112 assists made him the toast of the Sault Ste. Marie Greyhounds.

They called him "The Great Gretzky."

The nickname was no exaggeration.

The talent scouts with their wise old eyes and rancid-smelling cigars knew it as soon as they saw him working in back of the net, stick-handling in traffic, and laying off passes so soft a baby could catch them in his mouth and not get bruised. But the NHL had qualms about signing a seventeen-year-old *wunderkind* who had yet to graduate from high school. The soon-to-be-defunct World Hockey Association, bless its tacky heart, didn't know the meaning of qualms.

So in 1978, in a private jet flying somewhere over Alberta, a gadfly mogul named Nelson Skalbania gave Wayne Gretzky a four-year, one-million-dollar contract to play for the Indianapolis Racers. The contract was the foundation for a fortune, but it was also a ticket to the relative anonymity that still plagues him. He played just eight games with the Racers before they shipped him to Edmonton for fear his paycheck would sink them. It was the best thing that ever happened to the Oilers. Overnight, they had a hero to pack their arena and lead them into the NHL last season. All the hero had to do to hold up his end of the bargain was play center with sagacity beyond his years and keep his eyes open for potential assassins.

The former was easy, the latter more trying than Wayne Gretzky cares to admit. "There's always somebody banging on you," he says, "but it's not as dirty as people think." Dirty is one thing, however; embarrassing is something else. Simply put, Wayne Gretzky doesn't like to get hit, and usually he is quick enough to avoid it. But when somebody does tattoo him, he feels as if he has betrayed his talent. Not so long ago, he used to fling his sticks and gloves in the air and lie on the ice as if he had been struck dead. Now he bellyaches to officials. LINDBERG, MAYTAG, AND GRETZKY, said the sign that a man with answers erected in Buffalo recently. The question: "Name a flyer, a drier, and a crier."

But Wayne Gretzky can be forgiven his tears, real or manufactured, by anyone who has seen him put a puck in the net. Sometimes he seems to drop from the heavens, the way he did Wednesday night at the Stadium to score on a rebound off Tony Esposito's pads. Other times he brings back memories of Gordie Howe by changing hands on his stick as he booms up the ice, the way he did last year when he welcomed Olympic hero Jim Craig to the NHL with two goals.

He is still a kid, though. He was the league's most valuable player in 1980, but he says his biggest thrill of the season was playing on the all-star team with the immortal Howe. "I told him I was nervous," Wayne Gretzky says, "and he said, 'Don't worry, I am, too.'"

It is one of those memories Wayne Gretzky takes with him when he leaves Edmonton and heads into the States, one of those keepsakes that help him survive the losses and the strangers who aren't sure he's the Great One. Maybe that is further proof of what he is and what he isn't. One minute he is talking about Howe in the visitors' dressing room at the Stadium, the next he is walking into coach Glen Sather's office in search of a hair drier. "Come on, quit fooling," Sather growls at him. "You're no different than anybody else." The kid in Wayne Gretzky will have to leave. The man can stay.

Gretzky didn't remain anonymous in the States. He was traded to the Los Angeles Kings in 1988, and took them to the Stanley Cup finals in '93. He not only made the Hall of Fame, he made L.A. care about hockey, at least for a while.

Jimmy Connors
Blue Collar at a Tea Dance

Philadelphia Daily News
July 5, 1985

WIMBLEDON, England—The sport is so right for Jimmy Connors, and yet so wrong. He may be firmly entrenched in our consciousness as one more white-clad tennis champion performing the impossible for the rich and the royal, but there will always be something of the day laborer about him.

Look at the calluses on his hands, the sweat pouring from his brow, the ring around his collar. They aren't cause for shame. They are the essence of the man, for Jimmy Connors is an angel with a dirty face.

Not a saint, mind you. Nobody who has punctuated Centre Court blowups at Wimbledon by grabbing his manhood could ever fit that description. But in a sport where hunger for success and approval is in short supply, where quitters and cowards mince all over the idea of honest competition, Connors surely qualifies as an angel. Granted, the word itself will have him sputtering ten- and twelve-letter disclaimers, but he does have his standards and he does live up to them. And where is there another tennis player who can thump his chest and shout that his heart is as pure as his mouth can be foul?

Connors must look beyond the insular, insufferable world in which he lives to find kindred spirits. He must settle on sports like baseball and boxing, sports that would stain the All England Club with tobacco juice if they weren't splattering it with blood.

"I love to watch Pete Rose when he tries to get from first base to second," Connors says. "He may not always make it, but he's going to give everything he has time after time after time. There's always going to be a cloud of dust. It's always going to look rough."

And sometimes it can be rougher.

"I liked Joe Frazier leading with his face, getting beat up, getting bloody, and then coming up with a left hook. When I see somebody coming off with scars and marks and blood on them, I say that's my kind of guy."

Connors has nurtured an image that belongs in his East St. Louis, Illinois, birthplace, on the wrong side of the Mississippi River, rather than at a tea dance or a debutante ball. "I come off," he says, "and my shirt is ripped, my shorts are ripped, I'm bleeding, I'm scarred." It is his body that suffers, especially now that he is thirty-two, but it is his mind that carries him through.

And never underestimate what a strong mind can do. The one Connors possesses has thrust him into the men's singles semifinals at Wimbledon today while John McEnroe and Ivan Lendl, the top two seeds, are on the sidelines nursing their tormented psyches. What Lendl did in losing to France's unseeded Henri Leconte Tuesday was beneath contempt, an exhibition of spineless surrender that will not be dignified by further comment here. McEnroe, on the other hand, tried to fight everybody and wound up knocking himself out Wednesday when he had to contend with Kevin Curren's blistering serve. It was a sad thing to behold no matter how you feel about McEnroe's unfailingly bad manners, for here was the defending men's champion reduced to a quivering blob of protoplasm in straight sets by the anguish and insecurity he could no longer control.

"I'm not even sure if I played yet," McEnroe said after staggering off Centre Court. He thought he could beat the Fleet Street tabloids that snipe at him regularly, he thought he could survive without the comforting presence of actress Tatum O'Neal, he thought he could turn up the competitive fire that has been dimming inside him. He was wrong on every count. All he could do when he learned the sad truth was sigh wearily and say, "It's getting to be a little overwhelming to be No. 1 again."

This, remember, is the same John McEnroe who crushed Jimmy Connors in the final last year, who followed Bjorn Borg in a campaign of young Turks to turn Connors into an old man before his time. And now Borg is a twenty-nine-year-old retiree and McEnroe is a twenty-six-year-old basket case, and creaky Jimbo is wondering how they couldn't have loved the top of the mountain more than anything else in the whole blessed world no matter what personal price they had to pay for it.

"Being No. 1 is what the game's all about," Connors says. "You come in when you're a kid, you fight for a position, and you want everybody to think you're the best—the press, your peers, the people. You have to be your best day after day, but it's something I never minded when I was No. 1. It actually made me play better because there was so much expected of the one on top. You had to produce the magnificent, you had to get the oohs and aahs, but you were the only one up there. I always enjoyed that."

Maybe Connors realized how much it meant when he couldn't follow his 1974 Wimbledon title with another until eight years later. Maybe the realization came to him in one of his four losses in the finals or when he couldn't scratch and claw his way back to the top through players who were younger and stronger and blessed with serves that were Ferraris compared to his Model T.

But now it doesn't matter that he is a perpetual underdog against McEnroe and Lendl. They are gone and he endures. With two more victories, he can own the title that, even with his third seed, only the wildest dreamers gave him a chance of winning. The title, in case you haven't realized it, is what Connors came for.

Forget any notions you might have that he is excited by making the semis. "That's nothing to me," he says. Kevin Curren receives the same disdain, though the expatriate South African from Texas laid waste to McEnroe and rang up thirty-three aces against Connors here two years ago. "I hope he doesn't serve thirty-three aces again," Connors says, and his tone suggests that it won't happen, can't happen.

For he is one tough nut to crack and he has been hardened by age, hardened in ways that don't even allow him an isn't-the-kid-cute? smile when when Boris Becker's name gets tossed his way. "I don't think of Becker being seventeen," Connors says. "I think of him being a tennis player who's playing good tennis right now." A threat, if you will. A threat even if he has yet to prove that he can survive his status as the youngest player ever to make the semis and beat Sweden's Anders Jarryd. As such, Becker will get no free passes from Connors

Nothing personal. It's just part of the war Connors wages every time he sets foot on the court. He comes ready to raise a cloud of dust, to lead with his chin, to take his pound of flesh even if it costs him a pound of his own.

The scars show, of course, but why should they bother Jimmy Connors? He has been doing this all of his career, and besides, he's an old man now. Let the pretty boys worry.

John Carlos
The Olympic Ideal

Chicago Sun-Times
June 20, 1983

INDIANAPOLIS—He turns slowly and lets them look at him from every side, lets them see his long sprinter's body and his hell-bent-for-fun smile and the black corduroy hat on his shaven head. "Keeps the bugs off," he says when someone mentions the hat, and the laughter that swells in the night carries him back a decade. Or was it twelve years ago that he last saw Wilma Rudolph and Ralph Boston and Willye White and all the other Olympic heroes and heroines who were the best friends he ever had? He can't remember, so he shrugs and, vamping more outrageously than before, does another pirouette.

"See?" he tells his friends. "Still the same, still the same."

He isn't really, of course, and neither is the corner of the world he lives in, and we are all better for it. We are all better for John Carlos being who he is as well as who he was.

If it is pleasantly surprising to see him today, helping Los Angeles get its act together for the 1984 Olympics, it was profoundly disturbing to see him sacrifice himself fifteen years ago by defying the plantation-owner mentality that ruled amateur sports then. This cobbler's son from Harlem became an outlaw in 1968 with a single act of defiance on the victory stand in Mexico City. He received the bronze medal in the 200 meters, and when the band played the National Anthem, he bowed his head and raised his clenched, black-gloved left fist for black power.

Gold medalist Tommie Smith did likewise, and suddenly the world was given the message that the aborted black boycott of that Olympics had intended to deliver. Boos rolled down from the grandstand, and the two runners were expelled from the Olympic Village, and John Carlos rolled with the punches his demonstration inspired by saying, "White America would not understand."

It was if he knew that by 1983 there would be black men coaching our black Olympians, jobs and assistance for ghetto-trapped athletes, and a host of other changes that have come into being almost unnoticed. Maybe he even pictured himself at the U.S. Outdoor Track and Field Championships on a warm June night in Indianapolis, hugging the long lost friends, black and white, who never abandoned him. But only a dreamer could have imagined the words with which he greeted one and all: "Wait until the Olympics are on my turf."

John Carlos learned the virtue of putting up a bold front during his days of infamy. Even when he went home to Harlem, even when the door was closed and he was alone with his dying father, he held his ground. The only difference was that he whispered instead of shouting.

"The papers were writing bad about me, they really were," he says. "They were treating me the same as Rap Brown and Harry Edwards, and my father asked me, 'Johnny, why do you have to do those things?' I said, 'Pop, I'm really surprised. You know why. I have to do them because the situation isn't right.' He started crying when I said that. We was crying together."

Though John Carlos seldom let his tears be seen, they didn't dry quickly. Long after the '68 Olympics, life's sharp edges always seemed to be nicking him, drawing blood and causing pain. He signed with the Philadelphia Eagles as a wide receiver and was quickly sent packing, a fate that left him wondering if the scenario hadn't been a ruse to rob him of his amateur status. He ran for money in the International Track Association, only to leave after deciding he wasn't getting enough of it. He turned up at the 1976 Olympics, and when a sportswriter asked why he didn't go in, he said, "I don't have the bread."

His children heard the same reply when they came to him for money. "They was the ones who had it tough, not John Carlos," he says. "I couldn't even dress them the way my parents dressed me. And what could I tell them, man? That they was suffering on account of my principles?"

The question haunts John Carlos even though, at thirty-eight, he has achieved more success than the naysayers ever thought possible. He operates a youth club in Los Angeles that bears his name, hoping it will lure the best young athletes available, and he rarely engages in a conversation that doesn't eventually turn to L.A. and the '84 Olympics. "What we're telling people—black, white, yellow, whatever—is they got to have their package together," he says. He recruits minority stars from the past to spread the gospel in the city's public schools, and preaches that the Olympics are a once-in-a-lifetime opportunity.

The irony does not go unnoticed by the man in the pulpit. "You've got to understand it was never the Olympics I hated, the running and jumping and all that," he says. "The thing I hated was the politics behind it." The politics are still there, of course, but they have been leavened by a modest application of fairness and equality. If perfection is never achieved, at least his children will have that to console them for the lean times they endured.

"You know, the kids are getting old enough now where they can try to figure out for themselves whether I did right or wrong," John Carlos says. "They can have an intelligent discussion about what was happening back then and, who knows, some day they might even turn a page in a history book, they might even see a picture of their father."

It is better, after all, to have made history than mere trouble.

Johnny Kelley
The Elder

Chicago Sun-Times
April 20, 1980

BOSTON—They call him "The Elder" because there is another in a long line of Johnny Kelleys afoot at the Boston Marathon. The other Johnny Kelley is a kid who can't be more than fifty and couldn't possibly remember what Boston was like when there were only 284 souls brave enough to try it. No wonder he gets second billing as "The Younger" despite winning in '57 to break a string of eleven foreign victories and losing in '61 when a stray dog knocked his legs out from under him. He still isn't what Johnny "The Elder" Kelley will tell you he is in no uncertain terms: "I am the original."

Descendants of Pheidippides, patron saint of the fallen-arches brigade, may quibble over The Elder's choice of words, but no one can dispute his place in history. Here, for one thing, is a man who dared turn up his nose at the famed bowl of beef stew that used to be the reward for surviving the 26 miles, 385 yards from suburban Hopkinton to the Prudential Center. "I had some forty years ago and it made me very, very sick," he says. "Never again."

As if to appease him, the culinary geniuses catering this year's marathon have replaced the stew with yogurt. The mere thought of yogurt, however, turns him a shade of green that matches his last name. "Give me ginger ale," Kelley says. Give him ginger ale and give him his due, for Monday he will be running his 106th marathon and his 49th Boston, and when he pins that 72 on his shirt, it will be more than just a number. It will be his age.

The original, indeed.

More than anyone else, John Adelbert Kelley represents the spirit of Boston. It matters not that his second, and last, victory here came in 1945, giving him a string of failures equaled only by the Chicago Cubs. He runs for the pure joy of it, for the charge of matching strides with men and women less than half his age. "I suppose I should just be happy to finish," he says.

Like every other marathoner, he suffers along the way, but his suffering never diminishes the thrill for long. In fact, all it did last year was give him a chance to see a stranger capitalizing on his fame. Kelley saw the scoundrel two miles from the finish line, when he was gasping for breath and fighting the temptation to walk. He saw him but didn't really realize what was happening until he was holding a Johnny "The Elder" Kelley button featuring a picture of his own beaming mug.

"Would you believe it?" he says. "I'm out there hurting and some SOB is selling those things and making money off me."

Kelley's laughter gets the best of his indignation. He just wishes he'd thought of the button idea first. "Why should I complain about a guy making a buck?" he says. If that was his style, he would begrudge Bill Rodgers and Frank Shorter the way they have turned their marathoning fame into a marketable commodity. Instead, he says, "I wish I could have done what they're doing."

But in his day there weren't millions of runners clogging up America's sidewalks and wearing their shorts and sneakers everywhere except to church. Instead, runners were regarded as freaks. Kelley himself covered his tracks by finding work as an electrical maintenance man at Boston Edison, a job he kept until his retirement seven and a half years ago. The job stamped him as a practical man rather than as a freak who took up running as soon as he discovered he couldn't hit a baseball.

He was a little fellow then—five feet six inches and 129 pounds. Now he regards himself as practically elephantine. "One-thirty is just too heavy for me," he says. When he was young and trim, however, he lacked the savvy he possesses today. That explains why, in 1928, he neglected to turn his socks inside out, got blisters from the seams rubbing his feet, and had to surrender six miles short of completing his first Boston Marathon.

Things went no better when Kelley returned in 1932 and dropped out again. Then they got a lot better. In the next three years, he advanced from thirty-seventh to second to first. "The second man was two minutes behind me in '35," he says. "You know, I kind of expected it."

There are other happy chapters in the Johnny Kelley story, to be sure. His victory in 1945, when he was still a soldier, for instance, and his refusal to acknowledge Hitler when he was the only American to survive the marathon at the 1936 Berlin Olympics. "Hitler waved at me once," says Kelley, who finished eighteenth. "I didn't wave back."

If there has been a low point for him, it was Boston in '37. He came from out of nowhere in that one, and just as he was about to take the lead on Heartbreak Hill, he patted Tarzan Brown on the rump and unwittingly lit a fire under the mercurial Narragansett Indian. The next thing he saw was the cloud of dust Tarzan left him in on the way to a first-place finish.

And still Kelley endured. "I never thought about quitting after that," he says. "Why should I? I always figured I'd come back." And back and back and back, until there is no one like him.

Even down on Cape Cod, where he lives with his wife and smokes his cigars out in the backyard, the neighbors expect to see him running 350 days a year. "They get real mad if I run in the woods instead of past their houses," he says. So imagine how it is on marathon day, when there are upwards of six thousand official runners headed for downtown Boston and half a million free spirits lining the course.

"They love me, they really do," Kelley says. "They're shouting, 'C'mon, Kell, c'mon, old man.' And the runners, they're coming up to me and saying, 'Mr. Kelley, can I run with you a while?'"

It is then that he understands what he runs for—not a buck or a victory, but for the chills up and down his spine.

Ron Turcotte
Rider Down

Chicago Sun-Times
June 12, 1983

With a bounty he would rather have done without, Ron Turcotte has time to think about Secretariat now. When he was riding that mountainous chestnut to a Triple Crown and fame as perhaps the greatest racehorse ever, the world spun too rapidly for him to comprehend what was, let alone what might have been.

He had other horses to ride, planes to catch, pounds to keep off, and no matter how far Secretariat carried him, he never stopped to wonder how much ground they could have covered until they were out of chances to do so. But wonder Ron Turcotte does now that his fabled mount lolls in retirement and he sits in a wheelchair.

What Turcotte sees as he stares out his living room window is the leafy Canadian countryside where he grew up as one of fourteen children, a lumberjack's son who never imagined breaking his back when he was a teenager lighting out for the nearest track. What he sees when he closes his eyes on those solemn afternoons in Grand Falls, New Brunswick, is Secretariat thundering to more glory in races he never ran, burning track after track with the scorched-earth policy that reached its pinnacle in the Belmont Stakes ten years ago this weekend.

"It seems longer to me," Turcotte says. "Time passes kinda slow, you know."

So he envisions the splendor that never was, the splendor that was bypassed because Secretariat was syndicated before he turned three and ticketed for shipment to Kentucky's Claiborne Farm before anyone in racing realized he would become racing's most glorious performer. There was no turning back once the $6.8 million deal was done, but there was always the regret that the horse's loyal rider uses to punctuate his conversations.

"I don't think anybody ever saw the true Secretariat," Turcotte says. "People who hear that might tell you, 'This guy's crazy,' but I'm not making anything up. He was just coming into his own in his last two races. No other horse I ever rode compared to him—Tom Rolfe, Northern Dancer, Riva Ridge, Arts and Letters, none of 'em. Secretariat was just that much better. He had power and perfect balance, just like the best car you ever drove. He could run on the lead or lay back in the pack, just coasting until you touched him and he shifted gears. A two-year-old kid coulda rode him, that's how easy he was to handle. And him finished at three? If they woulda let him run until he was five, then you really woulda seen something."

As things stand, though, you will have to be satisfied with the memory of Secretariat making history in the Kentucky Derby, confounding the electronic timers in the Preakness, and waltzing off with the Belmont by thirty-one lengths. Sustenance will have to be found in the grand style with which he won $1.3 million and the lusty good humor with which his owner, Penny Tweedy, surveyed his massive chest before announcing, "He reminds me of a well-stacked girl."

Not that there weren't tough times, too—the abcess that likely cost Secretariat victory in the Wood Memorial and Tweedy's doubts about Turcotte's ability to make decisions in the saddle. But a decade later, the jockey insists that everything was beautiful, and the temptation to disagree vanishes when you remember the ugliness to which he automatically compares it.

On a July day at Belmont Park in 1978, barely half a dozen jumps out of the starting gate, Turcotte tried to steer a horse named Flag of Leyte Gulf away from trouble that wasn't of his own making. Tried and failed.

"Jeff! Jeff!" Turcotte shouted.

But the jock whose mount was drifting into him didn't respond until the collision that sent Turcotte lurching over his horse's head like a rag doll.

In the cloud of dust that rose as the horses tumbled and fell, he tried to get his breath and couldn't. He pushed in on his stomach and discovered that the muscles there were useless. "Don't touch me!" he screamed at the first men to reach him. He had seen the signs before on other fallen riders, and he knew what had happened. His back was broken. He was paralyzed.

Neither operations nor lawsuits have brought the feeling back to forty-one-year-old Ron Turcotte's legs, but the toughness that was his trademark as a jockey continues to manifest itself. "I still don't think race riding is that dangerous," he says. "I was always more worried about driving to the track." After all, the track was where good things happened to him, whether it was riding Tom Rolfe to a Preakness victory in 1965 or steering Riva Ridge to the winner's circle in the '72 Derby or letting Secretariat lay the foundation for the house that has become his shrine. There are walls full of pictures, mantels full of trophies, even a stack of posters to mail to the people who still write Turcotte about the horse that keeps his name alive.

"Do you have a few minutes to talk about Secretariat?" callers ask.

"That won't be long enough," he always tells them.

How could it be if he is to properly discuss the way he promised Penny Tweedy and trainer Lucien Laurin a Derby victory, then set a Churchill Downs 1¼-mile record in 1 minute, 59 and ⅖ seconds? And what about the gamble Turcotte took on the first turn in the Preakness, pushing Secretariat through the trap the competition had laid and on to the finish line so quickly that Pimlico's timers couldn't keep up with him?

Those are moments to remember, and yet they merely set the stage for the Belmont's 1½ miles and Secretariat's 2-minute, 24-second romp away from the pack and into legend. "I never realized how fast he was going," Turcotte says. "He was just galloping." Galloping? Flying seems a better description, flying so high that even ten years later the memory lifts the spirit and, however briefly, lets Ron Turcotte leave his wheelchair behind.

Buddy Delp
The Happy Anarchist

Chicago Sun-Times
May 5, 1979

LOUISVILLE—He is up from the sweatshops of thoroughbred racing, a claiming-horse trainer flaunting a fourteen-million-dollar
colt that the rich folks are just going to have to do without. His
suddenly exalted status produces too much of everything—glamour, interviews, friends he never knew he had—and he loves it
all. If he could get somebody to promise that the Kentucky Derby
would always be this way, he would come every year to strike a
blow for the common man. At the moment, however, Buddy Delp
is perfectly content with his one chance to be a happy anarchist.

Laughter is an infrequent visitor at Churchill Downs, but Delp
has discovered that there may be no better tool for giving the
track's denizens something to remember him by. When an emissary from ABC stopped at Barn 41 the other day to announce
the imminent arrival of Howard Cosell, the defiantly bald Delp
said, almost shyly, "I guess I'd better wear a toupee."

The emissary laughed as much as propriety allowed.

"Did you really think that sounded good?" Delp asked.

Moments later, as he entertained a flock of writers, the subject
of Cosell came up again. "Yeah, he's coming to interview me,"
Delp said. "I told him to bring me one of his toupees." The writers roared with laughter and Delp smiled triumphantly, secure
in the knowledge that it pays to polish your one-liners.

There is an audience starving for them. It consists of the two-dollar bettors who annually find themselves disdained by the Derby's bluebloods. Perhaps the truest measure of the ruling class's haughty demeanor is that even Delp's rowdy charm goes unappreciated. But, deep down, the aristocrats have to be wondering how God in his infinite wisdom could possibly allow this Philistine to train a horse as marvelous as Spectacular Bid.

True to form, Delp revels in the silent squirming. "I've raced here three times and won all three," says the amiable troublemaker, who saw his only Derby as a spectator in 1967. "After Saturday, I'll be four for four." That ought to get the fat cats right where they live. And how about this? "If Flying Paster is as good as Secretariat," he says of the big gun that has been imported from California, "then maybe we'll have a real race. Otherwise, you can forget about it." Delp goes on and on, piling candor atop humor, and when it is time to leave his audience laughing, he signs off with a poem only Muhammad Ali would claim:

> If Bid wins by two, that'll do.
> If he wins by five, we'll jive.
> If he wins by nine, we'll be fine.

The doggerel paints a between-the-lines picture of a racetracker more enamored of victory than horses. "Don't you forget it," Delp says. "I've spent a lot of my life hating those sons of bitches."

As the favorite in the 105th Derby on Saturday, however, Spectacular Bid enjoys special dispensation from Delp's wrath. For one thing, he has a well-advertised propensity for finishing first. But Delp is also sentimentally attached to Bid because the strapping three-year-old has given him a taste of honey.

"Every trainer that has paid his dues ought to have a horse like this one," Delp says. "Of course, until you get him, you don't know what you've been missing."

It took Grover "Buddy" Delp twenty-five years in the business before he found out the meaning of greatness. The first thing he noticed was Bid's endless energy supply. "You could run him to the Rocky Mountains and he wouldn't get tired," Delp says. Better yet, Bid used every tool he possessed to perfection and had no tolerance whatsoever for another horse's tail swishing in his face. Those who doubted it were set straight at the Florida Derby in March, when Bid banged into the starting gate, got roughed up at the ⅜ pole, and still won by four and a half lengths. Greatness, one had to assume, is an unflagging, unflappable horse.

In the past, Delp's steeds were always minus an important ingredient, usually talent. Still, Delp won races like the Massachusetts Stakes and became a dominant figure at the tracks in Maryland. He did it with horses that other people deemed expendable. And for every payday he enjoyed, he had a story to tell about having to unload some hayburner in Charles Town, West Virginia, just to make enough money to get home.

"Let me tell you another thing," Delp says. "I was in Laurel, Maryland, in '63, I guess it was, and a barn burned down one night and killed ten of my horses. Hell, I didn't sit around shedding any tears. I claimed three new horses the next day while the barn was still smoking. Thirty days later, I was the track's leading trainer."

That was in the hinterlands, though. The Kentucky Derby is what Bill Winfrey, the venerable trainer, once called "the race of America." The sport has no more important occasion, and the ruling class contemplated Delp's numerous rough edges and wondered if he would be able to stand the pressure. After all, he had punched out an exercise rider for galloping a horse too close to the rail and publicly excoriated Spectacular Bid's pubescent jockey, Ronnie Franklin, for assorted gaffes. Under the pressure of Derby Week, the naysayers expected Delp to crack like a cheap glass in hot water.

Instead, he has emerged as the star of the show. His only complaint concerns the workload that comes with training an extraordinary horse. "I got sixty-five horses back home in Maryland and they only keep me busy six days a week," he says. "With Bid, I work seven days. Hell, I haven't done that in ten years." He tries to frown, but he can't. He is having too good a time.

He can still phone his bookie and get bets down on the Washington Bullets. When he stops by the barn at night to check on Bid, there is always somebody around eager to shoot craps and drink beer. And despite all the frowns that have greeted his ceaseless self-promotion, he has yet to go without an audience.

"Nobody else is talking, huh?" he says. "That figures. They must know I could put Bid in the gate backwards and he'd still win."

There is no stopping Delp until every reporter's notebook has been filled and every radio guy's tape cassette has gone the distance. The truthseekers drift away slowly, reluctantly, for they know they will find no more agreeable subject. Behind them, Delp is asking, "Have I talked to everybody? Did you all get everything you needed?" It is the perfect refrain for a man who knows he may never come this way again.

Spectacular Bid won the Derby, and the Preakness, too. But he came a-cropper in the Belmont Stakes when he stepped on a safety pin the morning of the race and finished third. Delp, who would die in 2006, at seventy-four, returned to the world of claiming horses, still talking, still laughing.

Bill Shoemaker
A Million for the Shoe

Chicago Sun-Times
August 31, 1981

When it was over, someone called him Willie. With all due respect to the Willies of the world—from Mays and Stargell to Pep and Pastrano—it didn't sound right. It was too flip, too full of familiarity, and not tinged with enough respect. Maybe that is overreacting, but if you saw Bill Shoemaker do what he did Sunday, you might think the only thing anyone should call him is Mister.

They inaugurated the world's first million-dollar thoroughbred race out at Arlington Park, and Shoemaker filled it with style and grace and more electricity than it seemed possible for a fifty-year-old man to generate. On the grass, aboard a four-legged money machine named John Henry, he caught the competition from the rear and, hard as it is to believe, added still more luster to his legend with a photo finish for all time. The Arlington Million may never see another race like it, much less a jockey the equal of Shoemaker, and yet, when the starting gate opened, he looked like a good bet to get knocked on his reputation.

It didn't matter that John Henry was 11-10 to win or that his bank account is fast approaching Spectacular Bid's. The turf was soft from a week of August monsoons and the diminutive California bay had the twelfth post position in a twelve-horse field, which was like trying to run from Chicago to Milwaukee by way of Des Moines.

"He's a tough little dude, though," Shoemaker would say later. "The toughest little dude I ever rode in my life. He scraps, he fights, he don't give up."

No wonder the good, gray Shoe had big plans for getting out of the gate. He thought he could catch the opposition sleeping, angle toward the inside, and maybe even sneak into the lead right away. "I figured the worst I'd be laying was second or third," he said. But there were five other jockeys who must have read his mind. As they drove their horses toward the first turn, they formed a picket fence that kept John Henry wide and behind. All Shoemaker could do in eighth place was wonder if he was going to wake up Monday and read about Key To Content or Madam Gay or, worst of all, The Bart, a 40-1 shot.

"If you want to ride, you've got to take the good with the bad," Shoemaker said. "You go out there with a plan, and about 50 percent of the time it works. The other 50 percent is when you earn your money."

With six hundred thousand dollars of Arlington's million waiting for the winning horse, Shoemaker commenced scheming. It was an excruciating process, for by the mile pole, with only a quarter to go, John Henry was still no better than fifth. And he might have finished there, too, if Shoemaker hadn't noticed Lester Piggot, the lord and master of British riders, squeezing Madam Gay through the middle of the pack. "I just followed right along," Shoemaker said. "It looked like Lester had a lot of horse left, and I thought that if I got lucky, I might have a chance."

It was a masterful job of plotting in the saddle but a bad job of handicapping on the run. As soon as Madam Gay was out of the way, there was The Bart, and The Bart was pure trouble for the last precious eighth of a mile. Eddie Delahoussaye had the long shot running like his tail was on fire, and who knows, maybe it was. Whatever else was going on out there, John Henry and The Bart blended into one as they thundered across the finish line.

"Too close to call!" roared race caller Phil Georgeff. It was time for a photograph to decide what the human eye couldn't.

"How did you feel when you heard it was a photo finish?" someone asked Shoemaker in the interview room.

"I got butterflies," he said. "Of course I had 'em before the race, too."

They're what keep Shoemaker riding, those butterflies and the possibility that any time he puts on his silks, he might end up in a race like this one. If the great unknown didn't await out on the track, he would have been gone long ago, gone to savor the riches he has already reaped.

In the thirty-three years since he put his first victory on the board at California's Golden Gate Fields, Shoemaker has ridden thirty-three thousand races, won eight thousand of them, and made upward of eighty million dollars for his horses' owners. He has won ten Triple Crown races, inhabited racing's Hall of Fame for twenty-three years, and taken the reins of great horses from Swaps to Spectacular Bid. He has done everything there is to do, and yet, when they declared John Henry the Arlington Million's first winner, Shoemaker didn't act his age or his status. He was, in a word, delighted.

"That's probably the best race I ever rode in," he said. And John Henry was "a good horse, a great horse—no other kind of horse could have won this race." Suddenly, Shoemaker cared not that he can only ride three races a day instead of the nine of old. The same went for warming up with a few fast games of Ping-Pong, thereby avoiding the risk of taking two mounts before the Million. He had won another big one, and that was all that counted.

Now he could visit the winner's circle again, calmly accepting the handshakes of admiring men and the kisses of society-set women. He could even take a brief flight as he clutched the Arlington Million trophy when it was raised toward the heavens by Governor Thompson, at six foot six a whopping nineteen inches taller than the Shoe. And when the excitement was over, he could hoist a vodka and tonic and look forward to a morning flight back to Southern California and more racing. "I would have gone there tonight if there was a plane leaving," he said.

It was no knock on the available hospitality, just a statement of fact, one that makes you realize that Arlington Park relied on poetic license when it called the Million "the world's richest thoroughbred race." If you consider more than money, you can say the same of any race Bill Shoemaker rides in.

Shoemaker stayed in the saddle until shortly before his fifty-ninth birthday. Nobody ever rode in more than the 40,350 races he did, but he was not indestructible. In April 1991, as he was beginning a successful second career as a trainer, he was involved in a one-car drunk-driving accident that left him paralyzed from the neck down. He was in a wheelchair until his death in 2003, at seventy-two.

4

Arts and Letters

Red Smith
The Write Stuff

Chicago Sun-Times
April 27, 1984

This was always Red's time of year. Even when he was in his seventies and scrambling to stay ahead of his final edition, you could still find him out by the barns or the batting cage. He used to joke about the legs being the first to go, but when there was a rookie shortstop to be appraised or a precocious three-year-old to be worked at dawn, nobody dared spot him a stride.

Maybe he was fueled by the smell of new-mown infield grass or the way the sun warmed him as he kibitzed with grooms and hot walkers. Red never said, though. I guess he figured it was obvious.

The first time I found myself in a press box with him was the day Elocutionist won the Preakness, and I didn't really know what to do. I had written as best I could against the clock, but when I glanced over at Red, I couldn't stop myself from gawking. We used typewriters back then, and he was bleeding out his column a page at a time, sweating through his shirt the way everybody had predicted he would and crossing out whole paragraphs so he could pencil his new and improved thoughts in the margins. The result must have looked like a Rorschach test, but unscrambled and set in type in the *New York Times*, it would read like poetry no matter how much Red protested to the contrary. "You know," he said when he could stand and stretch at last, "I wasn't sure I could still go a mile and three-sixteenths."

Not a big man, I thought as I surveyed Walter Wellesley "Red" Smith.

But a giant.

In this business, we pride ourselves on not having heroes, on being able to report that the king has no clothes, and I am no different. Yet friends in other departments and other lines of work are forever accusing me of perjury. They can't imagine that I don't swoon every time Walter Payton bestows a quote on me or Reggie Jackson remembers my name. Much as I respect Payton and Jackson, though, they can never match the heroes I discovered writing about sports.

Maybe you will recognize some of their names: W. C. Heinz, John Lardner, Jimmy Cannon, A. J. Liebling, Jim Murray. Others, however, didn't have New York or Los Angeles as a launching pad to fame. You had to go to Philadelphia to read Sandy Grady, to Dallas for Blackie Sherrod, to San Diego for Jack Murphy. And they always made the trip worthwhile.

Each of them had days when he was the best in the business, but none had more of them than Red Smith. With prose as clear as the mountain lakes he loved to fish, Red made me fall in love with writing, not box scores. I am not the only one, either. Scratch a hundred other sportswriters of my generation and you may find that half of them live for the rare letter that says something they wrote made a reader think of Red.

He has been dead for two years, and yet he continues to tower over the profession. For as long as I live, I expect to hear colleagues recall how he worked until four days before his death at seventy-six and how he used his last column to lament the fact that he was going to be writing three times a week instead of four.

It is the stuff of legend, and friends and admirers continue to salute Red for it. There have been horse races named after him, and just a couple of weeks ago, a New York sports hangout called Gallagher's toasted his memory. The other night at Notre Dame, his alma mater, the elegant political columnist Murray Kempton delivered the second annual Red Smith Memorial Lecture. And at the Kentucky Derby next week, a writer will be honored with the Red Smith Award, which is not to be confused with the Red Smith Award that the Associated Press Sports Editors will hand out next month. Red would have been appalled by all the fuss, of course, and the awards would have made him laugh. The only thing he ever thought a wooden plaque was good for was kindling.

He deserved everything good that ever happened to him, though. Anyone could have deduced that after reading his account of Joe Louis's demise beneath Rocky Marciano's fists: "An old man's dream ended. A young man's vision of the future opened wide. Young men have visions, old men have dreams. But the place for old men to dream is beside the fire."

Red was at his peak then. It was 1951 and the *New York Herald Tribune* was still in business. But he wouldn't receive his Pulitzer until the *Trib*, like so many other writers' papers, had folded and he had spent five years in limbo waiting for the *Times* to hire him.

Though the unfairness of that scenario surely didn't escape him, Red never bellyached about it. It was as if he were determined to age gracefully while so many of the press box dwellers around him grew bitter, griping about snot-nosed ballplayers making more money than they deserved. He would field praise by telling whoever happened to be slapping him on the back, "Well, God bless. Don't let anything happen to you." And he would laugh off the shaking hands with which he raised his Scotch to his lips by saying, "Don't worry, it's an old Irish affliction."

And always he would tell stories. He told them about catches Joe DiMaggio made, about Citation and Coaltown dueling in the Derby, about Army-Navy football games that made the earth shake. Red remembered everything, and he seemed to take it as his duty to pass his memories on to a generation that would never see the St. Louis Browns lose a doubleheader.

Tom Seaver understands that. He once gave Red a ride to New York from the Connecticut town where they both lived, and the stories Seaver heard that day were still making him smile when he checked into the White Sox's training camp this spring. As he was getting acquainted with his new teammates, the subject of sportswriters came up—good ones, bad ones, and the hundreds of indifferent ones. It was a curious subject for a clubhouse conversation, but Seaver was prepared for it. "Did you ever know Red Smith?" he asked.

Now there was a sportswriter.

W. C. Heinz
The Professional

Los Angeles Times
March 1, 2008

I was thirteen the first time I read W. C. Heinz. I've never forgotten the story: "The Rocky Road of Pistol Pete." It was a bittersweet
look at Pete Reiser, undone by his own fearlessness when he was
the Brooklyn Dodgers' golden child and marooned years later as
a bush league manager with a bad heart and a rattletrap Chevy.

You wouldn't think a kid plowing through *True* magazine's 1958
Baseball Annual would care, but I did. And even today what Bill
Heinz wrote still gets me in the heart and the gut.

He was a master of the crystalline sentence, an understated
craftsman who put a human face on every subject from busted-
luck ballplayers and boxers to surgeons and dogface soldiers.
More than that, he was part of history. In the middle of the twentieth century, he stood shoulder to shoulder with Red Smith,
Jimmy Cannon, and the too-often-forgotten John Lardner as
they turned sportswriting into something approaching literature, like water into wine.

When Bill died the other day at ninety-three, after outliving all
the others and almost every newspaper and magazine he worked
for, you could look around and see his influence wherever words
still count for something. It's there in the books of David Halberstam and Elmore Leonard, and in the newspaper columns
of Jimmy Breslin. It's there, too, in the stylized journalism of a
new generation with no idea that Bill blazed the trail for them by

applying the tools of fiction—scenes, characters, dialogue—to his meticulous reporting.

For all I know, the seed for my own short, mostly happy life as a full-time sportswriter was planted when I read his Pete Reiser story. On my way to the press box, I came across more of his work in the old *Best Sports Stories* anthologies, and once I got where I was going, I heard about something else he'd written, a 1958 boxing novel he called *The Professional*. It was a revelation: a flinty-eyed yet profoundly compassionate study of a middleweight fighter and his aging manager as they chase a championship in a sport that crushes true hearts. The ending is so sad that Bill had to spend a day walking in the woods around his Vermont home to gather the courage to write it.

Ernest Hemingway, who admired *The Professional* as much as anyone, said you could read it only once. Ernest Hemingway was wrong. I've read it a half dozen times, always with the sensation of learning something new about an old friend. I've written about it, too. The first time I did, in 1992, Bill sent me a thank-you note that remains a prized possession.

But the important thing, to me at least, is what happened a few years later. I'd been working in Hollywood for nearly a decade by then, and a producer I knew got it in his head to turn *The Professional* into a movie. Walter Matthau had had the same idea and had gotten nowhere. Peter Falk fared no better. But the producer asked me to call this guy W. C. Heinz anyway, just to sound him out.

When Bill answered the phone, I introduced myself by saying he probably wouldn't remember my name.

"Sure I do," he said. "Every time I get depressed, I read that piece you wrote about *The Professional*."

The producer wound up taking a one-year option on the novel, but once again no movie came of it. Bill's disappointment was palpable—God, how he loved *The Professional*. There was nothing

I could do to buoy his spirits when I wrote a screenplay based on his stories about Lew Jenkins, a wild-haired Texan who drank and floozied himself out of the world lightweight championship and found redemption by fighting in the Korean War. Hollywood didn't buy that, either.

But Bill and I stayed in touch by letter and telephone. Though we never laid eyes on each other, never shook hands, sat down for coffee, or any of the other things friends do, I like to think that friends is what we were for the last dozen years of his life.

At first we talked about the obvious: politics, pro football, the invasion of TV by sports page gasbags. "All that lecturing, all that talking," he said. "What the hell is that about?"

In time, Bill revealed more of his inner self, starting with his frustration over the cataracts that would rob him of the sight in one eye and leave the other touch-and-go. I heard the grief in his voice in 2002 when he told me his wife, Betty, had died. And I could sense the unease beneath his rueful chuckle as he talked about his move to a care facility three years later. "If I'm not down-stairs eating," he said, "they come up to make sure I'm still alive."

Once in a while, he would mention that someone whose name I recognized had been up to see him—Halberstam or Ken Burns or Bob Costas. But there was never any talk about why he attracted such attention, just as there was never a word about his collaborating with Vince Lombardi on *Run to Daylight* or co-authoring *MASH*. Where others might have reveled in self-promotion, Bill cared only about doing a job right, treating it with respect. The essence of the man could be found in his ethos: "Don't admire yourself. Admire your work."

How fitting that, in Bill's final years, two collections of his journalism were published, his sportswriting in *What a Time It Was* and his World War II correspondence in *When We Were One*. There was no hiding how he felt about the pieces they contained, pieces dating all the way back to his days at the *New York Sun*. "I read them," he told me, "and I said, 'Hey, this is pretty good.'"

When he sent me a copy of *What a Time It Was*, it wasn't just autographed, it was personally copy edited. Failing eyesight be damned, he had tracked down every typographical error and corrected them all in blue ink and block letters as precise as his prose. That was Bill Heinz for you, a professional to the end.

A. J. Liebling
Joe

Chicago Sun-Times
December 5, 1980

On its bruised and bloody face, the fight racket seems as repug-
nant as a sport could be. There is the violence, of course—the
furious destruction of scar tissue, brain cells, even lives—and
there are also the little murders committed with ballpoint pens
in smoky back rooms. Promoters steal from managers, managers from fighters, fighters from the public. The evidence is in every gutbucket arena where a four-rounder was ever fought, yet
the heart refuses to heed what the head tells it.

When A. J. Liebling wrote about boxing as the "Sweet Science,"
he struck a note that rang as true as the one Rocky Marciano discovered by putting Jersey Joe Walcott to sleep with a one-punch
rhapsody. Alas, explaining this phenomenon, this puzzling love
affair, is as difficult as convincing an antivivisectionist that sleeping canines never know the difference.

But the reasons for adoring fistiana can be found if one is willing to sift through the all-too-well-publicized carnage. Boxing's
indestructible charm dwells in the dese-and-dose patois of a
trainer with a face like a baked potato, and in the street-smart ex-
istentialism of a ghetto kid who had just two choices in life—the
ring or the can. And if the sight of such rough-hewn noblemen
doesn't move you, doesn't make you understand how something
beautiful can flower in a sweat-sour gymnasium, then surely Joe
Liebling's prose will.

"It is through Jack O'Brien, the *Arbiter Elegantiarum Philadel-phiae*, that I trace my rapport with the historical past through the laying-on of hands," Liebling wrote. "He hit me, for pedagogical example, and he had been hit by the great Bob Fitzsimmons, from whom he won the light-heavyweight title in 1906. Jack had a scar to show for it. Fitzsimmons had been hit by Corbett, Corbett by John L. Sullivan, he by Paddy Ryan, with the bare knuckles, and Ryan by Joe Goss, his predecessor, who as a young man had felt the fist of the great Jem Mace. It is a great thrill to feel that all that separates you from the early Victorians is a series of punches on the nose. I wonder if Professor Toynbee is as intimately attuned to his sources. The Sweet Science is joined onto the past like a man's arm to his shoulder."

Only the daft or the sacrilegious would dare suggest that there has ever been a better paragraph written on boxing. It is funny, stylish, slyly irreverent, brimming with information, and, above all, affectionate. Those were the hallmarks of Liebling's work and they enticed the *Police Gazette* set to read his stuff in the usually forbidding pages of the *New Yorker*.

Seventeen years after his premature death at the age of fifty-nine, there are still those of us who won't be satisfied until we have devoured his every word not just on boxing but on war and food, politics and newspapers, Chicago and other foreign ports. We prowl secondhand bookstores hoping to discover a dusty copy of his beloved *Between Meals*, and we cherish the Lieblingesque nuggets we find squirreled away in the damnedest places. In New York, for example, there is a sportswriter named Stan Isaacs, an elfin scamp who in his formative years covered some of the same fights Liebling did. Their friendship remained a secret, however, until the teetotaling Isaacs invited Vic Ziegel, a scribe of the nonteetotaling persuasion, to meet him in a sleazy Eighth Avenue saloon.

"Stan," Ziegel said after he walked in and got a load of the dump, "why here?"

"Joe liked it," Isaacs replied.

That was all he had to say. To Ziegel, to anyone with good taste in boxing chroniclers, Liebling will always be Joe. He will always be the bald fat man whose feet jiggled merrily when he wrote a good line, the unpretentious adventurer who enjoyed an honest rainmaker as much as he did a commodious greasy spoon.

But until recently we never thought we would know any more about him; he seemed doomed to remain America's unacknowledged literary genius, cursed because he was a journalist instead of a novelist. And then Raymond Sokolov, nominally a food writer (how the perpetually hungry Liebling would have loved that), rescued him with a biography called *Wayward Reporter*.

The critics have debated the book's virtues loudly and not entirely favorably, but true Liebling devotees refuse to be deterred. There is much to know about their hero and now they know it—the good as well as the bad, the funny as well as the sad. Abbott Joseph Liebling was kicked out of Dartmouth for missing chapel once too often and fired by the *New York Times* for playing games in small print. He considered newspaper editors to be tools of the devil and nicknamed Chicago "The Second City" because he couldn't see any place finishing ahead of his native New York. He was a sucker for racehorses and women, and neither treated him well, especially the women. They left him with little for company except the gluttonous meals that eventually killed him—a tragic end for an affectionate soul.

If *Wayward Reporter* does nothing else for Liebling's memory, perhaps it will encourage people to hunt up *The Sweet Science*, the collection of his nonpareil boxing tapestries. Therein lies the true measure of the man called Joe. He could make you smile by describing a fighter "so hairy that when knocked down he looks like a rug." But when he studied the antique Archie Moore fruit-lessly trying to knock out Rocky Marciano, he refused to scoff. "Would Ahab have been content merely to go the distance with the White Whale?" he asked.

It takes a special talent to put words—and feelings—like those on paper. And no matter how beset by personal despair he may have been, Joe Liebling must have known what he was to the *New Yorker* and its readers. Quite simply, he was irreplaceable, as the late Jack Murphy, a splendid wordsmith from San Diego, discovered when he went knocking on the magazine's door.

"So what is it you'd like to write for us?" asked William Shawn, the editor.

"Boxing," Murphy replied.

"I'm sorry," Shawn said, "but we stopped covering boxing when Joe died."

In time the New Yorker *let boxing back into its pages. Murphy, Bill Barich, and its current editor, David Remnick, have all written memorably about the sport. But the champion, as I'm sure they would tell you, is still Liebling.*

Mark Kram
Poet and Provocateur

msnbc.com
June 25, 2002

It seems right to remember Mark Kram as a poet of the dark nights in sports. He wrote as though he believed that the best stories, like the best songs, are the sad ones, and sometimes he lived sad stories himself. He knew perhaps more than he should have about pain, failure, and disgrace, but given time and inspiration, he could transform them all into things of beauty. When you read Mark Kram, even when his subject was a crowd screaming for blood, you could always hear an old jazz band playing.

The idea was to write the way Edward Hopper painted: to capture in words the world of a one-eyed welterweight or a football cripple or a Depression-era refugee with HARD LUCK tattooed on his knuckles. Kram succeeded with a majesty that endured until his heart gave up on him in Washington DC, this month. The last piece he published before his death at sixty-nine, in the April issue of GQ, was about a boxer brought to New York for a fight he had no business taking, a fight that cost him his life. "Bee Scotland didn't have a chance in this velvet alley," Kram wrote.

Losers, lost causes, and long-shot players formed a holy trinity for Kram, who worshipped at no altar but that of good writing. Yet his best work was devoted to Muhammad Ali and Joe Frazier, two heavyweights whose rivalry transcended sports and mesmerized the planet. Ali brought magic, charm, and, yes, cruelty to their bloody equation, but it was the fierce, unpolished Frazier who forced Ali to find out just how brave and great a boxer he was. And Kram, more than any other writer, embraced the nobility that enabled Frazier to do so.

Just last year, in his book *Ghosts of Manila*, Kram made an elegant plea for the world to understand that the ex-slaughterhouse laborer nicknamed Smokin' Joe was every bit as great in his way as Ali. But Kram expended far more effort attempting to debunk Ali's legend beyond boxing, to knock him off his pedestal as a cultural and sociological force who raised black pride, championed an unpopular religion, and helped turn public opinion against the war in Vietnam. Sometimes angry, sometimes bitter, sometimes wrong (or so it says here), the result brought Kram, ever the provocateur, back to center stage.

For many of us, however—readers and writers who came of age in the sixties and seventies—his presence there had always been assured by his coverage of the third and final Ali-Frazier fight, the Thrilla in Manila, which moved him to take sportswriting where it has rarely gone. First, he found Ali at a victory dinner in the Philippines' royal palace: "The maddest of existentialists, one of the great surrealists of our time, the king of all he sees, Ali had never before appeared so vulnerable and fragile, so pitiably unmajestic, so far from the universe that he claims as his alone."

Frazier, meanwhile, was exiled in darkness that would lift only when his wounded eyes healed. "Another light was turned on, but still Frazier could not see," Kram wrote. "The scene cannot be forgotten; this good and gallant man lying there, embodying the remains of a will never before seen in a ring, a will that had carried him so far—and now surely too far."

Those words live on in a variety of anthologies, but they were written for *Sports Illustrated* in the wake of that 1975 fight. *SI* was where Kram did more than make his name; he established himself as the grandest stylist on a staff embarrassingly rich in talent. Indeed, it can be said that Kram's stablemates—Dan Jenkins, Frank Deford, Bud Shrake, Roy Blount—have all enjoyed greater long-term success than he did. Maybe they had more drive or better breaks, maybe lighter hearts or fewer demons. But for turning journalism into literature, there was no one whose dust Kram had to eat.

His passing received no mention in *SI*, though. There were obituaries in the *New York Times*, the *Washington Post*, and the *Sun*, in Baltimore, the city of his birth, but not a word in the magazine where he helped set the standard for excellence. The only possible explanation was that he left *SI* in disgrace twenty-five years ago, and that to say good-bye now would open old wounds.

The story of Kram's departure has been fiercely debated. Money, vulnerability, and ethics come to play in it. So does Don King, the Barnumesque boxing promoter who seems a comic figure until he has a hand on your wallet or your soul. Perhaps vindictive editors were involved, too. It all depends on your level of paranoia and your interpretation of guilt. Whatever really happened, Kram was left down and out for the second time in his life.

The first time was when he was a minor league baseball player, a kid second baseman in North Dakota laid low by a fastball that hit him in the head. Suddenly, his dreams were replaced by the fear that kept him from playing the game again. Without benefit of a college degree, he flimflammed his way into a job at the *Baltimore Sun*, educated himself with books of his own choosing, and began to develop the moody, visceral writing style that people would remember long after his days at *SI* were done.

They remembered what he wrote about a bibulous home-run hitter named Hack Wilson. And about the long gone days when sports traveled by train. And about the lunch-bucket guys who wouldn't abide anybody knocking their Baltimore when the 1966 World Series came to town: "They say it next to draft beer and a sports section opened to the racing page. From which the eyes never veer. Looking for a number or looking for a chance to make tomorrow different from today, or just looking. By bar light or kitchen light, by neon or track light, with racing page or scratch sheet, with money or no money."

Even when Kram had disappeared into the strange, anonymous world of writing books that are quickly remaindered and scripts for movies that never get made, there were magazine editors who couldn't forget his work. Rob Fleder, then of *Playboy*, was one. Dave Hirshey, then of *Esquire*, was another. They sought out Kram and brought him back to the glossy pages where he shined brightest. Tolerated his obstinacy and irascibility and came to grips with his fear of flying and his loathing of the pronoun "I." And watched him shake his fist at the world.

But the person who did the most for Kram's career was his son Mark, himself a high-minded craftsman for the *Philadelphia Daily News'* sports section. He stuck up for his old man, encouraged him, goaded him. Most important perhaps, the son never doubted him.

You could say Mark Jr.'s reward was all that his father accomplished in the last decade of his life—the consistently regal magazine pieces, the defiantly contentious Ali-Frazier book, the promise of another book, this one a meditation on fear. But there was something better than all that: the two of them in Memphis for the Lennox Lewis–Mike Tyson fight, kicking around the barbeque joints together, visiting Graceland, then driving out to the Mississippi crossroads where Robert Johnson is said to have done business with the devil.

The trip was Mark Kram's reward, too. When he went home, it was to die without warning, but also with a head full of good memories. After all the hard times, there had been laughter. After all the darkness, light.

F. X. Toole
One Tough Baby

Sports Illustrated
January 31, 2005

You come away from this movie called *Million Dollar Baby* feeling as though you just watched a hell of a fighter who never makes you think about all the rounds he sparred, all the roadwork, all the lonely hours before he wrapped himself in the crowd's roar. There's Hilary Swank as a hard-punching trailer-park refugee and Clint Eastwood as her never-seen-the-mountaintop trainer, two dreamers trying to fill the empty places in their lives with hardscrabble nobility. You've got Morgan Freeman, too, playing a washed-up main eventer who needs only his one good eye to see the size of their hearts, and how primed those hearts are for breaking. And it all seems so easy, with those glossy names and their Academy Award talent, and that's where *Million Dollar Baby* fools you, because easy is the last thing it ever was.

Getting the movie made was a four-year ordeal that didn't become a mortal lock even when Eastwood signed on in 2004 to star and direct. There was still all kinds of wheeling and dealing to be done after that—nothing as bad as Don King and Bob Arum eyeing each other's jugulars and reaching for their sharpest cutlery but enough to have everybody who loved the project back on their heels.

And yet they were in the fast lane compared with the writer upon whose short stories the movie is based. It wasn't just that F. X. Toole died before he could learn that *Million Dollar Baby* was finally in front of the camera. It was that his one shot at Hollywood represented a lifetime of waiting.

Toole spent his last twenty-two years working with fighters, tending their cuts, and mainlining the brutal, beautiful truth about boxing that he put into words he wasn't sure anyone else would ever read. He didn't sell his first story until he was sixty-nine. The San Francisco literary journal *Zyzzyva* paid him thirty-five dollars for "The Monkey Look," a story about a cutman's revenge on a fighter who's trying to cheat him. Toole took the editor a gooseberry pie, the kind his mother taught him to make. And that might have been that if he hadn't knocked out a New York literary agent with the pure American vernacular of his story, starting with the first sentence: "I stop blood." The agent, Nat Sobel, called and asked if he'd written anything else.

There was a long answer to the question, one that stretched over four decades, but the short one, the right one, can be found in *Rope Burns: Stories from the Corner,* the book that transformed Toole, at seventy, from literary tomato can to champion. It was 2000, and suddenly he was being praised in all the right places, doing readings and interviews, talking shop with big hitters like Joyce Carol Oates and James Ellroy. And love it though he did — nobody ever paid more dues — he always went back to the world in which he found Maggie Fitzgerald and Frankie Dunn and Eddie "Scrap-Iron" DuPris, the characters that were his alone before Swank, Eastwood, and Freeman climbed into their skin.

But nobody in any gym in Los Angeles knew an F. X. Toole. Then they'd hear about the guy's close-cropped white hair, and the beard and glasses and nice clothes, and the only old dude who fit that description was Jerry Boyd. Yeah, they'd been knowing Jerry Boyd since that day in '78 when he became the whitest white boy who ever set foot in the Olympic Gym before it got turned into a parking lot.

Boyd was forty-eight years old, and the writing game had him beat, and he was seeking sanctuary in a black and Latino province.

He looked around, and then he approached Dub Huntley, who had turned to training in the late sixties when a detached retina rendered him a former middleweight contender. Boyd wanted an education in the ring, and he was willing to pay. Huntley said it wasn't necessary, although he didn't think his charity would last long. "When I went home that night," he says, "I told my wife, 'I'm gonna run this white boy out of the gym.'"

Never happened. Huntley put Boyd through the hell he put every fighter through: punching mitts, big bag, speed bag, jump rope. But he couldn't make Boyd quit, and Boyd was nine years his junior, a middle-aged man with a head for boxing and the patience to teach others what Huntley taught him. Somewhere along the line, he learned how to care for cuts, too. And pretty soon Huntley had himself a partner in the corner, handling worthy L.A. fighters like Antoine Byrd and Hector Lopez. "I can't see things too good," Huntley says, "so Jerry saw them for me. 'Dub, he's dropping his hands.' Or, 'Dub, he ain't turning his feet.'" When you rely on a man that much and he never lets you down, the only thing you can do is become friends.

Huntley learned a lot about Boyd in their time together. Some of it had to do with Boyd's bad ticker and how open-heart surgery had sent him back to the Catholic Church. And some of it had to do with his three children and his three busted marriages, the second of which was annulled a week after the honeymoon. But mostly Boyd talked about living the kind of life that led to rum running and risking everything for a torch singer's kiss. He came out of L.A.'s South Bay as a gambling-den bootblack and studied acting in New York. He drove cabs and tended bar, fought bulls in Mexico—got gored twice—and had half his right ear bitten off in a street fight that ended when he almost ripped out one of the other guy's eyes. He worked as a private investigator and packed a gun because, as he told his oldest son, Gannon, "If somebody's going to take me out, I'm going to take them with me."

The only secret he seems to have kept was his writing. When he was finally a published author—after forty years of rejection slips for novels, short stories, children's stories, screenplays, stage plays, poems, and songs—he feared spooking his fighters and his P.I. clients. So he borrowed from Francis Xavier, the sixteenth-century Jesuit philosopher-saint, and actor Peter O'Toole, a rogue of longstanding. But his pen name didn't spare him a moment of truth in the gym.

He had dedicated *Rope Burns* to Huntley, calling him "my daddy in boxing," but Huntley wasn't sure what to think until he made his way through the stories and realized how much a part of them he was. Not just "Million $$$ Baby," but the others, too.

"Jerry had wrote down everything," he says.

It's awards season in the movie business, and *Million Dollar Baby* has already picked up a batch of them, the biggest so far being best picture from the National Society of Film Critics and Golden Globes for Swank's acting and Eastwood's directing. The one that really counts, though, is the Oscar, but while everybody waits for that big night in February, there's talk about an unofficial title: greatest boxing movie ever.

There aren't many contenders—and no, *Rocky* doesn't make the cut. A great boxing movie comes from a darker place than *Rocky* did, a place as real as a thumb in the eye and as unforgiving as a referee counting ten over a fighter whose dreams have just been savaged. You can see the essence of the species in 1947's *Body and Soul*, with John Garfield as an up-from-the-slums champion who defies the gangsters who own him and refuses to take a dive, saying, "What ya gonna do, kill me? Everybody dies." Thirty-three years later Martin Scorsese's *Raging Bull* stepped up beside it, more for the director's artistry than for any warmth generated by its subject, Jake LaMotta, a real-life fight-fixing, wife-beating middleweight champ. As Barney Nagler, the late blood-sport chronicler, said of LaMotta: "He was a prick the day he was born, and he'll be a prick the day he dies."

Fighters of that description and champions of any kind cannot be found in *Fat City*, John Huston's 1972 adaptation of the haunting Leonard Gardner novel that captured boxing at its tank-town bottom. The kid and the has-been at the movie's unvanquished heart look like losers consigned to the same sports-section agate as the denizens of *Million Dollar Baby*. But anyone who has spent time around the fight game knows you don't sneer at men and women who risk their lives every time they step in the ring.

Five years ago it became clear that Anjelica Huston had grasped the message of her father's movie when she called Al Ruddy, one of those unlikely Hollywood producers with a reputation for caring as much about a great yarn as he does about the bottom line. Huston had a short story she wanted him to read, "Million $$$ Baby," by someone named F. X. Toole. "If you don't cry," she said, "don't call me back."

Ruddy cried. And he called back. Then he tracked down Nat Sobel, the literary agent, and listened to stories that painted Toole as a wild Irishman who had boiled over when a deal to sell *Rope Burns* to HBO for a series of boxing movies blew up. No stranger to unhappy writers — Hollywood is overrun with them — Ruddy phoned Toole and invited him for a drink. "I don't drink," Toole said. "I'm in AA." But he made it to the Havana in Beverly Hills just the same and, Ruddy says, "We got plastered."

By the time they wobbled back outside, they had forged the beginning of a friendship that only got stronger until death intervened. Toole liked the fact that Ruddy had won an Academy Award for producing *The Godfather* — Toole had worked as a bouncer in a joint in New York alongside one of the movie's actors — but Ruddy's credits ran far beyond Don Corleone, to such hits as *The Longest Yard* and all the *Cannonball Run* movies.

Ultimately, however, Toole cared only for what Ruddy could do for his boxing stories. "You couldn't bullshit the guy," Ruddy says. "He was a Jesuit, a really hard-edged intellectual Catholic."

Armed with the forty-two pages of "Million $$$ Baby," Ruddy spent four years beating his head against the wall that Hollywood has made of a two-letter word: no. "I couldn't get anybody interested," he says, "and I'm talking about people who are friends of mine, people I've done business with for years. They'd tell me, 'Who wants to see a movie about two old grizzled guys and a girl fighter?'"

They were still balking when Eastwood agreed to direct and star, a load he swore he'd never take on again at seventy-four until he read the script that Paul Haggis had woven out of "Million $$$ Baby" and "Frozen Water," another story from *Rope Burns*. "It's a downer," Eastwood told Ruddy, "but, God, it's gorgeous." His sentiment echoed that of Swank and Freeman when they had signed on earlier. But sentiment counts in Hollywood only when it sells tickets. When Toole died in 2002, studios, including Warner Bros., Eastwood's home base, were still refusing to back the movie alone. Not until the Lakeshore Entertainment Group stepped up to go fifty-fifty with Warners on the thirty-million-dollar budget did Ruddy get his deal.

Then everything happened in a rush. Filming started last June and wrapped in August, two days ahead of the forty-day schedule. There was a drive to get the movie out by Christmas so it would qualify for the Oscars. And Ruddy entered the hospital for the prostate cancer surgery he had put off. He doesn't talk about it for public consumption now that he's back on the prowl for his next project, but word gets around, and when you hear it, you realize just how right he was for the movie. And for Toole.

No one can say for sure who the inspiration for Maggie Fitzgerald was. Jerry Boyd did see her, though—*after* he had written the story. It happened three years ago, when he was helping Huntley train a woman named Juli Crockett. Ever since she had climbed off the deck and won a bout in San Diego, he'd been telling Dub, "That white girl can fight." And then one day he was hanging around the L.A. Boxing Club, hard by a street called Hope, and he found Crockett reading Kierkegaard, the Danish existentialist champion. "Who are you?" he said.

She had a master's in experimental theater and designs on a PhD in philosophy, hardly subjects that Maggie would have wrapped her head around. But there were other connections. Crockett, from Alabama by way of Florida, had hillbilly roots like Maggie's, and they shared missing fathers, too. And the longer Boyd looked, the more he saw that she also had Maggie's build, hair, and smile. There was even a sad ending awaiting her in the ring, though nothing as tragic as Maggie's, just a shoulder and legs bum enough to make her quit. But before that happened, Boyd made up his mind about who she was. "I was the incarnation of this character he'd created," Crockett says. Sometimes life works backward that way.

☆ ☆ ☆

September 2002. Boyd and Huntley had a fighter on a card coming up in Vegas. When they walked to the parking lot behind the gym, Huntley thought they'd be talking about their guy's chances.

"I'm not going with you," Boyd said.

"You're not?"

"I want you to take care of business."

"You *know* I'm gonna."

"But, Dub, I want to tell you one thing: I love you."

Huntley comes from the South, and these were words he'd never imagined hearing from a white man. But Boyd was as good a friend as you get, no matter what kind of paint job he had. Looked out for Huntley when he was the only black man in a bar, brought doughnuts when they watched the fights at Huntley's place, took

Huntley and his wife to dinner at the Hotel Bel-Air—and they'd never been anyplace nicer than that.

"I love you, too," Huntley said.

Boyd was pacing in a tight circle now, saying, "I love you, I love you." Tears were streaming down the face of this man who never backed up even when his age said he should, and the sight unnerved Huntley. He could deal with a woman crying, almost expected it. A man was something else.

"You've always been my friend," Boyd said. "I swear to God I love you."

"I know you do."

"I love you," Boyd said. "I love you."

It was only when Huntley saw him next, comatose in a hospital bed, dying of pneumonia, that he realized Boyd had been telling him good-bye.

✯ ✯ ✯

The photo was taken when Jack Boyd was six or seven months old. Someday he will learn all about the man posing with him, the one who's wearing a floppy hat just like his. Jack is three now, he has had dinner and a bath, and he's asleep, unperturbed by the biblical rain pounding Southern California. His father is on the phone talking about how maybe he'll read some of Jack's grandfather's stories to him when he's six or seven. "The easier ones," Gannon Boyd says. Jack can tackle the tougher stuff when he's in high school, and his father can explain F. X. Toole. And then there will be *Million Dollar Baby*, with the crotchety old trainer who has a taste for lemon pie and hectors his priest and gives his heart to the fighter he loves like a daughter. Jack's father will help him sort it out, let him know it's not a chapter from his grandfather's life. But it is—and Jack should always remember this—the essence of his grandfather's soul.

5

Sweet Scientists

Marvelous Marvin Hagler
The Proud Warrior

Philadelphia Daily News
April 16, 1985

LAS VEGAS—Blood cascaded down Marvelous Marvin Hagler's nose, leaving a stripe thick enough to divide a highway. And yet the sight and feel of the relentless crimson ooze moved Hagler in a way that bore no relation to anything modern, automated, or federally funded. Suddenly he was jerked out of 1985 and back into a time when warriors wore loincloths instead of boxing trunks and did their hunting without benefit of eight-ounce gloves. He was a primitive and that splash down the middle of his face wasn't blood. It was war paint.

The more it flowed, the more savage Hagler became. And the more savage he became, the more you wondered if this hellish explosion hadn't been building inside him for all of his thirty years. Or is he really thirty-two, the way Thomas Hearns kept insisting? For all Hearns knew, Hagler might have been born two thousand years ago if the violence that poured out of him last night was any measure. And there was no time for Hearns to renew the debate now.

He was trapped inside the third-round nightmare that would end his dream of becoming the world's middleweight champion. The roar of the crowd had moved him to try slugging it out with Hagler, and now it was an angry, unbearable hum in his ears. Every time he tried to take a step to safety, Hagler was there punching him—punching, punching, punching until the spidery challenger must have thought he was trapped in a thunderstorm of leather.

This wasn't the way anyone expected Hagler to fight. Hagler was supposed to be cautious in the early rounds, jabbing, moving in and out, a conservative who would make Ronald Reagan look like a socialist by comparison. That was why the champion had looked so bad in groping to a decision over Roberto Duran thirteen months ago. That was why Hearns's stock had skyrocketed when he caught Duran on the rebound and splattered that vicious little wharf rat across the canvas like a bad painting. But it counted for nothing now as Hagler turned the gaudy outdoor ring behind Caesars Palace into the kind of hellhole the beautiful people aren't supposed to know about.

As Bo Derek, Joan Rivers, and a host of TV stars who aren't worthy of the name gaped and gawked, the champion woke up memories of dingy arenas where the air is solid cigar smoke, human flesh is the leading commodity, and the showers never work. It can be a miserable business, the fight racket, and maybe Hearns forgot that inescapable truth when he got a load of the money he and Hagler were making. The price tags on this one were $5.6 million for the champion and $5.4 million for the challenger, and you can get your head turned around by a payday like that. You can think you are better than you really are. You can think your sweat doesn't stink. And if you do, your thoughts aren't worth a penny.

"Tommy is very cocky," said Hagler, who knows that fortunes don't come easily, "and I had something for him."

Make that some *things*.

The first of them was a leaping right hand that sent Hearns reeling across the ring. Then there was another right that sailed over gloves that were barely at half-mast and bounced the challenger's brain around the inside of his noggin. Hagler punctuated the barrage with a left hand that missed—what an irony for a great southpaw puncher—and then he went back to his right for the last time. Hearns was done.

He lay on the canvas with nothing moving except his heaving chest as referee Richard Steele stood above him, tolling his destiny. At nine he was up, but it didn't matter. "His eyes were glazed and his legs were wobbly," Steele said. There was no point in pushing the issue beyond 2:01 of the third round. Thomas Hearns was finished and Marvelous Marvin Hagler was still champion.

"Yeah, I'm still the champion," he said. "But I had to fight like a challenger."

And he was magnificent.

So was Hearns—for a while. Maybe he was just setting himself up for what matchmaker Teddy Brenner called "a tomahawk followed by an ax." Maybe he was just giving Sugar Ray Leonard, the only other man to beat him, an opening to belittle him "for thinking he could knock everybody out." But the first round that he and Hagler wove last night was a tapestry of violence—beautiful, beguiling violence.

They went for each other's throats, and they refused to retreat. If Hagler was rattling Hearns's ribs, Hearns was hammering Hagler's head. If Hearns was making Hagler taste blood, Hagler was filling Hearns's mouth with a fist. Back and forth they went, never pausing for a break, never looking for a break. The result wasn't Pryor and Arguello. It wasn't Ali and Frazier. It wasn't Robinson and LaMotta. It was all of them rolled into one.

Just as he had said he would, the five-nine-and-a-half Hagler turned into a giant. He was giving away four years in age, three and a half inches in height, and three and a half inches in reach, and none of it mattered. He got cut on the forehead in the first—"A butt," grumbled one of his trainers, Pat Petronelli—and that didn't matter, either. He was getting bigger and bigger, and as the round thundered to an end, he whacked Hearns with a left that drove him into a neutral corner and widened his eyes with surprise and unwanted knowledge. Now the challenger knew who the boss was.

"Marvin took away Tommy's right hand, that was the key," Petronelli said. "He ran right through that right hand, and when he knew he could do that, he knew he could do anything. He took away Tommy's legs and he took away Tommy's heart."

The only thing that could have stopped Hagler was his own blood. It poured from the gash in his forehead, and there was more to come when Hearns opened the scar tissue under his right eye. The ring physician studied the damage between the first and second rounds, and the referee did likewise at the start of the third. But Hagler—the single-minded destroyer who had WAR written on the baseball cap he wore throughout training—never paused in his attack. "I was afraid they might stop the fight," he said, "but you know, when I see blood, I turn into a bull."

So Hagler raged and Hearns fell in the round he had predicted for the victory that eluded him. The challenger wound up helpless in the referee's arms and the champion moved within three of Carlos Monzon's record of fourteen successful title defenses. And that was as it should have been. "I hope Tommy will say I'm the better man now," Hagler said. Whether the loser did or didn't hardly mattered, though. The rest of the world knew the truth—the world that Hagler rules as king of the middleweights.

Never mind that this was the sixty-fifth fight of his career. He had never been royalty before. But when he walked into his postfight press conference, he was embraced by the new major domo at Caesars Palace. And everything around him seemed musical, even the sound of promoter Bob Arum introducing the sagging Hearns while he, Marvelous Marvin Hagler, donned his championship finery in the sanctuary of his dressing room. Hagler was moving at his own pace now, deciding when he would step back outside into the loving glow of the television lights, enjoying it all so much that he scarcely noticed the stretcher he passed on his way out the door and into the night. No stretchers for him. Only a chariot would do.

Sugar Ray Robinson
He Gave Style a Name

Sport
December 1986

The name lives because of the man who wore it first and best.
He made being called Sugar Ray a badge of honor and a symbol
of high style, and the rush to bask in his reflected glory is like
nothing sports has ever seen. Every Snider need not be a Duke,
nor does every Stan have to be the Man, but if you are a Ray and
young, gifted, and black, Sugar is in your destiny. Look at Leonard, look at Seales, look at Richardson—each a Sugar Ray, each
fated in his own way to chase a legend who will never be caught.
For there really is only one Sugar Ray. The original. Sugar Ray
Robinson.

He was a world champion once as a welterweight and five
times as a middleweight, and even if you never saw him with a
crown atop his head, you knew Robinson was special. He put his
name in lights over a Harlem nightclub and double-parked his
pink Lincoln Continental wherever he pleased. He surrounded
himself with an entourage before anyone knew what an entourage was, had his locks tended home and away by his personal
barber, pulled out of a dozen fights at the last minute, and once
showed up three days late for a national television appearance.
How did he dare? The roar of the crowd told Sugar Ray Robinson it wasn't any dare at all.

He knew his place in boxing's stratosphere and he cherished
it with a zeal that should make all the latter-day Sugar Rays glad

they never had to tangle with him. So should the rascals who pass themselves off as just Sugar, for Robinson didn't cotton to them, either. When he fought George "Sugar" Costner in 1950, Robinson interrupted the referee's pre-fight instructions to say, "Listen, Costner, there's only *one* Sugar, and that's me. So let's touch gloves now, man, because this is your last round." And it was. Flat on his back lay just plain George.

As Robinson made his way from dressing room to ring, admirers in arenas around the world reacted as if they were iron shavings and he was a lodestone. From a distance, his magnetism could be traced to his regal bearing. "The guy moved like a prince or a king," says Angelo Dundee, who twice marched Carmen Basilio off to battle the Sugar Man. Up close, the attraction may have been that Robinson looked more like a movie star than someone who would risk his profile in 201 professional fights. Muhammad Ali may have anointed himself Dark Gable, but it was Sugar Ray who looked the part. "The women," says Ben Bentley, the venerable Chicago fight publicist, "were aghast."

Maybe Bentley is trying to enhance his reputation as a malaprop artist here. Then again, *aghast* may be the perfect word, considering that Sugar Ray forever flirted with scar tissue against Rocky Graziano and Kid Gavilan, Fritzie Zivic and Sammy Angott, not to mention Jake LaMotta, who lost four of his five bouts with Robinson and came away sputtering, "I fought Sugar Ray so many times it's a wonder I didn't get diabetes."

Robinson was a majestic figure in the ring, up on his toes like a ballet dancer, maneuvering his opponent this way and that, calculating every punch he threw. "An architect," Bentley calls him. Barney Nagler, the fight racket's reigning historian, concurs by saying, "He could build a house and then he could wreck it." Sometimes Sugar Ray did the damage with a left to the body, sometimes a right to the chin, but always there was artistry that, Nagler says, "spoiled you for every fighter you saw afterward."

When Robinson embarked on his twenty-five-year career in 1940, there were no world champions with eight fights, no multimillionaire champions who couldn't take up half a column in *The Ring Record Book*. A fighter had to be a fighter, and Robinson measured up handsomely. "He didn't get a shot at a title until his seventy-sixth fight," says Teddy Brenner, the erstwhile Madison Square Garden matchmaker. "How many of these guys today even have seventy-six fights?" Better yet, think how few of them could survive the gauntlet Robinson ran in 1943, when he lost for the first time as a pro, to LaMotta, and came back to beat bullish Jake in a rematch twenty-one days later—after pausing to pick up a victory against Jackie Wilson. Want to say they don't make them like Sugar Ray Robinson anymore? Go ahead, because they don't.

★ ★ ★

On such a foundation rests the case that, pound for pound, Robinson was the greatest prizefighter ever. He was a better welterweight than a middleweight, but it was as a middleweight that the world watched him longest. And though he pushed his tenure in that division far beyond his prime and passion, he still provided moments that haven't faded yet.

The cutoff point, according to Brenner, was his ill-fated run at Joey Maxim's light-heavyweight championship on a stifling night in 1952. The heat leveled referee Ruby Goldstein first, then it sucked the life out of Sugar Ray. It was the only time in his career he was knocked out. "After that," Brenner says, "he was just a good fighter masquerading as Ray Robinson." There were scrapes with the Army and the IRS, championships won and lost, retirements and comebacks, dalliances with show business and basketball's Harlem Magicians, and, ultimately, an extended fade-out that found Robinson sticking his head out of the shower in places like Tijuana and Steubenville and asking, "What's that cat's name I fought tonight?"

With Sugar Ray's name, of course, the story was different. Sugar Ray's name always sparkled like the biggest diamond at Tiffany's no matter what happened to the man himself. When you see him today, for instance, 65 years old, sad and sickly, protected by a wife who never lets strangers get too close, you can't believe it's possible. Only if he were still called Walker Smith could your eyes be telling the truth. But he left Walker Smith behind when he swapped AAU cards with a retired fighter back home in Detroit long, long ago and began the creation of Sugar Ray Robinson, who was like no other.

Joe Louis
Larger Than Life or Death

Chicago Sun-Times
April 13, 1981

He probably never realized how dank and dimly lit the basement hallway was. On his way to the ring, everything in Chicago Stadium must have been a furious blur—his handlers surrounding him protectively while he stared at the floor and contemplated the violence that was about to come pouring out of him. And as he returned to the dressing room tasting the fruits of victory again, he made people wonder if he even noticed that his magic filled the hallway with the candlepower it lacked. Maybe that was why it seemed drearier than ever Sunday. Joe Louis was dead.

The news arrived as you waited outside the Boston Celtics' dressing room, poised to wade into another victory celebration and swathe another hero in rococo prose. It is a strange business, this deciding who's to bless and who's to blame, who's a story and who's history, but with Joe Louis, there was never a question.

He was a champion for all time, a man who was remembered as the sleek, sleepy-eyed Brown Bomber even when he was up to his thick neck in unpaid taxes and the demons in his mind were telling him that the walls had ears.

The last of his sixty-six years on earth trapped him in a wheelchair, left him leaning on a nurse who could dab the sweat off his brow, but the people who saw him being rolled up to ringside for the fights in Las Vegas never varied in their reaction. "Hi, champ," they would say, just the way the awed and the innocent did when he was the greatest heavyweight who ever laced on a pair of eight-ounce gloves. The thick middle didn't matter; neither did the cowboy hat that hid his bald head. Until his heart gave out, Joe Louis managed to retain the magnetism that was best illustrated when he ventured onto the Soviet side of the Berlin Wall in 1967, long after his first fight, and watched his guide aim a camera at him.

"No pictures, no pictures!" shouted a Soviet lieutenant, rushing over in a haughty rage.

Then he recognized the object of his imperiousness.

In a minute, all the lieutenant's soldiers were taking Joe Louis's picture.

There couldn't have been a more natural response, for Joseph Louis Barrow Jr. was bigger than boundary lines, bigger than color lines, bigger than any barrier that ever confronted him. The unlettered son of an Alabama sharecropper, he became a champion that America's white power structure wasn't ready for. Only Jack Johnson before him had been black, and Johnson had been written off as a self-destructive aberration. But Joe Louis was different. "He came forth," the Reverend Jesse Jackson once said, "and the cotton curtain came down."

Nothing and nobody could withstand the power in his fists. He beat Buddy Baer and Tommy Fall, Jersey Joe Walcott and Two-ton Tony Galento—beat them so badly that Galento was moved to pugilistic hyperbole. "He musta used an ice pick," growled fat Tony. And the beauty of Joe Louis was that he didn't deny his greatness, didn't try to hide behind artificial modesty. Just remember what he said as he prepared to stalk the clever, courageous Billy Conn: "He can run, but he can't hide." The man wasted neither words nor punches. But his gift didn't flower until after he had lost to Hitler's pet heavyweight, Max Schmeling, and heard the cry of Aryan supremacy.

They met a second time after Joe Louis had won his championship, and in Archery, Georgia, the black hired hands at Earl Carter's farm gathered round the boss's radio to listen. The fight ended in one round with Schmeling stretched on Madison Square Garden's hallowed canvas and Joe Louis vindicated. Swiftly, quietly, the hired hands went back to their shacks. "All the curious, accepted proprieties of a racially segregated society had been preserved," Earl Carter's son Jimmy wrote years later as he pursued the presidency. They were preserved, that is, until the hired hands were alone, and then there came a shout of joy that Jimmy Carter heard all night long.

At last, Black America had a hero whom white people couldn't ignore. Joe Louis was a great athlete and more. He never ducked a challenge, provided psychological relief from the Depression, answered the nation's call to duty during World War II. And all the while he was showing his brothers and sisters by skin that it was possible to rise above the hate and squalor that was supposed to be theirs for eternity.

It was for other pioneers to integrate schools and get blacks on the voting rolls—to move to the front of the bus, if you will. What Joe Louis announced was that the future would not be monochromatic. When it finally arrived, though, he had become a tragic figure. His millions had been squandered, he struggled with drugs and the Internal Revenue Service, and he fought to keep his sanity. The best job he could find was as a greeter at Caesars Palace, and though the gawkers still called him champ, they told themselves he didn't matter anymore.

Maybe all of us did until his big heart began short-circuiting three years ago, and it became obvious that Joe Louis was not forever. Suddenly, there were high-rollers in Vegas willing to fly him to the world's foremost heart specialists. Frank Sinatra snapped his fingers and every bright light in Hollywood turned

out for a banquet in the champ's honor.It was as if everybody realized we were about to lose an irreplaceable natural resource.

The inevitable finally happened Sunday, just as you knew it
would the night you saw Joe Louis on the dais next to Sinatra,
shivering in a wheelchair, waiting for someone to pull a blanket tight around him. He was helpless, and yet he wasn't. As a
fighter and a human being, he had been something that even
death won't erase. He was too big for it, just as he was too big
for life. What better way, then, to remember him? The candle is
out, but the light still shines.

Tony Zale
Raise Your Glass to a Teetotaler

Chicago Sun-Times
April 30, 1984

So the champion's people rolled into the gym and what they saw was not the Tony Zale who would wage such unforgettable wars against Rocky Graziano, and become the first middleweight since Stanley Ketchel to win the world title twice, and hear Frank Sinatra praising him from a Las Vegas stage. What the champion's people saw was a boxer who bore a much closer resemblance to Anthony Florian Zaleski, the mill worker from Gary, Indiana, who could change his name but not the fact that he once lost three straight fights to guys you never heard of.

He was on the road to nowhere in 1940 and he was getting there fast. "A durable opponent, that's what he was becoming," says his old friend Ben Bentley. Opponent is boxing's way of describing someone who isn't supposed to have any more future than a filet mignon in a logging camp.

To watch Zale in the gym even in his glory days was to wonder how he ever won a round, much less a fight. His lack of elegance had nothing to do with deception or sloth. It was just one of those things. But the champion's people didn't take that into account when someone suggested that their man, Al Hostak, could get some useful non-title exercise against Zale. "This is what they said," Bentley says. "They said, 'Do you think the commission would approve it?'"

Bentley looks at Tony Zale sitting there listening in a stuffy room in a South Side gym, and then he looks at Zale's wife, Philomena. "Am I telling the truth?" he asks. "Is this a true story?"

Zale nods that it is.

Philomena starts to say something.

But Bentley says, "Lemme finish the story," and now there is no stopping him. He was the publicity man at the Stadium and Marigold Gardens when boxing was big in Chicago and Tony Zale was establishing himself as somebody. He was there when Zale won a ten-round decision over Hostak and the champion's people demanded a rematch, for the title, on their turf in Seattle. "It was a fatal mistake," Bentley says. Zale, suddenly aware of the potential in his fists, didn't risk waiting for any out-of-town judges to put the National Boxing Association crown on his head. He knocked out Hostak in the thirteenth round.

"So they're on the plane back from Seattle, right?" Bentley says. "And they run into this terrible storm. The baggage is flying around and people are heaving, and Art Winch, who was one of Tony's managers, he's down on the floor with his crucifix, praying. He figures it's all over, and he looks back behind him and there's Tony doing the crossword puzzle. If I'm lying, I'm dying. That right, Tony?"

"I look at it this way," Zale says, smiling as serenely as anyone can after ninety fights. "God's will be done."

There is a beauty about his philosophy that belies the savagery with which Tony Zale hammered out his reputation. Though he dealt in pain—former champion Billy Soose said Zale's body shots were "like having a hot poker stuck in you"—he tempered the deeds that put him on pages 659 and 660 of *The Ring Record Book* with a beguiling sense of decency. Never is that more apparent than in the tale behind his latest honor.

When the seventy-year-old Zale is inducted into the Chicago Sports Hall of Fame Thursday night with hors d'oeuvres and high-flown oratory, he will have gotten there the way he wanted to. "The right way," Philomena Zale says. The wrong way, as far as her husband is concerned, would have been to go into the hall when a beer company sponsored his big night. For he was never a drinker and he always told the kids he trained to lay off alcohol. Damned if he was going to be a hypocrite just to get his name on another plaque.

"Why, when they put Tony in the Boxing Hall of Fame, they had movie stars there," his wife says. "He's in the Polish Hall of Fame, too, and one up in Canada and another one in New York, and they're trying to get him in New Jersey. But to be in all the other hall of fames and not the one in Chicago was not flattering. He had to stick up for what he believed, though. If he had gone chasing after it, it wouldn't have been of no value."

Now Tony Zale has two kinds of satisfaction. First, he can sleep nights knowing that he is being honored by the Chicago Park District, which still employs him as a boxing instructor. Second, he can take pride in knowing he has been honored at last by the city where he fought his first amateur bout, and tried out for the 1932 Olympic team, and achieved greatness by holding up his end of the most glorious series of fights the sweet science saw in the forties.

Oddly, the only fight Zale lost in his three world title bouts with Rocky Graziano was the one they had in Chicago. It came after Zale had knocked the Rock kicking in New York, and it ended with Graziano in a rage because he thought his bleeding purple balloon of a right eye had forced the referee to stop the festivities in the sixth round. When he finally realized he had been declared the winner by technical knockout, Graziano celebrated with a unique turn of phrase: "I like Chicago. They trut me good."

Zale, of course, had plans for treating Graziano badly. "Somebody asked me right away if I wanted a rematch," he says, "and I said, 'Sure, I'll knock him out in three.'" Zale did, too. He starched

Graziano in Newark and secured his place in boxing history by regaining the championship. He made a friend out of Graziano as well. "Oh yes," Philomena Zale says. "Rocky still calls, and when they do appearances together, Rocky makes sure Tony gets the same price he does."

The equal money is a compliment and a sign of affection, but to hear Zale talk about a chance encounter he had with Sugar Ray Robinson is to wonder if everything must have a price tag. The year was 1950, Zale was retired, and there was Sugar Ray, pompadoured, preening, and seemingly primed for action. "He saw me," Zale says, "and he said, 'Hey, Tony, they offered me a lot of money to fight you. Thank God I didn't take it.'"

"You would have destroyed him," Philomena says.

And Tony Zale, who has always relied on God's will, just smiles.

Paddy Flood
One of a Kind

Chicago Sun-Times
April 1, 1983

It was easy to get the wrong idea about Paddy Flood. He dressed like he was just out of stir and his language would have made a dockworker blush. When he fired up a cigarette, he left it dangling from a corner of his mouth, the smoke swirling into his eyes and giving him a sinister squint that matched his broken nose perfectly. A memorable figure, Paddy, and the amazing thing was, you knew exactly how he looked just by listening to him on the phone.

"You mother lover. You egg sucker."

This was the way Paddy began a lot of long-distance conversations in 1977, when sportswriters around the country began to realize that he and his partner, Al Braverman, had discovered a new way to mint money. They were bamboozling promoter Don King and ABC-TV's Roone Arledge with a bit of hocus-pocus called the U.S. Boxing Championships, and when they called their critics, they remained true to form. They reversed the charges.

"You're gonna be buried in the desert," Paddy cooed more than once to the *Las Vegas Sun*'s Mike Marley. "You're gonna be out at some testing site and nobody's gonna find you, not even the buzzards."

"Paddy, Paddy," Braverman would cry in anguish. "Wait a minute, Paddy. You're out of line. Now, Michael, you know we love you. We know you love boxing. And what you have to realize is, anything that's wrong is because of this egg sucker King. See, Paddy? I told you Michael's not a bad kid."

"He's an egg sucker," Paddy would mutter.

"See, Michael?" Braverman would say. "I've got him cooled off already."

It went on that way for weeks, and after the initial shock wore off, Marley actually looked forward to his regular dose of good guy, bad guy. When he moved to New York for a turn at the surrealistic *Post*, he liked the idea of being on Paddy Flood's turf and took it as a badge of honor when Paddy spit at him the first time they met. If that sounds implausible, Marley destroyed all doubts the other day when he called from his new digs at ABC and said, "Every time people remember Paddy, they'll laugh." From this point on, remembering is all anyone can do. Paddy Flood is dead at forty-eight.

He had always suffered from jackhammer headaches that he never talked about much, and Sunday one of them flattened him while he was watching Larry Holmes at work on television. Twenty-four hours later, Paddy's doctors were calling him the victim of a massive brain hemorrhage, and his favorite fighter, Mustafa Hamsho, was falling to his knees and wailing with grief.

The outpouring of emotion would have touched Paddy, but he never would have admitted it. "Foggin' cuckoo," he would have grumbled, just the way he did when Hamsho crowed that he was ready to die in his futile quest for Marvelous Marvin Hagler's middleweight championship.

That was a large part of Paddy Flood's appeal as a manager and trainer, though—he cared about his fighters enough to make them care about him. They bled and he held their hands when they got stitched up. None of them won a title, but most of them had a few decent paydays and then went on to be solid citizens, even cops, like Irish Bobby O'Brien. And the unlucky ones? Paddy looked after them, too.

Every time dazed and dreamy Ray Elson wandered into New York's Grammercy Gym, Paddy would slip him a fin and think about the night Elson lost a middleweight war to Victor Galindez in Madison Square Garden. Paddy was out watching the next fight when his sawed-off cornerman, Tony Canzi, tugged at his sleeve. "You gotta talk to Elson," Canzi said. "He's taking a shower and his girlfriend is in there with him."

A lopsided grin split Paddy's face. "Hey, Tony," he said. "The kid just fought his heart out. Let him go."

No one had to tell Paddy Flood what kind of business he was in. He knew only too well. "It's the most treacherous, dirtiest, vicious, cheatingest game in the world." And the wise guy from New York's Upper East Side survived because he sank to the occasion when he had to and laughed at the bums in power the rest of the time. "You know what I tell Bob Arum and Don King?" he once said. "I tell them, 'You oughta be in the gas chamber, both of youse.' What the fog, they know it. It's just a big foggin' joke, boxing, that's all."

So Paddy took nothing seriously—not the sharp operators who moved in from other dodges, not the ex-convict heavyweight he punched out for menacing Mustafa Hamsho, not even Chuck Wepner's woebegone attempts to keep his dukes up against Muhammad Ali. "I'm blocking punches," Wepner announced in his corner and Paddy stopped mopping up the blood to say, "Yeah, I can tell you're blocking them—with your nose. If it wasn't for your nose, your face would be taking a helluva beating."

It should come as no surprise, then, to hear that Paddy didn't genuflect at the thought of death. Even when he was lying in his wife's arms on the next to last day of his life, he was mumbling about taking a nine-count, getting up, and fighting to a draw. He just wasn't ready for the obituary page, nor, to be honest, was the obituary page ready for him.

"These newspapers really must love this," he said when he looked up from his paper one morning.

"What's that?" his unsuspecting straight man asked.

"You know, how these egg suckers die in alphabetical order every day."

God, we're going to miss him.

Sugar Ray Leonard
The One-Eyed Man

Chicago Sun-Times
September 17, 1981

LAS VEGAS—After all those miles and all those smiles, Sugar
Ray Leonard wasn't pretty anymore. He was a one-eyed man in
an ugly fight that had nothing to do with the glitz and glamour
that have become his calling card. There had been a time when
he could have avoided this grim marathon, a time in the sixth
and seventh rounds when he could have added Thomas Hearns
to his list of victims. But the moment had passed and Hearns
had escaped, and now Sugar Ray Leonard, his handsome face a
scowling bruise, was struggling for survival.

It was the thirteenth round Wednesday night, and the catcalls
had begun to fill the outdoor stadium behind Caesars Palace.
There were twenty-five thousand people baking in the remnants
of another hundred-degree afternoon, each of them seemingly
intent on proclaiming Hearns a winner and Leonard a loser. In
those opening seconds, you could see why as Hearns kept jabbing and moving and Leonard kept looking for a place to throw
his right hand and never finding it. The frustration smoldered in
his one good eye, smoldered almost hypnotically.

Then it was gone.

And so was Hearns.

The bomb that caught him was a right to the head that he never
saw. Suddenly, the hit man from Detroit was on Queer Street,
weaving under a flurry of lefts and rights, bouncing from one side

of the ring to the other until Leonard bulled him through the ropes and onto his back. Hearns escaped without getting charged with a knockdown thanks to the largesse of referee Davey Pearl, only to find himself back on the second strand thirty seconds later.

"Off the rope," Pearl shouted.

The weary, wobbly Hearns refused the order with a shake of his head. He would not move until Pearl started counting, and he would never be the same.

Maybe the fight should have ended there, maybe Hearns should have been spared more punishment and Leonard the reason to deliver it. But that is not the way the sweet science operates, not when the guy getting his brains scrambled is ahead on the judges' scorecards by two, three, and four points. So on the beating went into the fourteenth round, on until Leonard had Hearns helpless against the ropes once again, on until a minute and forty-five seconds were gone and Pearl had no choice but to say that Hearns was undefeated no more.

Sugar Ray, the sweet slugger from Palmer Park, Maryland, was the winner by dint of a technical knockout and a quality he had never before had to use so heavily.

"I had to dig down in my guts," he said when nine million dollars, a 31-1 record, and both of the world's welterweight titles were his. "I knew I was behind. I knew I had to keep the pressure on. There wasn't anything I could do but find out what was inside of me."

Leonard was looking at the world through dark glasses. Under normal circumstances, you would have called them the trappings of America's busiest athletic celebrity. But on a night that found Muhammad Ali, Burt Reynolds, and Charo shoulder to shoulder at ringside, Leonard had bigger things to worry about than his image. "I suffered a slight injury to my left eye during workouts," he said, "and Hearns kept jabbing it." By the fifth round,

Sugar Ray had a mouse the size of a small bagel. By the twelfth, it was a question of whether he could see at all. And even when Hearns had been dragged back to his dressing room, Leonard still squinted painfully at the glory surrounding him.

There had never been a fight like this, financially if not artistically. With three hundred million people around the world watching on closed-circuit television and pay TV and who knows how many more waiting for the delayed videotape, the Leonard-Hearns showdown could gross as much as forty million dollars by the time the last penny is counted. Add to that the six million dollars that the Caesars crowd paid for tickets ranging from fifty to five hundred dollars and you have the makings of a grand welterweight coronation.

The bookmakers had predicted the occasion would belong to Hearns. After being on the short end of the gamblers' good faith until two days before the fight, the snake-quick 145-pounder became a 6-5 favorite to add Leonard's World Boxing Council title to the one he already owned from the World Boxing Association. It made you wonder if the wise guys knew something the rest of the world didn't. When you saw Leonard enter the ring timidly Wednesday night, your doubts turned to outright fears.

For the first five rounds, the six-foot-one Hearns was in command, stinging Leonard with his jab and keeping his shorter opponent at bay with his vaunted seventy-eight-inch reach. Unable to get inside where he wanted to operate, Leonard had to fight outside, and he paid for it in pain. Not until the sixth round could he solve Hearns' surprisingly good defense, and then he did it with a vengeance. A left hook to the head inaugurated the assault, and after that, there was no telling what Leonard was throwing, just that he was throwing everything.

"He did something nobody ever did before," trainer Angelo Dundee said. "He was a better puncher than Tommy Hearns."

The record book shows that Hearns had thirty knockouts in his thirty-two victories, and thirty knockouts is a whopping figure until you realize that he had never fought anyone like Sugar Ray Leonard. Nor had he ever fought so long in such withering heat. No wonder he was in trouble again in the seventh, no wonder his long legs looked like rubber. But the greatest wonder of all was that Leonard, master strategist though he is, let Hearns off the hook.

It could have been fatal when you think back to how Hearns rallied in the next three rounds, keeping Leonard off balance with his jab and becoming the stalker once again. In the far reaches of the stadium, the faithful from Detroit started chanting "Tommy, Tommy!" before the twelfth, and Hearns leaped off his stool to wave them on. Little did he know what Leonard had in store for him one round later.

Afterward, the fight judges would marvel at the savage beauty of Sugar Ray's surprise attack. They would talk about the lifeless glaze that came over Hearns' face when Leonard finally found the room to throw the combinations he had been saving all night. He used them until they were wretched excess and then he just banged away with his right hand. Twenty-three unanswered punches, one judge said. Twenty-eight, said another. The debate would range long into the night, and when it was over, there would be only one point everyone could agree on. Sugar Ray Leonard, the one-eyed man, never missed his target.

Ray Arcel
A Touch of Class

Chicago Sun-Times
June 19, 1980

MONTREAL—It was a glimpse of the future and Ray Arcel refused to believe it. He had left the fight racket with his head caved in nearly two decades before, and now, on an autumn night in 1972, he was back in Madison Square Garden for the first time since then, just catering to a whim, nothing more.

He had come to see the main event—that much he remembers. But the pugs who were in it have long since been forgotten, both of them replaced in his memory by a scrawny Panamanian upstart who steamrollered his opponent with one punch and raced directly to the corner where Arcel's wife was sitting. They shook hands, the boxer and the lady who had never seen him before, and off to the side, Ray Arcel did something he thought was beyond him in a fight palace of any description. He smiled.

"People don't realize how good Roberto Duran can make you feel," he says now. "But right away I told myself, 'This isn't some ordinary street urchin. This kid's decent. He's very decent.'"

The retired trainer's kind words, however, were supposed to be the signal of two ships passing in the night.

Hard experience had taught Arcel not to dream that eight years later he would have Duran knocking on glory's door for the second time in his career. But that is precisely the case, for Friday night the erstwhile lightweight champion will attempt to dethrone Sugar Ray Leonard, the king of the World Boxing Council's welterweights. It is a classic story of an aging fighter seeking the recognition that has always eluded him, and the tale is made all the more enchanting by the presence of Arcel, who is eighty-one years old and getting younger by the minute.

True to form, he refuses to acknowledge his status as a geron-tological marvel. "Everybody keeps coming up and telling me how much they want to meet me," he says. "Who the hell am I? I'm a bum." The last person who believed that was the strong-arm man who dented his skull with an iron pipe.

The year was 1953. Arcel was out of the training dodge then, busily putting together *The Saturday Night Fights* for television as an antidote to the wretched excesses of Frankie Carbo, Blinky Palermo, and the rest of boxing's riffraff. There were faster ways to make a buck, but Arcel was content to mine the talent he found in the outposts beyond New York City. So it was that he went to Boston on Yom Kippur, spent the Jewish holy day worshipping in a temple near the arena, and walked outside to meet the cru-elest surprise of his life.

"I was just taking a little recess, you know," he says, "and I saw the manager of one of the guys fighting for me that night. So we're standing there on the corner talking, and all of a sudden, *bang!*"

When the pipe crashed down on him from behind and Arcel sagged to the sidewalk, a chill fell over boxing. This wasn't another fast-talker from New York, you see; this was a gentleman who gave the sport grace, dignity, and, most of all, a sense of history.

To trace Ray Arcel's career, you must go back to 1917, when he was an undersized preliminary boy fighting for the most el-emental of reasons: "I came from the only Jewish family on a block of Italians." Greatness eluded him, but he did get to know Benny Leonard's cousin. And not long after that, he got to know Leonard himself. And not long after that, he was training the mesmerizing lightweight in his comeback. Before Leonard was done, he had become the first of the eighteen champions Arcel has called his own.

The number is so astounding that it overwhelms the memories Arcel carries around in mint condition. Memories of a heavyweight who couldn't outrun him when he was fifty. Memories of a washed-up journeyman who upset a hotshot in Detroit and was embraced by the notorious Purple Gang. Memories of Angelo Dundee, Sugar Ray Leonard's trainer, carrying towels in the forties. All kinds of memories, but the people want champions, so Arcel delivers.

Let's see, there was Tony Zale and Barney Ross, Jim Braddock and Billy Soose, Frankie Genaro and Ezzard Charles. The list goes on, but Arcel stops at Charles. "He had Rocky Marciano beat, you know," he says. "Ripped Marciano's nose wide open. I thought they were going to stop the fight. But Freddie Brown fixed the cut up and Marciano came out and put Charles on ice."

Arcel shakes his head, a half-smile playing on his face.

"Funny, huh?"

Funny because now Freddie Brown, at seventy-one, works in Roberto Duran's corner, too, and he is there because Arcel couldn't stay retired. Arcel tried, though. He was clean for eighteen years after his battered head mended, contenting himself with his job as a purchasing agent for an alloy company. But that didn't matter to Carlos Eleta, the Panamanian millionaire for whom he had trained fighters after World War II. "Carlos wanted me to come down and work with a couple kids he had," Arcel says. "You know how they are in Panama: When they see you on the street, they don't shake hands, they shadow box." That is a roundabout way of admitting he couldn't say no to Eleta.

It was Arcel's good fortune, although no one realized it at first. The second kid in Eleta's stable was the little jawbreaker from Madison Square Garden, the one named Duran. He did not hit it off immediately with Arcel. "I remember telling Eleta, 'You are going to make me hate you,'" the trainer says. "He had given me a colt to ride and I'd never even been on a horse."

In time, Arcel learned. Oh, Duran still calls him and Brown "the crazy Americans," but the respect is there. It grew out of the patience the ancient cornermen had with this child of the Panama City streets, and the respect they have shown for his ability. "It wasn't anything we taught him," Arcel says. "He had it and it came out of him. The kid was another Jack Dempsey."

In a sport nourished by exaggeration, the temptation is to shrug off the comparison as just more bushwah. Yet something about Arcel moves his sincerity beyond reproach. Perhaps it is his refusal to be kept away from Montreal by age. "I'll be with Roberto until he packs it in," the old man says, and the pay will be the same as always. It will be nothing, because Ray Arcel figures the fighter has already rewarded him with greatness.

Roberto Duran
A Man of Stone

Chicago Sun-Times
June 15, 1980

MONTREAL—The legend does not serve Roberto Duran well. He has soared to the heavens of boxing, a sport in which simply escaping the gutter is an accomplishment, but the spotlight has done little beside capture his shadow. To people who should know better, Duran has remained a runty Panamanian savage who can drop a horse with one punch and has suffered loss after loss to the English language. And no doubt he would have gone to his athletic dotage neglected and misunderstood were he not where he is now, blinking in the reflected glory of Sugar Ray Leonard.

It shouldn't be like this, of course, this stealing into the public consciousness because a fighter five years his junior, with less than half his experience, deigns to give him a shot at the World Boxing Council's welterweight championship. Life isn't always fair, though, and the fight racket never is. So Duran must squirm indignantly while Leonard, back in Montreal, the scene of his Olympic triumphs, plays the lord of the manor.

Most of the time, the Sugar Man handles the role with consummate grace and intelligence, but every now and then the temptation to gloat and preen becomes too much to resist. Witness his act in New York at the press conference announcing the fight that will earn him ten million dollars and Duran two million. He stood tall on the dais and glared down at the opponent everyone in the room expected him to respect grudgingly.

"I want to kill you," Leonard said.

Duran did not need an explanation.

Even now, two months later, with the fight just five days away, he bristles at the thought of such insolence, such macho posturing. There is no calming him with Leonard's innocent plea that he was only trying to speak the little assassin's language. Indeed, there is nothing to do but flinch at the thoughts of vengeance those ill chosen words have aroused.

"If he wants to kill me," Duran says, "he has to stand up and fight."

A cold smile twists Duran's face into a death's head. It is the same smile so many of his victims have seen before he sent them reeling to the canvas, jaws unhinged, senses unraveled.

"How in hell is Leonard going to stand up and fight?"

Now Duran's eyes dance crazily.

"He'll be running once he feels my punch."

It is not for nothing, after all, that Roberto Duran is called *Manos de Piedra*. He has just what his nickname says he does—Hands of Stone—and if you doubt it, you need only think of the damage he has done while winning sixty-nine of seventy fights and knocking out fifty-five targets. "If the foundation crumbles," says the man in charge of demolition, "the building will come down." Lord, how he loves that sight, loves to break his opponents into small pieces and dance on the rubble.

When the once great Carlos Palomino fell before him, he sneered, "Quit. You don't got it no more." When Ray Lampkin got carted off to the hospital, the victor shouted that next he would get in shape and, yes, "kill him." Heartless cruelty perhaps, but in the Panama City slum where Roberto Duran grew to manhood, heartless cruelty was an impregnable defense against street-corner extinction.

He was a fighter from the start. Fighting went with carving out the turf where he shined shoes, peddled mangoes, and danced in saloons. He played the drums, too, and maybe he would have been the star of his high school band if he had survived that long in academia. But the third grade was it, and his hair-trigger right hand—what else?—was his undoing. He was thirteen years old.

Two years later, he stepped into the ring as a professional for the first time with a jockey as his manager and a zest for violence as his foremost weapon. The jockey soon vanished, selling Duran's contract to a millionaire sportsman named Carlos Eleta for the magnificent sum of three hundred dollars. The zest for violence remained, waiting for Duran to put together his two-fisted attack and flee Panama for Madison Square Garden. When he finally arrived there, in December 1971, the crowd belittled him as a skinny fraud until he knocked Benny Huertas still as death for six minutes. From that night on, people began to understand what Duran's hands were made of.

The stone in them destroyed everyone blocking his way, made him into the lightweight champion of the world, turned him into his native land's tax-exempt hero. But in the United States, where the money was, the coast-to-coast infatuation with heavyweights proved too much to overcome. "Small guys can't raise any hell," Muhammad Ali said. Duran happily proved otherwise until he ballooned into the welterweight division and became the butt of cruel jokes and insidious whispers. Since then, his knockout punch has disappeared and, at times, so has his enthusiasm.

"When you're fighting smear cases and you're the best fighter around," says Ray Arcel, the mouthpiece for Duran's brain trust, "it's hard to be interested."

Now that has changed. At twenty-nine, with the end rapidly closing in on him, Duran finds himself faced with a challenge so all-consuming that he doesn't care whether he steps into the ring as a two-to-one underdog or takes home only one-fifth as much money as Leonard. "I no happy for the money," Duran says. "I happy for the fight." Happy because this is his one real chance to wear another crown, to prove his greatness and to win the love he has been denied throughout his career.

On the surface, the need for love would seem totally foreign for Duran, and yet to see him being honored as one of the two fighters of the decade was to see the thing that could get him past Leonard. Never once did he fret that the New York boxing writers were abusing propriety by calling him Ali's equal. He had chills running down his spine, and he let it be known. "I speak English because I am learning from my teacher," he said. "I am glad to be here. I thank you very much for this reward." For just a moment those crazy eyes of his were calm and the room was quiet. For just a moment, you could tell what Roberto Duran will have on his side Friday night. Emotion.

He Cramped His Own Style

Chicago Sun-Times
January 27, 1982

Good times never last long enough and bad ones always last too long. Barbershop philosophers can explain the phenomenon in a minute, but Roberto Duran gives the impression that he doesn't hang around barbershops. He has a head of inky black hair that he combs straight back, hair so wild and shaggy that it must be modeled after his pet lion's mane. The ragged pompadour suggests a man in a hurry, and Duran certainly was that until he got trapped by a moment's indiscretion.

Just a moment, nothing more. Oh, he may have thought about quitting earlier in the fight that rewrote his life. Sugar Ray Leonard was carving the macho right out of him that November night in 1980, hitting him at will and making him swing wildly and laughing with delight. Never in his fierce, crazy life had anyone done that to the urchin revered at home in Panama as Hands of Stone. But when Duran finally did something about it, when he decided that two minutes and forty-four seconds of the eighth round was as long as he could stand to be humiliated, the good times stopped and the bad ones began.

He meekly waved his right fist and uttered the words that haunt him still: *"No mas!* No more!" They echoed through the funky streets outside the Louisiana Superdome and on into boxing's infamous history. True, Duran has argued ever since that he was done in by stomach cramps, not cowardice. But it doesn't matter. He failed himself and his image when the world was watching, and in that fleeting instant, the good he had done for a far longer time in a far lesser light was rendered inconsequential.

Suddenly, he was the fight racket's answer to Roy Riegels, who ran the wrong way with a Rose Bowl fumble; and Tracy Stallard, who got nailed to the cross of Roger Maris's sixty-first home run; and Ralph Branca, who fed Bobby Thomson the gopher ball that cost the Dodgers a pennant. Duran had done something so memorably bad that its brevity didn't matter. And now it has lived so long and thrived so relentlessly that it seems he never did anything else.

How else can you judge our reaction to his assault on Wilfred Benitez's WBC junior middleweight championship? They will fight in Las Vegas Saturday night—age against youth, savagery against subtlety, scowl against smile—and the chemistry should be all you are thinking about. But it isn't, and Duran knows it, and everyone around him knows it. They can tell at a glance that you are thinking about his fall from grace, if you are thinking about him at all.

"A tremendous tragedy, a great tragedy," says Ray Arcel, his eighty-two-year-old trainer. "I don't condemn him for what he did in New Orleans. But it was a tremendous tragedy."

In the fifteen months since then, there has been no place for the tale of how Duran was born to the slums of Panama City and how he shined shoes, caught fish, and fought off the thugs who tried to prey on him. Once, he was a success story fashioned by his fists, a street child whose incomparable punch made him the pet of Panama's president and its richest man. He flattened a horse with a straight right and almost killed the poor devil who opposed him in his Madison Square Garden debut. He was a pro at fifteen, the world's lightweight champ at twenty-one, the world's welterweight champ at Leonard's expense. He was truly Hands of Stone and then, in the rematch he sneeringly granted Sugar Ray, he showed his public what it never suspected he had—a heart of mush.

Even Arcel, who guarded him paternally before that debacle and has returned to do so now, wept bitter tears in the long hours afterward. "Duran quit," the old man said, and the quaver in his voice fueled resentment. It was as if Duran had betrayed the people who thrilled at his rage, painted him as the embodiment of violence, and bet their ranches on him. Now they were going to get him. They were going to make him pay for not being what they imagined him to be. And most of them haven't let up yet.

The reaction is human enough—who among us has not dreamed of revenge of one kind or another?—but it fails to take into account that maybe Duran is human, too. He doesn't always show it, of course. Indeed, you can find him in Las Vegas sneering at reporters who ask him about the night he quit and why he thinks Leonard should give him another shot at the welterweight title. The studied surliness is vintage Duran, yet it may also mask the desperation that has come to mark his life.

At thirty-one, eight years Benitez' senior, his powers are slipping away faster than he discovered them. Though he snarls at the suggestion, surely he must know it is true. It has been happening since his insatiable appetite pushed him into the welters, a weight class where his knockout punch lost its authority and his reputation began to lose its luster. Leonard drove that point home, but, lest you forget, so did Zeferino Gonzalez before that and Nino Gonzalez and Luigi Minchillo afterward. Now the lethal Benitez awaits him with a dose of punishment, but no one begs Duran to turn back before it is too late, no one offers him the kindness that soothed Muhammad Ali and Joe Louis and so many other fallen champions.

In one sense, that may only be fair, for Duran never offered anyone mercy. Violence was his key to boxing's kingdom and so it shall also be his destruction. The violence he suffers, however, comes not just from the men he fights but from the public he betrayed on a night that should be nothing more than a line in the record book. For a moment, he forgot he was Roberto Duran and waved the white flag of surrender. He waved it until he realized his mistake, but by then there was no escape. His shame would last him a lifetime.

Larry Holmes
His Time and No One Else's

Philadelphia Daily News
March 18, 1985

LAS VEGAS—He showed up peddling a dream. He brought it to newspaper sports departments from New York to Washington a decade ago, hustling like a carny barker and promising to become the world's heavyweight champion. Everyone who shook the hand that was always there for shaking thought, "Sure, kid." They had seen a hundred others just like him, and heard a hundred other stories about young fighters who didn't want to live in housing projects anymore and were tired of wasting away in a job at a car wash. And what made this kid different anyway?

Larry Holmes showed us.

He outgrew his cheap leather jacket and the body-and-fender man who was his manager, and he waited until he could get his shot at Ken Norton and win the title. He jumped into the swimming pool at Caesars Palace to celebrate that night in 1978, and when he emerged, he began a reign of greatness that only Joe Louis ever surpassed. And yet it was hard to give him his due, for he followed in Muhammad Ali's wake, and he had a propensity for walking into ominous right hands, and he had the nerve to insist that he could tell the time on his body clock better than anybody else. Larry Holmes wouldn't quit when the world beyond Easton, Pennsylvania, was urging him to. He had to knock out young David Bey here the other night, and then ask us to believe he is all but through with the International Boxing Federation title—on his terms.

Belief is the least we owe him.

After forty-seven professional fights and thirty-four knock-outs, eighteen title defenses, and thirty-five birthdays, maybe he really is tired.

Surely there was fatigue in his voice as he looked over his shoulder at Bey in their post-fight press conference and told the kid what awaits him if he gets to the top. "You're gonna have to go through the same stuff I did, somebody calling you names, challenging you," Holmes said. "The closer the fight gets, you ain't gonna be able to eat, you ain't gonna be able to sleep. All you gonna do is worry about that sucker coming after you."

No sooner was Bey out of the way, in fact, than World Boxing Association champion Greg Page was in the winner's face. Refusing to blush for having lost to Bey last August, he hauled his porcine form into the ring and began demanding a showdown with Holmes. And if it hadn't been Page, it would have been Pinklon Thomas, the World Boxing Council's champion, or Tony Tubbs, who has emerged as the hottest item in an ordinary crop of young heavyweights, or maybe even some character who is known only to his mother and his probation officer.

The routine has become standardized and predictable, and Holmes is as much to blame for that as anyone. It was he, after all, who set the tone for champ-baiting with the way he went after Ali.

Now he is at a different stage of his career—the twilight—and he neither seeks nor nurtures further challenges. He simply wants us to accept his fifth declaration of retirement as gospel truth. Had he been this adamant after his bloody, awkward effort against the undistinguished James "Bonecrusher" Smith four months ago, he would have found an agreeable audience. But he was so overwhelming against Bey, so strong and smart, that you have to wonder if he didn't become his own best argument against riding into the sunset.

Holmes made promoter Don King, who controls Thomas and Page, concede that he is indeed "the undisputed heavyweight champion of the world." What's more, he forced a lot of critics who wanted him out two years ago to concede that he could fight two more instead.

"Yes, I think he could do it," said Holmes's wise old trainer, Eddie Futch, "but I also think he'd be taking lumps he never took before. That's the problem when you reach Larry's age—everything starts to catch up with you. Those kids coming up through the ranks would keep getting better and better. And Larry wouldn't."

The ethic of the fight racket, however, requires the greatest warriors to be carried out on their shields. That was why there was such a stir when Roberto Duran surrendered meekly to Sugar Ray Leonard. Better he should be sent pitching to the canvas face-first and unconscious, the way he was by Thomas Hearns. There is almost something cleansing about seeing violence repaid with violence. And yet it was the saddest spectacle imaginable when Holmes beat Ali like a disobedient pup. Surely Holmes remembers that night, and hates his memories of it, and sees no reason to run the same risk himself.

His bank account tells him he is safe. He can joke about buying a Rolls-Royce for his two-year-old son, and he can say he will retire June 9, the seventh anniversary of his reign as champion, if no one comes up with the twenty-five million he wants for fighting Gerry Cooney or the three million he wants for fighting Michael Spinks. And he can afford to be as silly or as serious as he wishes.

"How do you want to be remembered?" someone asked him the other night.

"As one of the guys who saved his money," he said.

What a splendid epitaph in a sport where squandered fortunes are as common as broken noses. But it is not enough for Larry Holmes. And when he has disregarded caution, when he has been getting himself in the mood to do harm to another challenger, he has told us so himself. In those moments, it hasn't mattered that Eddie Futch ranks him just behind Joe Louis and Ali and just ahead of Joe Frazier. Holmes would certainly cherish such a place in history, but he wants to hear more than the sound of one hand clapping. He needs something to make up for the neglect that has dogged him throughout his championship run, the neglect he suffered because he lacked Ali's flash and Cooney's complexion.

"*Time* magazine," Holmes snorted when he discovered a reporter from that august publication at one of his pre-Bey workouts. "You know what *Time* magazine did when I was fighting Looney Cooney? They was ignoring me and writing about him. All these years I been heavyweight champion and they couldn't think of nothing to say about me."

For the longest time, Holmes was obsessed with such shabby treatment. The result was a bitter, nonstop rage that robbed him of his appeal. But now that boxing has come to mean less to him, now that he takes more joy from running hotels and restaurants than he does from separating other men from their senses, the demons no longer control him. "You can talk all you want about Ali and Joe Louis and Rocky Marciano," he says, "but they did what they had to do in their time. I've done what I had to do in my time. You understand that? *My* time." And that is where he leaves it.

As his long good-bye draws to a close, Larry Holmes has come to an understanding with himself. Pride keeps him from asking us to do the same, but there is no question about what he deserves after so many years of war.

Peace.

Muhammad Ali
No Garden Party

Chicago Daily News
September 29, 1977

NEW YORK—It had been a long time coming. Even Muhammad Ali, who is seemingly beyond blushing, must have been embarrassed by the delay. But at last there was a heavyweight championship fight that deserved the name.

The explanation for this startling development was so simple you would think someone would have thought of it before. What it boiled down to was that the other half of the human equation involving Ali was not Richard Dunn, a butterfly waiting for his wings to be picked off, nor was it Alfredo Evangelista, the walking Spanish omelet. It was Earnie Shavers, a brave man, a stubborn man, a tough man. And he was exactly what Ali needed to prove he can still deliver the quality on which he swears he has cornered the market—greatness.

True to form, Ali waited as long as he could before doing it Thursday night. For twelve rounds, he stuck just enough stiff left hands in Shavers's face to turn it an ugly purple and pile up the points he needed to walk out of the Madison Square Garden ring wearing his crown. Then he woke up as Shavers tried desperately to knock him out.

The thuggish-looking challenger, 211 pounds of muscle packed under a shining dome, stormed out for the thirteenth round and clouted Ali upside the head. "Hell, yeah, he hurt me," Ali said later. "He hurt me four or five times."

At least one more of those jolts came seconds after Shavers's first bomb. The rest came in the hailstorm that was the fourteenth.

Ali started the round by trying to show Shavers he hadn't been stunned. The ploy didn't work. Shavers went right back at him, tying him up against the ropes, banging away on Ali's kidneys, and chucking him under the chin on the break. Then Shavers really got down to business.

He sent a looping right hand to Ali's head. And another. And another. Ali went stumbling backward into Shavers's corner looking dazed, ready to be finished. But Shavers didn't move in. He stood ten feet away and stared at Ali as if it couldn't be true that he, Earnie Shavers, who just two years ago was fighting in dumpy gyms for a thousand grubby dollars, could have done such a thing.

"I thought he was faking," Shavers said afterward in the gentle, almost fluty voice that seems foreign to the rest of him. "He's a pretty good faker."

The problem was, Ali wasn't faking. "I was out on my feet," he said.

In Ali's corner, Angelo Dundee, the brains of the outfit, kept telling the champ it didn't matter. Dundee had a man in the dressing room watching the round-by-round scores as they were flashed on television, and he knew that Ali had the fight won if he could stay upright.

That was all Ali had to do. You had to wonder if he was up to it when Shavers raced out and popped him with the nastiest left he had the strength to throw.

Ali struck back with a left of his own. Shavers was more startled than hurt. Ali pumped two more lefts into his face. Now Shavers was hurt. Ali didn't need anyone to shout the news to him from his corner. He unlimbered the right hand he uses primarily for signing checks and rammed it upside Shavers's head. He was going for the kill. In a round that began with him in danger, in a round where he had to do nothing more than survive, he was putting on his greatest show since he and Joe Frazier gave us the Thrilla in Manila.

"He never hurt me bad," Shavers insisted. "I wasn't hurt."

If the round had lasted thirty seconds longer, Shavers would have known the truth. He would have been knocked out.

The brilliance of those final three minutes made a lot of things palatable afterward. You listened to Dundee say it was "the best fifteenth round I've seen in a long time," and you agreed with him.

"This is just Muhammad Ali," he said. "Muhammad always finds a way. He summons something up from out of nowhere and comes back. He's too much for all of us."

Even Ali, when he finally faced the press an hour and five minutes after he left the ring, had to be listened to seriously when he delivered his usual paean to himself. "I'm a courageous man," he said. "I have a whole lot of heart." Yes he does, and that is not all.

He has the ability to make us forget. Sad to say, there was much to be forgotten in this fight. There was the sleepwalking Ali did in the early rounds. There was the swing he took at Bundini Brown, his longtime good luck charm, after the fifth for telling him he should cut the comedy. There were the boos Ali heard when he tried to cover up some seventh-round soft-shoeing with a little showboating. And there were the boos Shavers's trainer, Frank Luca, is sure to hear for not being cagey enough to monitor the scoring on TV the way Dundee did.

It seems like an awful lot to be erased by just one round of boxing, just three minutes out of the lives of two men. But it happened, and when it was over, you realized something. Annoying as Muhammad Ali can be, you are going to miss him when he's gone.

Marching Off to Slaughter

Chicago Sun-Times
September 12, 1980

An old man's dream ended. A young man's vision of the future opened wide. Young men have visions, old men have dreams. But the place for old men to dream is beside the fire.
—RED SMITH, writing in 1951 after Rocky Marciano knocked out Joe Louis

Someone should show Muhammad Ali the pictures from that October night. They came out of Madison Square Garden bearing the awful truth about what happens to former heavyweight champions who forget their best is behind them. In one frame, Joe Louis is on his knees. In the next, he is outside the ropes, propped on one elbow. Finally, he is on his back, giving the world a lasting portrait of the bald, the paunchy, and the hopeless. He was thirty-seven, one year younger than Ali is now.

It would behoove Ali to think of that as he approaches October 2 and his first act of legal violence in two years. He should understand there is every chance that history will repeat itself in Las Vegas when he raises his fists against Larry Holmes, the king of the World Boxing Council. And maybe, God forbid, history will take a turn for the worse.

Remember, we are not going to see the Muhammad Ali who vanquished Leon Spinks in 1978 and walked away with an unprecedented third heavyweight title. The Ali now preparing to appear before us will be older and slower, and if he is not fat, he is odds-on to have stretch marks as a reminder of the blubber he has shed. But mere physical deterioration is not the greatest thing we have to fear. It would be wisest for us—and for Ali—to heed the warnings that his mind no longer sends messages to his muscles as fast as it used to, that the words that tumble out of his mouth ceaselessly are beginning to trip over one another.

Alas, we have no say in the matter and Ali has no apparent interest. He will not let himself be talked into retreat, even by those dearest to him. He has made a career of crusades, and now he gets a crusade that means far more than fighting tank-town exhibitions or even rewriting foreign policy for the Carter administration. The only question that remains is whether his inspiration stems from simple vanity or the eight million dollars promoter Don King is paying him to fight Holmes in the parking lot at Caesars Palace.

"The parking lot," King proclaims, "is symbolic of the humble beginnings of these two gladiators."

What poppycock.

If there is anything symbolic about the arena that has been erected where Cadillacs and Continentals usually dwell, it is that such places are usually the sites of the meanest, grimmest brawls imaginable. Just think of how many middle-aged men have forgotten themselves, yelled at young thugs in flashy cars, and wound up getting stomped bloody for their lack of diplomacy.

The fear in these quarters is that the loquacious Ali has become irreparably middle-aged himself and that Holmes, eight years his junior, couldn't care less about it. "I ain't gonna let Porky beat me," the champion says. Porky? It is Ali who is supposed to bequeath the demeaning nicknames on his opponents, not vice versa. But there you have the unfortunate truth: Holmes has thrown down the gauntlet and Ali is a poor choice to do anything about it.

Perhaps his chances would be better if he had not shot for the moon in his first fight out of retirement. Indeed, when he announced his intention to return to the ring last March, the sentiment here was wholeheartedly positive because he was making noises about meeting Big John Tate before he tried Holmes on for size. Unfortunately, Tate lost his World Boxing Association championship to Mike Weaver, and Ali lost his taste for adventure. If he fought Weaver and fared poorly, he might be denied his shot at Holmes. Ergo no eight million dollars. Ergo no test fights against lesser competition.

What awaits us then may be a mismatch on the order of cockroach versus heel. In one corner will be Holmes, undefeated after thirty-five fights and still close enough to the peak of his powers to be the most dangerous heavyweight in captivity. In the other corner will be Ali, two years away from throwing his last punch in anger and five years away from his last great fight, the Manila Thrilla against Joe Frazier. The longer you look at the two of them, the better Marciano-Louis seems, and Marciano-Louis was hardly the Hundred Years' War.

At bottom, the fight served as a steppingstone toward a championship for the relentless young punching machine from Brockton, Massachusetts, the one everybody called the Rock. But surely Louis couldn't believe that. He had lost his title to Ezzard Charles just a year before, and in the months since, he had fought eight times, each time facing a little tougher foe, each time telling himself he was regaining the sharpness of his youth.

Marciano needed just eight rounds to convince Louis otherwise, to point the old man toward his dreaming place beside the fire. "I'm real glad for myself," the Rock said when the deed was done, "but I'm real sorry for him." Louis had been knocked down by one left hook, knocked out by another, and knocked out of the ring by a right to the neck. For those long seconds that he lay on the ring apron, he was as sad and pitiful a sight as the fight racket has ever seen. But he did get up eventually, and he did walk back to his dressing room, however slowly.

Pray that Muhammad Ali does so well.

The closest thing to an execution I ever covered was the Ali-Holmes fight. Knowing that I had predicted such a beating for Ali gave me no satisfaction. I was outraged at the leeches in his camp who eagerly marched him out to face Holmes. But an even more loathsome figure was Ali's manager, Herbert Muhammad, who watched his meal ticket get his brains beat out before allowing Dundee to stop the fight. I like to think there's a special corner of hell reserved for Herbert Muhammad.

Ali! Ali! Ali!

GQ
April 1998

I remember a night in New York and Muhammad Ali doodling on a paper placemat, his heavyweight glory behind him and the bittersweet future daring him to step toward it. There would be a banquet later, then an award ceremony, and he would fall asleep between the two. Before he did, he nudged me and gestured at what he had wrought with a felt-tip pen and a water glass. It was a globe, complete with continents. "I used to be champion of all that," Ali whispered in a gentle rasp. Suddenly, I felt the way the nation, and maybe the entire world, would feel eleven years later when he carefully made his way out into the Atlanta night to light the Olympic torch. And yet, as I think about his words now, it seems that Ali, of all people, was understating the case. He was so much more than a champion.

He beat the kind of giants the fight game no longer breeds— Sonny Liston, Joe Frazier, the young and thuggish George Fore-man—but the true measure of the man was that he instinc-tively knew what to do afterward, when power and glory were his. No hiding behind the millions he earned, no morphing into the monster that success makes of so many in and out of sports. That would have been too easy, and Ali chose no easy paths in his life outside the boxing ring.

He shed the name Cassius Clay as if it were a slave master's shackles, he found peace in a religion that confounded the heartland's sensibilities, and he declined to wage war on a country that hadn't come looking for a fight. This was a free man in every sense, one who could inspire black Americans when pride became their rallying cry in the sixties. He taught them to believe in themselves, and he taught the rest of us to believe in him. And he made the nation laugh while he was doing it, gleefully tormenting Howard Cosell, performing magic tricks for delighted strangers, and astounding the future pooh-bahs at Harvard with what remains both history's shortest poem and the best description of his impact on society: "Me. / Whee!"

Transcending his sport, transcending all sports, Ali became the first truly global athlete. He took championship fights out of the traditional fleshpots and deposited them in Third World countries whose faraway villages needed no electricity to get word of his greatness. It didn't matter that he ruled the planet in those dark days before ESPN and marketing deals and the other phenomena that have turned his successors into international products instead of mere sports-page swashbucklers. He had himself, and that was enough. At the end of a century in which our relationship with sports has evolved from pastime to preoccupation, you can look as long and as hard as you want and never find anyone who is the equal of Muhammad Ali.

Only four men come close to matching his impact, which may seem a harsh judgment considering the multitude of heroes and champions we have anointed. But this counting is not solely about affection (Willie Mays and Mickey Mantle) or awe (Jim Brown and Wilt Chamberlain), nor is it about one bright, shining moment (Bobby Thomson) or even a career burnished with relentless excellence (Joe DiMaggio and Joe Montana and so many more). It is about all those things and the rare athletes who somehow climbed still higher to write their names so large that they actually forced a seismic shift in society.

The first was Babe Ruth, who drank bathtubs full of gin and bashed enough home runs to single-handedly save baseball from ruination after the Black Sox scandal. Seven decades later, his name is still evoked as a symbol of power, size, and strength, although never so colorfully as when Japanese soldiers taunted their American foes during World War II by shouting, "Fuck Babe Ruth!"

Joe Louis dealt in muscle, too, when he ruled the world's heavyweights and set the myth of black inferiority to crumbling. "He came forth," Jesse Jackson once said, "and the cotton curtain came down." But Louis never talked about it; silence was his style. It was the same proud silence that Jackie Robinson kept when he was breaking baseball's color line. Once that first season in Brooklyn was history, though, a different Robinson emerged, his voice suddenly as slashing as his style on the diamond. A lifetime of rage poured out of him, filtered by the Ozzie-and-Harriet fifties but still a harbinger of the thunder that Ali would shake down. Michael Jordan shows no sign of knowing about such righteous anger, for he is the ultimate modern athlete, a well-spoken, well-groomed tool of commerce as much as he is a force of nature when the Chicago Bulls absolutely need to win. No one has ever played better basketball than he does, and he may even have surpassed Ali in terms of worldwide impact. But Jordan uses his clout to peddle sneakers and star in unwatchable movies with Bugs Bunny, leaving the very distinct impression that he has the social consciousness of a baked potato.

Ali towers above the competition, despite his own dalliances with show business and roach-trap commercials. What may surprise you is that it isn't heart and soul that elevate him, though he possesses those qualities in abundance. It is, rather, intellectual courage, a rare concept in the nation's locker rooms, where the heaviest thinking tends to involve how many bimbos you can fit on the head of a pin. Though neither scholar nor autodidact,

Ali was not afraid of ideas, of the things that hang in the air un-seen, daring those who know they're there to do something with them. He took the dare, just as Robinson did before him, and he made more of it than any athlete ever has or maybe ever will.

Of course, his intellectual courage would mean nothing to us if he hadn't proved his physical courage first. He did it in our cru-elest sport. Boxing kills some men, and it scrambles the brains of others, and an army of doctors will tell you that it cursed Ali with Parkinson's syndrome. He used to joke about punchy fight-ers, saying no one would ever catch him walking on his heels and conducting his conversations in mumbles. There is a sad irony to his humor now that he moves through life in slow motion, but he couldn't have survived in the ring if his mind had been cali-brated any other way.

No heavyweight ever traveled a road more fraught with peril than Ali did. Even the second-tier contenders in his era made you realize how soft Mike Tyson and Evander Holyfield have had it. Just think of those old wallopers: Earnie Shavers, Doug Jones, Jerry Quarry, Jimmy Ellis, and the surprisingly memorable Ken Norton, who not only defeated Ali but broke his jaw in the pro-cess. Ali came back to avenge himself against Norton (barely), and he beat the rest of them, too, because that is what champions do.

He called himself "the Greatest," though when it comes to as-sessing modern-day prizefighters, that title may be too rich for those who embrace the savage artistry of Sugar Ray Robinson, a champion as both a welterweight and a middleweight. But as far as heavyweights go, only Joe Louis and Jack Johnson deserve to keep Ali's company in the same sentence, and Ali was bigger and faster than either of them. Lord, could he move. And that isn't the half of it. He could take a punch, a virtue admittedly with a severe downside, and he could improvise in the middle of a fight like Rodney Dangerfield in a club full of hecklers. If vic-tory lurked somewhere with a microbe's cunning, Ali would track it down, ever the sweet scientist. He did it when his right hand was dynamite and when it barely qualified as a popgun. He won as a big-mouthed kid from Louisville clinging to his gold medal from the Rome Olympics, and he won after losing prime time in his athletic life for refusing induction into the armed forces. He went through all those changes, and he never lost sight of the fact that he was a showman as well as a render of concussions. So it was that he fought some of the most memorable fights ever, fights that were the stuff of high drama, fights that riveted even those in our midst who take no joy from watching men deviate one another's septums.

He was still Cassius Marcellus Clay Jr., so easily dismissed as more prankster than contender, when he plucked the heavyweight crown off baleful Sonny Liston's noggin in 1964. What a wild ride that was, starting with his driving his bus onto the lawn of Liston's Denver home in the middle of the night to challenge the head-breaking ex-convict he called "a big, ugly bear." Came the weigh-in in Miami and his pulse rate more than doubled while he and his goofy shaman, Bundini Brown, shouted his trademark slogan: "Float like a butterfly, sting like a bee!" But he was doing neither when he came howling back to his corner at the end of the fourth round. He had been blinded by the caustic goo slathered on Liston's bum shoulder—no one ever identified it more precisely than that—and he wanted out. Fat chance. Angelo Dundee, the amiable pragmatist working his corner, did what he could to wipe away the goo and thrust Ali back into combat. Hell, this was for the championship. Two rounds later, Liston quit in his corner and Ali climbed the ropes to shout, "Eat your words!" at the sportswriters who had said he didn't have a prayer. It would not be the only time he gave them religion.

Still, the general reluctance to believe in him endured until he fought Liston again fifteen months later in a hockey rink in Lewiston, Maine. When they were finally in the ring, everything changed in, oh, let's call it a minute. That was all the time it took Ali to find an opening to throw what was either a perfect punch or the excuse Liston needed to take a dive. The fight racket's historians may never stop debating the right hand that couldn't have traveled more than four inches. But know this: No matter how loudly Ali challenged him once he went down—"Get up and fight, sucker!"—Liston stayed that way until the referee counted ten over him.

George Foreman was the other classic bully Ali left hoist on his snarl. Big George hardly fits the description now that he has assumed the role of boxing's jolly, cheeseburger-eating uncle. But in 1974 Foreman reveled in the meanness he had exported from Houston's bloody Fifth Ward. He was the undefeated champion by then, and after the way he had laid waste to Joe Frazier and Ken Norton, it looked as if he would rule until he grew bored or got locked up. Going to Zaire for his "Rumble in the Jungle" with Ali seemed an annoying formality. He grumped and glowered every step of the way, while Ali charmed the Africans he embraced as long-lost kin. Foreman's disposition didn't improve any when the fight had to be delayed six weeks after he was cut in a sparring session. Worst of all, he and Ali had to put up their dukes at four in the morning to accommodate the closed-circuit crowd back home—hardly a mood enhancer.

But the ultimate indignity for Foreman was the way Ali flummoxed him once they finally climbed into the ring. Ali even had a name for the flash of inspiration that struck him when he realized he didn't have the legs to dance for fifteen rounds. He called it the "Rope-a-Dope." Starting in the second, he leaned against the ropes and let Foreman blast away at his forearms and elbows. Nobody could believe what was happening, least of all Dundee, who had assumed until now that he was on the same wavelength as Ali. But this was a singular thinker at work, and by the sixth, what had seemed madness was being hailed as genius. Foreman

310 | SWEET SCIENTISTS

didn't have anything left—the danger in his punches had been used up. All that remained for Ali was to knock him out in the eighth so he could walk into the dawning day and do magic tricks for the African kids who had come to love him.

The fights that best defined Ali, however, were the three with Frazier. Here was Smokin' Joe, a sharecropper's son who punched his way from a job in a slaughterhouse to a heavyweight title of his own, and the purity of his vision in the ring touched something deep in Ali. When they did battle—and what transpired between deserves no less noble a phrase—it was never about money or a championship or any of the other things for which men beat one another senseless. Something far more personal was at work. It was as though, someone once said, Ali and Frazier were fighting for "the championship of each other."

Frazier hated Ali, and not without reason. Ali called him "ignorant." Ali called him "gorilla" and "Uncle Tom." Ali called him the white man's hope, when every aspect of Frazier's life had been shaped by his being poor and black. So it doesn't take much to imagine the rage with which Frazier stalked Ali the first time they fought. The year was 1971; the place was Madison Square Garden; the atmosphere was unlike anything you can possibly imagine for a fight today. The entire nation was swept up by the anticipation of what would happen between the undefeated Frazier and Ali, whose only loss up to this point had come at the hands of the U.S. government. Fifteen rounds later, Frazier had beaten Ali's handsome face lopsided and won a unanimous decision. But Ali salvaged something from the wreckage: respect. He found it in the final round, after Frazier dropped him with a left hook that Ali's unborn children must have felt. The easy thing would have been to lie there and be counted out. Ali couldn't do that, even though the fight was almost over and winning was out of the question. He climbed back to his feet and got punished some more. If there had been questions about his courage, they were answered right there.

Ali-Frazier II barely registers in memory. Neither man was a champion at the time, and the pre-fight scuffle they had on national television, with Howard Cosell ducking for cover, was in its bizarre way more interesting than the fight itself. But Ali won the unanimous decision this time, leaving them even and setting the stage for the legendary "Thrilla in Manila." Not that anyone anticipated greatness when the fight was made. Frazier was in small pieces after Foreman demolished him to take away his title. Ali had been coasting since he, in turn, had waylaid Foreman in Zaire. When he reached the Philippines, change didn't seem imminent. Just riding herd on his entourage, which numbered half a hundred and ran to the exotic, seemed a job that would have stymied Patton. And then there was his second marriage, crumbling while he frolicked publicly with Veronica Porche, the icy beauty who would become the next Mrs. Ali. But the sight of Frazier boring in on him one last time snapped everything back into focus.

It was a fight in three acts—classic Hollywood structure. When the curtain went up in the sweltering Araneta Coliseum, Ali greeted Frazier with a boxing lesson that lasted for the first four rounds, sticking and moving, even giving him a dose of his own left-hook medicine. Frazier ate one punch after another until his time arrived, and then, from the fifth round until the eleventh, he gave Ali a beating of biblical proportions. Ali tried to cover up against the ropes, but Frazier hammered his arms and body until they went soft and left his head an unprotected target. Asked afterward how he felt, Ali said, "Next to death."

Somehow he survived. Reaching down into the well of fury and courage that only Frazier could drive him to, Ali summoned three of the most magnificent rounds of his career. He pounded Frazier relentlessly, hammering the sweat off him in sheets, knocking his mouthpiece flying, and turning his face into a Halloween mask of lumps and bruises and blood. There would be no fifteenth round for Frazier; he stayed on his stool when the bell called him to action. In the winner's corner, with everyone who hadn't thrown a punch going nuts, Ali celebrated by sitting on a stool, wondering if his heart would explode.

If he had only stayed there, he might not be in the muzzy limbo where we find him now. Surely Frazier had inflicted enough damage to last Ali the rest of his days, just as he in turn had done to Frazier. But Ali was a fighter, and fighters fight, so he marched off to war for six more years. The low point was the beating he incurred in 1980 at the hands of Larry Holmes, once his sparring partner and before that a housing-project kid who was only too happy to stow away on the champ's bus. The last traces of Ali's boxing genius were pillaged that night in the parking lot outside Caesars Palace, and the prevailing emotion afterward was true sorrow. At the end of the line, Ali had achieved a state of grace with the public he had amused, agitated, enlightened, and sometimes simply scared to death.

Grace, however, was a long time coming, for he wasn't always an easy icon to love. There was, for one thing, the anger that poisoned his early fights, an anger far beyond whatever a boxer needs to function in that Darwinian environment. The beatings he inflicted on Floyd Patterson and Ernie Terrell for calling him Cassius Clay were cruel, even barbaric, and his ugly baiting of Frazier was mean-spirited and, far worse, completely unjustified. He was just as cruel to the wives who had to put up with his relentless philandering, although it would have taken a eunuch to resist the temptation he faced daily. But none of that roiled public sentiment as much as his entrance into the Nation of Islam, which smacked of nothing less than a black man's version of the Klan. In one instant, he was the Louisville Lip, sure to get busted open by Liston; in the next, he was the unlikely champion and Elijah Muhammad, the crusader who decried white devils, was bestowing a Muslim name on him. Whites, both devils and otherwise, suddenly looked at Ali as if he were the one who had sprouted horns and a tail.

It was only the beginning of the spiritual gauntlet he had to run. When he responded to his draft notice by saying, "Man, I ain't got no quarrel with them Vietcong," his world was turned upside down. There would be no conscientious-objector status for him on religious grounds; instead he was hit with the loss of his championship and a federal conviction in 1967 for refusing induction into the army. As far as boxing went, the next three and a half years vanished, but Ali persevered, touring college campuses to speak out on Vietnam, race, and religion. John Kennedy had been assassinated, and Bobby Kennedy and Martin Luther King were fated to cross paths with lunatic killers, and still Ali forged ahead, working the same territory as those brave souls. The FBI shadowed his every step, but that didn't stop him, either. He kept on telling the truth as he—an unlettered, basically apolitical man—knew it. And the truth set him free.

The sixties took care of the rest. It was a time for rebels, for Bob Dylan with his protest songs and Eugene McCarthy with his crusade against the war, and Ali was a perfect fit. The kids who delighted in scorning most everything else were the first to flock to the light he gave off. Their elders would follow in the years ahead, moved in part by the Supreme Court's unanimous decision to overturn his conviction, but primarily because he was able to move beyond the rage that had been so necessary. Then the holdouts embraced him the way they never would Jane Fonda, the sixties' other great celebrity rebel, or the contemporary athletes who think they honor his legacy by strutting and running their mouths.

No matter how his late-arriving admirers looked at him, Ali proved impossible to resist. Profile left, he was a three-time champ with a place in history outside the ring and a black man who, even at his most amusing, never let himself be hamstrung by the white man's world. From the right side, he was the movie-star handsome scamp who billed himself as "Dark Gable" and the deadpan joker who, when a pair of his boxing gloves were enshrined in the Smithsonian, asked, "You gonna put a rug in here?" Taken straight on, he was the dreamer who wanted to open soup kitchens for the poor around the country and the soft touch who had a thousand-dollar-a-day habit when it came to handouts.

Every time the spotlight that was always on him moved, it seemed to reveal something new about Ali, something worth study at the least, admiration at best. Yet all those angles and all those facets led to a single conclusion, and it endures to this day: He was exactly who he was put on earth to be. One of a kind. One for a century.

Source Acknowledgments

"Concrete Charlie," *Sports Illustrated*, September 6, 1993

"The Poetry of Silence," originally published as "Man of few words, but poetry in motion," *Chicago Daily News*, November 21, 1977

"A Country Boy Can Survive," originally published as "Bradshaw does what comes naturally," *Chicago Sun-Times*, January 22, 1979

"A Win, and a Coach, for All Time," originally published as "Staggering: Bryant bears win record," *Chicago Sun-Times*, November 29, 1981

"A World of Hurt," originally published as "Hampton's aches just a pain," *Chicago Sun-Times*, December 2, 1983

"Me and the Tooz," *Sports Illustrated*, February 2, 2004

"The Other Side of the Story," originally published as "Matuszak is a guy his mother can love," *Chicago Sun-Times*, December 13, 1981

"Runaway," originally published as "Riggins a chip off old blocks," *Chicago Sun-Times*, January 31, 1983

"A Kid Among Legends," originally published as "Young Marino Joins the Legends," *Philadelphia Daily News*, November 27, 1984 (Reprinted with permission of Philadelphia Newspapers, LLC.)

"Easy to Underestimate, Hard to Beat," originally published as "The MVP? None Other Than Joe Montana," *Philadelphia Daily News*, January 21, 1985 (Reprinted with permission of Philadelphia Newspapers, LLC.)

"Boola! Boola!," *GQ*, September 1986

"Out of the Past," originally published as "Living Is Easy for a Boy of Summer," *Baltimore Evening Sun*, October 9, 1974 (Reprinted with permission of the Baltimore Sun Media Group. All Rights Reserved.)

"The Man, Forever," originally published as "Stan still 'The Man' for all seasons, *Chicago Sun-Times*," September 21, 1982

"The Ego Is a Lonely Hunter," originally published as "Reggie's ego a lonely hunter," *Chicago Sun-Times*, October 13, 1978

"Pete Belongs in Cooperstown," *GQ*, September 1995 (Copyright © 1995 Conde Nast. All rights reserved. Originally published in *GQ*. Reprinted by permission.)

"On Second Thought," originally published as "A belated apology to Ryan from a reformed 'hit man,'" *National Sports Daily*, July 3, 1990

"Old Too Young," originally published as "Bench—what a way for benchmark career to end," *Chicago Sun-Times*, August 24, 1983

"The Earl of Baltimore," originally published as "Has Weaver sworn off sin?" *Chicago Sun-Times*, August 16, 1981

"The Toughest Loss of All," originally published as "Mauch Returns from Indifference," *Philadelphia Daily News*, March 8, 1985 (Reprinted with permission of Philadelphia Newspapers, LLC.)

"More a Ghost Than a Legend," originally published as "Keeping track of Dick Allen," *Chicago Sun-Times*, February 8, 1982

"Hard Game, Hard Man," originally published as "Frank Robinson: A vintage blend," *Chicago Sun-Times*, August 1, 1982

"Honored To Be a Hero," originally published as "'Bawlmer' keeps babbling about Brooks," *Chicago Sun-Times*, July 31, 1983

"Mr. Cub Remembers," originally published as "Ernie, you'll always be a Young Timer," *Chicago Daily News*, August 5, 1977

"Bionic Man I'm Not," *Sport SCORE*, May 9, 1979

"Family Tradition," originally published as "Inevitably, 'So long Yaz' draws closer," *Chicago Sun-Times*, August 28, 1983

"Spaceman," originally published as "A spaceman who never comes down to earth," *Chicago Sun-Times*, April 9, 1978

"Bird with a Broken Wing," originally published as "Bird still flies, but on a wing," *Chicago Sun-Times*, April 26, 1978

"The Slugging Seraph," originally published as "Steve Bilko," in *Cult Baseball Players: The Greats, the Flakes, the Weird, the Wonderful*, ed. Danny Peary (Fireside/Simon & Schuster, 1990)

"Lipstick on a .407 Batting Average," originally published as "Brett gets bright lights, .400 in sight," *Chicago Sun-Times*, August 29, 1980

"The Pirates' Patriarch," originally published as "Willie Stargell: The perfect patriarch of Pittsburgh's Family," *Chicago Sun-Times*, October 18, 1979

"And a Rookie Shall Lead Them," originally published as "Valenzuela: The start of a new age," *Chicago Sun-Times*, October 23, 1981

"Good-bye Doesn't Come Easy," originally published as "An adieu to Oriole No. 22," *Chicago Sun-Times*, May 21, 1984

"A One-Way Ticket to Obscurity," *Sports Illustrated*, September 5, 2005

"The Pistol's Parting Shot," originally published as "Pistol Pete: Parting shot full of sorrow," *Chicago Sun-Times*, September 24, 1980

"Sky King," originally published as "Sky king—Erving plots 76ers' course," *Chicago Sun-Times*, April 18, 1983

"The Ultimate Celtic," originally published as "The super natural basketball player," *Chicago Sun-Times*, April 26, 1982

"No Way To Treat a Legend," originally published as "Legend as big as dreams from the Big House," *Chicago Sun-Times*, December 7, 1979

"Sunday's Jester," originally published as "McGuire's fragile side handled with care," *Chicago Sun-Times*, February 15, 1981

"Only the Good Die Young," *Philadelphia Daily News*, December 7, 1984 (Reprinted with permission of Philadelphia Newspapers, LLC.)

"Borderline Case," originally published as "Gretzky: A borderline case," *Chicago Sun-Times*, February 6, 1981

"Blue Collar at a Tea Dance," originally published as "Connors's spirit sets him apart," *Philadelphia Daily News*, July 5, 1985 (Reprinted with permission of Philadelphia Newspapers, LLC.

"The Olympic Ideal," originally published as "John Carlos still demonstrates the Olympic ideal," *Chicago Sun-Times*, June 20, 1983

"The Elder," originally published as "Boston's long-running free spirit," *Chicago Sun-Times*, April 20, 1980

"Rider Down," originally published as "Memories of Secretariat a soar point for paralyzed Turcotte," *Chicago Sun-Times*, June 12, 1983

"The Happy Anarchist," originally published as "Buddy Delp was here," *Chicago Sun-Times*, May 5, 1979

"A Million for the Shoe," originally published as "Shoe: Million's body and soul," *Chicago Sun-Times*, August 31, 1981

"The Write Stuff," originally published as "Red Smith: The write stuff," *Chicago Sun-Times*, April 27, 1984

"The Professional," originally published as "W. C. Heinz got to the heart of the story," *Los Angeles Times*, March 1, 2008 (Los Angeles Times copyright © 2008. Reprinted with permission.)

"Joe," originally published as "Liebling means love—of boxing," *Chicago Sun-Times*, December 5, 1980

"Poet and Provocateur," originally published as "Unsung poet of all the dark nights," msnbc.com, June 25, 2002

"One Tough Baby," *Sports Illustrated*, January 31, 2005

"The Proud Warrior," *Philadelphia Daily News*, April 16, 1985 (Reprinted with permission of Philadelphia Newspapers, LLC.)

"He Gave Style a Name," originally published as "Sugar Ray Robinson," *Sport*, December 1986

"Larger Than Life or Death," originally published as "No one could hold a candle to Joe Louis," *Chicago Sun-Times*, April 13, 1981

"Raise Your Glass to a Teetotaler," originally published as "A whale of a tale about Zale," *Chicago Sun-Times*, April 30, 1984

"One of a Kind," originally published as "Paddy Flood: Voice of the cuckoo gone from boxing jungle," *Chicago Sun-Times*, April 1, 1983

"The One-Eyed Man," originally published as "Leonard saves face with TKO," *Chicago Sun-Times*, September 17, 1981

"A Touch of Class," originally published as "81-year-old trainer has ticket to immortality," *Chicago Sun-Times*, June 19, 1980

"A Man of Stone," originally published as "He's a man of stone," *Chicago Sun-Times*, June 15, 1980

"He Cramped His Own Style," *Chicago Sun-Times*, January 27, 1982

"His Time and No One Else's," originally published as "Holmes Has Earned a Long Rest," *Philadelphia Daily News*, March 18, 1985 (Reprinted with permission of Philadelphia Newspapers, LLC.)

"No Garden Party," originally published as "No Garden Party for Ali," *Chicago Daily News*, September 30, 1977

"Marching Off to Slaughter," originally published as "Ali Still Fast? Yes, Aging Fast," *Chicago Sun-Times*, September 12, 1980

"Ali! Ali! Ali!" *GQ*, April 1998